THE STRATEGIC QUADRANGLE

THE STRATEGIC QUADRANGLE

*Russia, China, Japan, and the
United States in East Asia*

MICHAEL MANDELBAUM

EDITOR

COUNCIL ON FOREIGN RELATIONS PRESS

NEW YORK

COUNCIL ON FOREIGN RELATIONS BOOKS

If you would like more information on Council publications, please write the Council on Foreign Relations, 58 East 68th Street, New York, NY 10021, or call the Publications Office at (212)734-0400.

Library of Congress Cataloging-in-Publication Data

The Strategic quadrangle : Japan, China, Russia and the United States
 in East Asia / edited by Michael Mandelbaum.
    p.   cm.
  Includes bibliographical references (p.   ) and index.
  ISBN 0-87609-168-0 : $16.95
  1. East Asia—Foreign relations.   2. East Asia—Strategic aspects.
I. Mandelbaum, Michael, 1946–   .
DS518.1.S68   1994
327.5—dc20   94–40867
                                                                   CIP

95   96   97   98   99   EB   10   9   8   7   6   5   4   3   2   1

Cover Design: Kuan Chang

CONTENTS

ACKNOWLEDGMENTS

This volume is part of the Council on Foreign Relations Project on East-West Relations, which is supported by the Carnegie Corporation of New York. The project originated under the auspices of Professor Seweryn Bialer and the Research Institute on International Change at Columbia University, with assistance from the United Nations Association and the U.S.-Japan Foundation. An initial conference, cosponsored by the Samuel Bronfman Foundation, was held in 1989. The chapters were later presented as papers at a symposium on "The Strategic Quadrangle in East Asia," held in Washington, D.C., on November 3 and 4, 1993. The views expressed are those of the authors alone.

The editor is grateful to all those involved in the production of the volume, especially Audrey McInerney for organizing the symposium and supervising the publication of the book.

Introduction

MICHAEL MANDELBAUM

The Strategic Quadrangle—that part of the globe encompassing East Asia and the western Pacific where the political and economic interests as well as the military forces of the United States, Russia, the People's Republic of China, and Japan all intersect—has been, with Europe, one of the two centers of international politics in this century.

As in Europe, great powers have confronted one another directly there. And like Europe, it has been the site of the world's most productive economies. As in Europe, the history of the Strategic Quadrangle since 1945 can be divided into three distinct periods: the first, when the Cold War was most intense, from the late 1940s to the early 1970s; the second, when the Soviet-American rivalry still dominated the politics of both regions but was more more relaxed and less urgent, from the early 1970s to the early 1990s; and the third, post–Cold War era, which began with the collapse of the Soviet Union at the end of 1991. It is this third, current period that is the focus of this book.

THE POST–1945 HISTORY

In each of the three periods the politics of Europe and the politics of the Strategic Quadrangle in East Asia were similar but not identical. In the first, both regions were divided into two camps, with the United States and its allies—the most important of which in Asia was Japan—on one side and the forces of communism, led by the Soviet Union in an increasingly shaky partnership with the People's Republic of China on the other.

In Asia, as in Europe, divided countries became flashpoints for larger conflicts. In Asia, however, these conflicts broke into open, bloody, and protracted hostilities, first on the Korean peninsula in the 1950s, then in Vietnam in the 1960s. In Europe, the division of Germany, while the cause of several tense confrontations, never triggered a war.

Indeed, the starting point of the first stage of the post-1945 history of East Asia was June 25, 1950. On that date the Communist regime of North Korea attacked the South. The United States sent troops to the Korean peninsula, under the auspices of the United Nations, to prevent the northern forces from conquering South Korea. At the same time President Harry Truman ordered the American Seventh Fleet into the Taiwan Strait, interposing it between the Communist government of the Chinese mainland and Chiang Kai-shek's Kuomintang, which had fled to the island of Taiwan from the mainland a few months earlier in the wake of its defeat by Mao Zedong's forces. The United States thus effectively committed itself to defending Taiwan.

On November 25 Chinese forces crossed the Yalu River, the border between Korea and China, and entered the war. The conflict ended in a bloody stalemate, with Korea divided at the thirty-eighth parallel three years later.

The Korean War and the Cold War in Asia were extensions of the conflict in Europe, at least in American eyes. North Korea, China, and later Vietnam were seen in Washington as part of a single Communist bloc, all allies and instruments of Moscow. This view was not entirely the result of a hyperactive anti-Communist American imagination. The Soviet Union did provide substantial military assistance to China and North Korea when they fought the United States in the 1950s and to the Vietnamese Communists in their war against the Americans in the 1960s and 1970s. Moreover, in the decade between the Korean and Vietnamese conflicts, war between the United States and China was a recurrent possibility. On several occasions during the 1950s, mainland forces bombarded Kuomintang-controlled islands in the Taiwan Strait. The United States threatened to retaliate, hinting that it would use nuclear weapons.

What had begun in Korea ended in Vietnam, where Communist forces prevailed, driving out the United States and conquering all of Indochina. The end of that war marked the beginning of the next historical period in the Strategic Quadrangle; but this period was not dominated, as the outcome of the Vietnam War suggested it would be, by the Communist bloc. Contrary to American fears of a "domino effect," the rest of Asia was largely unaffected by the Communist conquest of Indochina. Particular national features and internal balances of power turned out to have far greater influence in shaping the regimes and the policies of other Asian countries than the result of the war in Vietnam, Cambodia, and Laos.

In fact, the United States, which had been beleaguered in East Asia from the 1940s to the 1970s, assumed a comfortable, even privileged position in the 1970s and 1980s. During this second post-1945 period, the politics of the Strategic Quadrangle once again diverged from those of Europe, but this time in that East Asia was a less polarized, more tranquil place. In the second half of the Cold War, Europe remained frozen in a hostile stalemate between the two opposing camps. In the Asia-Pacific region, by contrast, the balance of military forces and political power changed significantly and in ways favorable to the United States. This was because of two major developments in the region that were without parallels in Europe.

One was the shift of the People's Republic of China from alliance with the Soviet Union to alignment with the United States. The schism between the two great Communist powers broke into the open at the end of the 1950s as a result of divergent national interests and leadership tensions reflected in contrasting interpretations of Communist dogma. In 1969 the two fought a series of minor skirmishes over a disputed island in a river that formed their common border in the Far East and over disputed territory in Central Asia. Alarmed at the prospect of a wider conflict against a much stronger power, China sought a measure of protection by moving to end its long estrangement from the Soviet Union's great adversary, the United States. After public gestures of reconciliation and a series of secret diplomatic initiatives, a new Sino-American relationship was sealed with a visit by the American president, Richard Nixon, to Beijing in February 1972.[1]

There followed improved political relations, expanded economic ties, and even military cooperation between the two nations. They did not become full-fledged allies, but after 1972 China was clearly closer to the United States than to the Soviet Union.

The second major development in East Asia was what is sometimes called the postwar economic miracle in the region. By the beginning of the 1990s, this development overshadowed everything else that had happened there since 1945. An extraordinary surge of economic growth transformed largely agricultural and in some cases quite backward countries into producers, indeed exporters, of the most modern, sophisticated products, raising their standards of living dramatically.

In the 1950s and 1960s Japan's economy recovered from the destruction of war and grew at an impressive rate. The Japanese economic momentum continued in the 1970s and 1980s, creating the world's second largest economy and leading to enormous trade surpluses with the rest of the world in general and with the United States in particular. In the 1970s South Korea, Taiwan, Singapore, and Hong Kong also began to manufacture automobiles, consumer electronics, and other high-technology consumer goods.

All of these countries were politically allied or aligned with the United States. Their successes strengthened the coalition that the United States led. As they prospered, they became more stable politically and, in the cases of Japan and South Korea, more formidable militarily.

High rates of economic growth were a feature of postwar Europe, both eastern and western, as well. But the European economic successes had a far more modest impact on the international politics of Europe than Asian economic progress had in Asia. The most impressive growth came earlier in both sectors of Europe— during the first half of the Cold War. In the West, it occurred in countries that had been prosperous before the war. In East Asia outside Japan, prosperity was created where previously there had been poverty. The countries' economic performance involved a new and startling development rather than simply the resumption of a pattern interrupted by World War II. It thus served as a powerful example for the rest of the world.

The economic performance of eastern Europe was an equally impressive counterexample. Growth tapered off after the 1960s. During most of the second half of the Cold War, the Communist economies of Europe stagnated. This fact helped to discredit communism in general and paved the way for its downfall. The economic successes in East Asia in the 1970s and 1980s, coupled with the failures in Communist Europe, played a major role in bringing the second historical period to a close and ushering in the third. They had a particularly powerful impact on the two Communist powers of the Strategic Quadrangle.

The leaders of China and the Soviet Union could hardly ignore the fact that the most dynamic economies on the planet were not Communist ones. In Beijing and Moscow, the recognition dawned—sooner in China, later in Russia—that, if the trends of the postwar period continued, especially those that gained momentum in the 1970s, the rest of Asia would soon outstrip them economically. Without serious changes, the two Communist giants were destined to become economic and ultimately political backwaters, with sluggish agricultural sectors and inefficient industries saddled with the obsolete technologies of the first half of the twentieth century. The example of the Asian economic miracle thus played a role in the decision to institute sweeping reforms in China in the late 1970s and in the Soviet Union a decade later. That example thereby contributed to the events that led, in 1991, to the end of the Soviet Union.[2]

Both before and after the disintegration of the Soviet Union, the two principal developments of the second post-1945 period in East Asia affected its strategic configuration. China was aligned, but not allied, with the United States and Japan. Even before its diplomatic tilt toward Washington, Beijing had declared that it would chart an independent course in foreign policy; on many issues the Chinese identified not with the United States but with the nonaligned countries of the Third World. By the early 1970s, therefore, while Europe was still divided into two military and political blocs with the United States and the Soviet Union at the center of each, the international politics of East Asia had become, for some purposes, triangular, involving the Japanese-American partnership, the Soviet Union, and China.

Moreover, the American-led coalition in East Asia was not as tightly knit as its counterpart in Europe. Washington's efforts in the 1950s to build an Asian alliance similar to the North Atlantic Treaty Organization (NATO) in Europe did not succeed. Instead, the United States maintained a series of bilateral security relationships in the Asia-Pacific region. The security treaty with Japan was the most important of these, the one that most closely approximated the American association with Western Europe through NATO. Yet the Japanese-American relationship differed from that of the United States and its European allies. Japan was more populous and culturally more distinct from the United States than any one of them. The Japanese also felt less directly threatened by the Soviet Union. Unlike the Germans, they did not confront a large, Soviet-led army on their border that was poised to move tanks and troops at a moment's notice. Thus an American army was not stationed in Japan as it was in Germany. Although Japan's attitude toward the Soviet Union was anything but cordial, many Japanese considered the modest complement of American forces in their country to be not so much a shield against Soviet power as a concession to the United States in exchange for which Japanese exporters received access to the American economy.

In the 1970s and 1980s, moreover, Japan became an economic giant and ultimately the world's largest creditor. While still an American ally under the Japanese-American Security Treaty and closely tied to the United States in economic terms, it was no longer simply an American client or protectorate. In the world economy Japan had become a major independent force.[3] Thus, by the end of the 1980s, in the Asia-Pacific region there were four major powers. The appropriate geometric metaphor was neither two opposing blocs nor a triangle; it was a quadrangle.

While both East Asia and Europe have been affected by the great revolutionary upheavals that brought the Cold War to an end, these effects seem at first glance more pronounced in Europe than in the Strategic Quadrangle.

In Europe, a comprehensive agreement on nonnuclear armaments (the Conventional Forces in Europe accord of 1990) and the dissolution of the Warsaw Pact in 1991 led to the withdrawal and demobilization of tens of thousands of troops and hundreds of thousands of pieces of military equipment. East Asia has seen neither comparable negotiated reductions nor the dissolution of a great military alliance.

In 1989 revolutions removed Communist governments (or at least longtime Communist leaders) in Poland, Hungary, Czechoslovakia, East Germany, Bulgaria, and Romania. These governments (with the partial exception of Ceaucescu's in Romania) had been puppets of the Soviet Union. When Moscow signaled that it would no longer support them, they collapsed. In Asia, by contrast, Communists remained in power in China, Vietnam, and North Korea. None had depended as heavily on Soviet support as the European Communist regimes. The Chinese Communists had earned some credit with the Chinese people by the success of Deng Xiaoping's economic reforms, and Vietnam was beginning similar economic innovations; but North Korea had not departed at all from Stalinist political and economic practices. All survived first the radical reforms of Mikhail Gorbachev and then the official disappearance of the Communist Party of the Soviet Union.

With the end of communism and the collapse of the Soviet Union, not only the politics but also the very map of Europe changed. New sovereign states appeared. Russia was suddenly separated from Europe by a series of independent countries, the largest and most important of which was Ukraine, with a population of 52 million.

In East Asia, by contrast, independent Russia extends to the Pacific Ocean, just as the Soviet Union did. What had once been Soviet Vladivostok, Sakhalin, and Kamchatka are now Russian, as they were before 1917.[4]

In Europe, the conclusion of the Cold War ended the division of Germany. In East Asia, Korea remained divided and territorial disputes involving China and Japan persisted as well. Beijing continued to regard the island of Taiwan as a Chinese province illegally occupied by a rebel government. Tokyo continued to consider the four southern islands of the Kurile chain, which the Soviet Union had seized at the end of World War II, to be Japanese territory.

But appearances can mislead. The end of the Cold War did bring change to the Strategic Quadrangle. It affected the internal politics of all four countries and injected a degree of uncertainty into the policies of each toward the other three. The extent of the change varied considerably among the four, however, as the four chapters in this volume make clear.

THE CHAPTERS

Russia has changed the most. It has been transformed from a multi-national empire to a nation-state that, while still enormous and still peopled by non-Russians, is geographically smaller and ethnically more purely Russian than at any time in the last three hundred years.

This and other political and economic changes have left Russia, as Chapter 1 by Robert Legvold makes clear, in a state of internal political flux and economic disintegration. It is so consumed with its own difficulties that its presence in East Asia for the near term is likely to be negligible. For Moscow, foreign policy will principally involve dealing with the former Soviet republics that are now independent or quasi-independent states, which Russians call their "Near Abroad."

Because the new Russian republic does not consider any of the other three powers of the Strategic Quadrangle to be an adversary, and because its internal upheavals have crippled its armed forces, the Russian military presence in the Far East does not cast a menacing shadow over the region as it did in the days of the Soviet Union. At the outset of the post–Cold War era, Boris Yeltsin, like Mikhail Gorbachev before him, aspired to participate fully in the commerce of the region; but the internal economic transformation of Russia that would make that possible is certain to be a protracted affair.

Russia is weak. Weakness circumscribes its relations with the other three powers of the Strategic Quadrangle. Russia no longer threatens them, but its weakness is also an obstacle to reconciliation. Yeltsin and Gorbachev would probably have liked to return the four Kurile Islands to Japan, if only so that Japan, out of gratitude, would be generous with economic assistance to Russia. But the trauma of losing first the Soviet empire in Eastern Europe and then, after 1991, territories that had been Russian for centuries created a nationalist backlash that prevented Yeltsin from ceding yet more territory—even small, rocky, more or less insignificant specks of land far from Europe.

Russia's internal weakness could also influence East Asia if the effects of Russian economic collapse, ethnic strife, nationalist irredentism, and nuclear proliferation—none of which is certain but all of which are possible—were to reach beyond the country's borders. For the foreseeable future, if Russia is a major force in the Strategic Quadrangle, it will be, as Legvold puts it, not as a player but as a problem.

Of the four countries, China has been the least changed by the end of the Cold War. Its great shift in course had come a decade earlier, at the end of the 1970s. Deng Xiaoping launched a program of economic reform that moved the Chinese economy to even higher levels of marketization. The reforms have enjoyed extraordinary success. Economic growth has surged. China is a far wealthier country as a result.

The overwhelming fact of Chinese economic growth has three consequences for the politics of the Strategic Quadrangle. First, as David M. Lampton notes in Chapter 2, China has perhaps the clearest vision of the desirable short-term future of the region of any of the four major powers. Ironically, it is a classically capitalist vision, emphasizing trade, investment, and the separation of economics from politics. "To get rich is glorious," a slogan from the early days of Deng's economic reforms, captures the essence of what China seeks: political and military détente and economic cooperation with the other three powers in order to sustain the remarkable economic performance of the decade and a half following 1979.

Second, success has bred confidence among China's leaders, despite the Tiananmen episode and the collapse of Communism in Europe. They not only favor the course they have set but believe that they can keep to it despite the objections, and perhaps obstacles, presented by the United States.

Third, Chinese growth will be a central feature of the politics of the Strategic Quadrangle over the long term. As the three other powers gaze into the future, they know they will have to come to terms with its consequences: a richer, more powerful, and perhaps more ambitious China. Their policies will increasingly take this prospect into account.[5]

The revolutionary changes in Russia were largely the result of the collapse of communism, of which the end of the Cold War was a by-product. The sweeping changes in China were due to the economic reforms of the 1980s. The changes in Japan were more modest. But as chapter 3, by Mike Mochizuki, notes, they were hardly inconsequential and unlike what happened in the other two countries, change in Japan was largely provoked by the end of the Cold War. The disappearance of the Soviet-American rivalry introduced an unfamiliar and unwelcome strain of uncertainty into both its domestic politics and its foreign policy. During the conflict, Japan had enjoyed several decades of stability in both arenas, based on the domination of the Liberal Democratic Party (LDP) at home and the alliance with the United States abroad. The end of the Cold War undermined both.

Indeed, it ended LDP dominance. In 1993, the party split apart and a new, shaky coalition government took power for a few months before collapsing and being replaced by an even shakier one. What had been an immobile political system during the Cold War seemed destined for a period of instability, without enduring, predictable alignments and with government by shifting, fragile coalitions.[6]

As for relations with the United States, although the Security Treaty remained in place, the Japanese could not be certain that, absent the Soviet threat, over the long term America would continue the policies in the region that had relieved Japan of the need to conduct an independent defense policy. This was so in part because the Japanese-American relationship was under mounting strain from trade disputes that had been suppressed by the need for political solidarity during the Cold War but had become increasingly important in the United States in its wake.

If the end of the Cold War brought upheaval to Russia while leaving China firmly committed to existing policies, its legacy to Japan was discomfort. The Japanese aspired to perpetuate the conditions of the second half of the Cold War, under which, like the

Chinese, they had flourished. But they had reason to be less confident than the Chinese that they could manage this.

Nor was the prospect of taking the initiative in shaping post–Cold War East Asia a comfortable one for Tokyo. Since 1945 Japan had been, by choice and temperament, a follower rather than a leader internationally, with a foreign policy devoted almost entirely to promoting exports while lacking any broader definition of the country's interests or responsibilities.[7]

The end of the Cold War had a more modest effect on the internal affairs of the other democracy of the Strategic Quadrangle, the United States, than was the case with Japan.[8] But it conferred upon American foreign policy a wider array of choices than either the other three countries in the Strategic Quadrangle confronted or than the United States had faced during the previous four decades. In that period a clear hierarchy of purposes had governed what the United States did in the region. At the top of this hierarchy was security: American policies flowed from the confrontation with the Soviet Union.

With the end of the Cold War, two other traditional American public purposes, never abandoned but always less important than security during the Cold War, came to the fore: democracy and prosperity. The disappearance of the Soviet threat and the rise of these two goals created a new agenda for the United States in the post–Cold War Strategic Quadrangle, an agenda that, as I show in Chapter 4, has become a source of friction with the other countries.

The frictions and disagreements that it has generated, with the exception of the unresolved conflict on the Korean peninsula, are not the sort that will lead to war. But they are serious enough that, even with the threat of war in abeyance, East Asia has become a place that, for the United States, is marked by conflicting goals, acrimonious disputes with longtime friends, and a general lack of clarity about the nation's purposes in the region.

According to Richard H. Solomon, the greatest uncertainties and possibilities for future conflict will be with America's relations with China. In his Conclusion, Solomon foresees that both the United States—as the world's sole surviving superpower, even if a reluctant one—and China, for historical, cultural, and economic reasons, will make active efforts to shape the politics of post–Cold

War East Asia. On a variety of economic, political, and security matters the two governments already have significant disagreements, not to mention their profoundly differing approaches on human rights issues. This will lead, at best, to a Sino-American relationship that is a mixture of cooperation and conflict, one less confrontational than the Soviet-American rivalry after World War II, but also one less cordial than Sino-American relations during the 1970s and 1980s. At worst, relations between the world's largest country and its most powerful state could deteriorate into a new form of "cold war," serving as a major source of tension in East Asia into the twenty-first century.

REGIONAL ISSUES

Post–Cold War Europe may be thought of as a region. Indeed, the sense of the continent as, for some purposes, a single unit goes back at least to the Congress of Vienna of 1815. After 1945 an international and, in limited ways, supranational economic organization—the European Community—was created in the western part of the continent. Similarly, a permanent peacetime military alliance, NATO, which was transatlantic in scope, was established.

The history of regionalism in East Asia is shorter and thinner. Japan's forcible efforts to organize an economic and military bloc in the first half of the 1940s—known in English as the Greater East Asia Co-Prosperity Sphere—were thwarted, also forcibly, by the American armed forces and are not fondly remembered by anybody. After 1945 such regionwide organizational structures as developed there were centered on the United States. The successful economies of the region depended on access to the American market; the principal security arrangements were a series of bilateral pacts between the United States and various countries of the region, of which the Security Treaty with Japan was by far the most important.

With the passing of the Cold War, sentiment in favor of more extensive and more formal regional cooperation than had been practiced in the past could be detected around the Pacific rim.[9] The end of the dominant military and ideological rivalry in concert with the dramatic expansion of trade and capital flows within the region had, it seemed, given rise to the kinds of common purposes that organizations are created to serve.

At the outset of the 1990s, therefore, several initiatives to build organizations for security and economic issues in East Asia were undertaken. After the regular meetings of the foreign ministers of the Association of Southeast Asian Nations (ASEAN), issues of regional security began to be discussed. The forum for Asia-Pacific Economic Cooperation (APEC) brought its members' heads of state together in Seattle in November 1993.

The ASEAN postministerial meetings and the APEC summit, however, illustrated the limits to formal regional cooperation. Each was a forum devoted strictly to discussion, Neither had any authority to make decisions, and none of the countries involved was prepared to urge that either organization acquire this authority. ASEAN, moreover, centered on Southeast Asia rather than on the heart of the Strategic Quadrangle, to the north.[10]

Strong regional organizations including all of East Asia or even encompassing the Strategic Quadrangle are not likely to be created in the near future. The four major powers of the region are far more diverse than the great powers of Europe ever were.

On the most important indices of international capability they are not at all alike. While the United States is a major military power and a formidable international economic power as well, Russia is a military but not an economic presence, Japan is an economic but not a military giant, and China is neither but, with the combination of its size and growth rate, has the potential to achieve great-power status in both arenas sometime in the next century.

The four are markedly dissimilar in other ways as well. There are differences of demography: China, the world's most populous country, is several times larger than any of the others. There are differences of economic status: Japan and the United States are the most technologically advanced countries in the world and their citizens enjoy high standards of living; Russia is dominated by the large but now backward industries of the first stages of the industrial revolution; and China, despite an urban population that is enormous by the standards of other countries, is still mainly a nation of peasants.

Not least important are differences of geography. The European great powers shared the same landmass. The powers of the Strategic Quadrangle do not. China is firmly planted on the Asian mainland, but Japan is an offshore archipelago, Russia's center of political and economic gravity is in Europe, and the United States is part of Asia economically but not geographically.

Thus, while Europe will increasingly be influenced by the politics of continent-wide institutions, the future of the Asia-Pacific region will be shaped by the individual national policies of its major powers, which are the subjects of the chapters in this book. For the remainder of the twentieth century and beyond, the international relations of East Asia will emerge from the politics of the Strategic Quadrangle.

Notes

1. On the evolution of Chinese security policy, see Michael Mandelbaum, *The Fate of Nations: The Search for National Security in the 19th and 20th Centuries* (New York: Cambridge University Press, 1988), chap. 6.
2. It is not fanciful to impute an important role in the collapse of the Soviet Union to South Korea. While the Communist rulers in Moscow could rationalize their country's failure to close the economic gap with the United States, Western Europe, and even Japan, when a formerly barren and backward country that historically had scarcely seemed worthy of notice emerged as an industrial dynamo, with a more sophisticated commercial industrial base than the motherland of socialism, they could no longer ignore the serious economic shortcomings of the Soviet Union.
3. Testimony to its independent status was its ongoing and increasingly acrimonious dispute about trade with the United States. See below, pp. 178–184.
4. The breakup of the Soviet Union has affected the borders of one other country in the Strategic Quadrangle. China has new neighbors. What were once Soviet Central Asian republics are now independent Kazakhstan and Kyrgyzstan. This has created a potential problem for Beijing. Some of the Muslim peoples of Central Asia—the Uighurs and Mongolians in particular—live on both sides of the Chinese border with the new countries. Chinese authorities are concerned about the rise of Islamic and national consciousness among these peoples, which could lead to movements for autonomy or even independence in the large, sparsely populated regions of Xinjiang and Inner Mongolia, where Muslims outnumber Han Chinese. See Ross Munro, "Central Asia and China," in Michael Mandelbaum, ed. *Central Asia and the World* (New York: Council on Foreign Relations, 1994), pp. 225–238.
5. In some ways China's recent experience—political stability (with the important but short-lived exception of the democracy movements of 1989) and economic success—has been the opposite of Russia's. In other respects, however,

the two countries are similar. Both have moved away from the orthodox communism of the Stalinist and Maoist varieties, albeit at different speeds and with different short-term results. This has entailed considerable change in both countries. While the impact of the end of the Cold War on Chinese policies has been modest, the effects of Deng's economic reforms on Chinese society have been immense. The sheer volume of change these reforms have produced—measured in opportunities created, social mobility provided, and wealth accumulated—surely rivals that in any ten-year period in any country at any time in history.

The movement away from communism has had two similar political consequences in Russia and China. The once all-powerful central government has lost its grip on the country in both cases. China's regions have achieved considerable economic autonomy; this is happening in Russia as well. Finally, in neither country is political stability assured. The potential for instability in Russia has been evident since the collapse of communism; in China, no orderly mechanism for political succession is in place and the country's political prospects when Deng's generation finally passes from the scene are uncertain.

6. At the same time, the Japanese recession in the early 1990s called into question some of the social bases of postwar Japanese politics, such as lifetime employment in its large industrial enterprises.

7. For a view of Japan as a "reactive state," see Kent E. Calder, "Japanese Foreign Economic Policy Formation: Explaining the Reactive State," *World Politics* 40 no. 4 (July 1988).

8. It had some effect. Bill Clinton, the governor of a small state with virtually no experience in foreign policy, could almost certainly not have been elected president during the Cold War. Postwar presidential elections before 1992 were occasions for full-blown debates about American foreign policy. In 1992, America's relations with the rest of the world were hardly mentioned.

9. For an inventory of the possibilities for regional organization, see Hisayoki Ina, *A New Multilateral Agenda for the Pacific: Beyond the Bilateral Security Networks* (Washington, D.C.: The Johns Hopkins University School of Advanced International Studies Foreign Policy Institute, 1993).

10. Its discussions on security in July 1993 did include representatives of the United States, Japan, China, and Russia as well as Korea.

CHAPTER ONE

Russia and the Strategic Quadrangle

ROBERT LEGVOLD

After a hundred years and a long detour through Soviet power, Russia returns to Asia, but with nearly nothing the same. Russia arrived at the end of the nineteenth century as a troubled but ambitious power, at the peak of its imperial drive. Russia at the end of the twentieth century is also troubled, but weak and alone, without an empire, internally preoccupied, and, for the time being, struggling toward a democracy that it has never known. East Asia too recalls little of the earlier era. It no longer constitutes merely a distant theater of a European-based international order; China is no longer the helpless object of Japanese, Russian, and European depredations; Korea is no longer anyone's colony; and Japan is no longer an insular, unrequited imperial power. And the dynamic among nations is no longer a competitive scramble for extraterritorial privilege, ports, railways, and colonies. No longer do the great powers calculate the ebb and flow of influence in Asia in terms of an intricately poised (European) balance of power. No longer is war or even the sinking of significant parts of another state's navy in peacetime (as the French twice did to the Chinese in the nineteenth century) a normal, even casual recourse of policy. History, therefore, comes back as a stranger.

In challenging historical analogy, I am not dismissing certain underlying and enduring geopolitical realities in East Asia. Whatever is to become of the region ultimately depends, as it has for the last two centuries, on the fate of three major powers—China,

Japan, and Russia, three-quarters of the Strategic Quadrangle—and on the stability and tranquility of their mutual relations. Great upheaval in any one of them or grave tension between any two of them will alter politics for everyone in the region and outside.

Second, continental Asia, a landmass dominated by Russia and China, occupies the physical and strategic core of the area, a core that radiates effects first through the subregions that jut from it—the Korean peninsula and Southeast Asia—and then, inevitably, to the great surrounding archipelagos. Third, although over time the comparative strength, cohesion, and dynamism of the core versus the periphery has varied, today, as at the end of the nineteenth century, the core is weak and unsure of itself, while the periphery is solid and self-confident, providing both an anchor for the international politics of the area and vitality to its international economics[1]

Yet amid these enduring facts, both the context and the content of the Asian Strategic Quadrangle has turned into something fundamentally different—not, however, because of the return of history nor because of a still more popular, related explanation that locates cause in the collapse of bipolarity and the return of multipolarity. Bipolarity, of course, did matter in East Asia. The East-West standoff and the larger global U.S.-Soviet competition deeply influenced the character of international relations in the region, even though Asia, from the moment the Sino-Soviet conflict erupted in the mid-1950s, lost the sharp structural clarity of Europe during the Cold War. Albeit blurred, the lines of bipolarity cut through East Asia, from the thirty-eighth parallel to Indochina, where, for two decades, first the French and then the Americans warred against communism and its surrogates. Above all it underpinned the Sino-American relationship—both in the 1950s, when the two struggled against one another, and in the 1970s, when the two struggled alongside one another. It also inspired the U.S.-Japanese security partnership, which in turn, affected the entire Asian landscape.

Nearer our own day, the ascent of vibrant, mutually dependent market economies partially eclipsed the cruder, underlying military competition between socialism and capitalism. Yet even then the security and economic dimensions remained intertwined. To the end, the global rivalry between the two superpowers echoed in East Asia, augmented and complicated by the conflict between Beijing and Moscow. Regional tensions on the Korean peninsula and to the south never broke free of these larger contests. The shifting military balance in Northeast Asia continued to compete effectively among the new and swelling concerns of national policymakers.

What in the first instance transformed the context and content of the Strategic Quadrangle, therefore, was the force that transformed the content of bipolarity. This force was the revolution in Soviet foreign policy effected by Mikhail Gorbachev and his colleagues between 1986 and 1989. What they wrought yields the first of the three theses argued in this chapter: Even had the Soviet Union survived, the Strategic Quadrangle would have been, indeed was, profoundly altered by the metamorphosis in Soviet foreign policy, a reorientation that took place before bipolarity collapsed. The Soviet Union, of course, did not survive, and its demise produced still another convolution in Asian international politics. This leads to the second thesis: The transformation of the Strategic Quadrangle has gone through two critical stages, and the effects of each need to be understood.

The third thesis bears directly on the current, post-Soviet Russian phase, and, also contests the prevalent focus of much of the thinking about international politics beyond the Cold War. Nearly all of the images or theories of an emerging international order depend on a traditional preoccupation with war and peace. But war and peace may not be the defining juxtaposition in the new international politics, at least not for the great powers, including China, Japan, Russia, and the United States. The issue may be the vitality of the international environment rather than its stability, national welfare rather than national security, economic prosperity rather than peace.

More than a decade and a half ago, Doak Barnett argued that a sturdy equilibrium had come to characterize relations among East Asia's four great powers.[2] Neither war nor any major upsetting of the balance among these decisive players seemed likely or even possible. Despite the considerable asymmetries in the kinds and quantities of power possessed by the four, despite the uneven pattern of alignment and antagonism among them, and despite their differing aims (with two of them, China and the Soviet Union, wanting to change the balance of power and the other two wanting to preserve it), little that any one of them cared or dared to do threatened the emergent order. The need to cooperate mixed with the impulse to compete, economics chipped away at the utility of military force, and the quest for dominance was sure to meet adequate resistance from the other three, not a cowardly readiness on the part of any of them to join the bully. A new and stable multipolarity was already emerging in Asia, replacing the bipolarity of the first two postwar decades.

Into the new era both multipolarity and equilibrium survive. Everything that Barnett said of the earlier period applies with equal or greater force today. More than ever each of the four powers has compelling stakes in its relations with the remaining three, stakes that coexist with, complicate, and, in good measure, counterbalance the sources of friction and fear in these relations. Less than ever does any of them see any of the others as an enemy or is any of them racing to amass arms against another. The U.S.-Japanese relationship remains the only alliance, and is welcomed more than ever by the other two. More than ever each of the four counts as a separate and independent player. And as much as ever none of them has the power, nor apparently the inclination, to destroy this equilibrium—Russia least of all.

Which leads to the essential point about a post–Soviet Russia in Asia. Russia's relevance is not likely to be a factor affecting the basic equilibrium in East Asia. Nothing Russia might do seems capable of impairing or redirecting the basic dynamic among the other three powers. If one thing stands out in the analyses in this volume, it is how seemingly marginal Russia and its new neighbors have become to the central concerns of the other three powers, even of the United States in Asia. The post-Soviet states, contrary to their hopes, have largely ceased to be relevant on the main avenues of East Asian international relations.

Yet, this misses the new potential significance of Russia and the other post-Soviet states for Asia. Their way back into the preoccupations of Asia's great powers surely will not be as a result of their power and influence, but of the trouble into which they can slide. If, for any number of reasons, order within or between these societies collapses, the misery and mayhem likely to follow will not halt at the old Soviet borders. Given the scale and importance not only of Russia but of Ukraine and Kazakhstan, the effects of either a breakdown in the civil peace or of interstate conflict—refugees, crime, gunrunning, and the tendency to suck others in—will be magnitudes greater than the sad instance of Yugoslavia. The former Soviet Union is the one region of the world capable of affecting the welfare—albeit not the peace—of East Asia through its own escalating troubles. Hence, to return to the question of basic perspectives, the essence of the Russian challenge is not Russia as a player—the focus of most current theory—but Russia as a problem; not Russia's actions, but Russia's condition. What a far cry this is from our habitual ways of thinking about international politics and, in particular, our long-settled view of Russia's predecessor, the Soviet Union.

SOVIET ROOTS

To understand how much has changed, it helps to reconsider the essentials of the Soviet encounter with East Asia. At the same time, for all the change, the roots of contemporary Russian policy are in this experience. For both reasons, therefore, I devote some space to the Soviet era, particularly, the critical last years under Gorbachev.

In contrast to Russia's faded influence, Soviet policy played a central role in shaping the postwar international setting, including relations in East Asia, and, in turn, that policy was much shaped by the international setting. First, and most fundamentally, the long and deep alienation of the Soviet Union from the West and a Western-dominated international system constituted a critical, constraining influence on relations among nations. The Soviet leadership, for all of its cynicism and narrow self-preoccupation, saw itself as the natural, permanent, and honorable foe of what all of its members down through Konstantin Chernenko preferred to call the imperialist powers. As a result, they invited from—indeed, imposed on—international politics, including politics in East Asia, an irreducible level of belligerence. Even if, as I believe to be the case, Stalin's successors were not acting principally to wield domination over an ever-expanding empire or merely to aggrandize the Soviet state, their notion of international reality guaranteed limitations to cooperation and permanence to rivalry.

Because of these biases, rooted in an ultimately unreconcilable value system, the competition with the United States had none of the pliability and impermanence of earlier great-power contests. Nor could Moscow have the expediential and flexible attitude toward the allies of the United States held by nineteenth-century predecessors toward the friends of enemies. For the same reason the stakes in the falling out with an apostate Chinese leadership were graver than historical grudges, disputed borders, and massed armies. Each threatened not merely the territorial integrity or strategic interests of the other, but the very legitimacy of the other's system.

The Soviet Union's permanent estrangement both reinforced and redirected the effect of bipolarity. States were not merely caught in the field of force of one or another superpower. Allies of the United States were kept where they were also by the nature and purpose of the Soviet Union. Allies of the Soviet Union, reluctant as they were, came to be as they were and their subordination as thorough as it was not simply because of great Soviet power, but also because of peculiar Soviet concepts.

Indeed, in Asia, the structure of international politics all along had been more complex than the starker bipolarity of Europe. Rather than two competing systems, Asia's international order was a clutter of triangles. By the late 1970s economics had begun to cut through this fragmentation and meld the region into a less chaotic whole. To the Soviet Union, however, until the Gorbachev era, economics mattered less; more important was Asia's elaborate political-military geometry.

For no country more than the Soviet Union did the underlying structure of Asian international politics revolve about a complex, interconnected set of triangular relationships. Because few other countries thought about the contours of East Asian international politics in these terms, the point may seem strange. The most obvious and famous of the triangles linked the Soviet Union, China, and the United States, but the Soviet-U.S.-Japan triangle was also important. In addition, five others also helped to shape Soviet policy: (1) the Sino-Soviet-Japanese triangle; (2) the Sino-Soviet-

North Korean triangle; (3) the Sino-Soviet-Vietnamese triangle; (4) the Soviet-Vietnamese-ASEAN (Association of Southeast Asian Nations) triangle; and (5) the Sino-Soviet-Indian triangle.

Thought of from this perspective, certain things stand out. First, China's centrality: China, and only China, played a role in nearly all of the triangles. Not even the United States figured in so many of the relationships critical to the Soviet Union in Asia. Second, the full set of triangles that impeded, shaped, and invigorated the policies of Gorbachev's predecessors varied greatly in importance, all of them overshadowed by the crucial Sino-Soviet-U.S. triangle. Indeed, the others owed much of their dynamic to the course of events in it.

Third, because over the years triangle was added to triangle, Asia became increasingly complex and challenging for the Soviet Union. The major turning point occurred in the 1970s. Until then the underlying geometry of Asia was much simpler. At the most, through the 1960s, one could speak of four triangles, and of these one—that among the Soviet Union, China, and North Vietnam— had emerged only in the last half of the decade.[3] Of the other three, only two—the Soviet-Japanese-U.S. and the Sino-Soviet-Indian triangles—had a significant bearing on the course of East Asian events. The third triangle—among the Soviet Union, China, and North Korea—remained an appendage of the Sino-Soviet conflict and largely an affair within the world of socialism.

In the 1970s, however, this changed not only because more triangles were added, but because they included a new kind of triangle, one giving the West access to the turmoil among the socialist states. The Sino-Soviet-U.S. triangle merged what until then had been two separate sets of Asian relations—virtually two local international systems. Coupled with the proliferation of lesser triangles, the new Sino-American relationship made life far more difficult and challenging for the Soviet policymaker.

CHINA: THE CENTRAL PIECE

Much as the United States was the primary focus of Soviet foreign policy globally in the postwar era, China served as the core of

Soviet policy in Asia. Ever since the triumph of the Chinese Communist revolution in 1949, Soviet leaders had viewed Asia from behind the rocky northern plains of China. While (socialist) China was not to the rest of Asia what (socialist) Eastern Europe was to the rest of Europe—namely, a pressure point in the politics of the West and, at the same time, a vulnerable glacis of Soviet security—it was a permanent Soviet preoccupation.

At the time the Chinese Communists prevailed in 1949 two critical shifts in the fortunes of Bolshevism occurred, each of which would shape the subsequent course of Soviet foreign policy. To the west, the Soviet Union conquered Eastern Europe and imposed socialism. To the east, revolution conquered China and left in its wake socialism no less in the Soviet image than in Eastern Europe. Both developments vindicated the strength and possibilities of Russia's own, now increasingly imperial, socialist revolution. Both, however, also guaranteed its long-term transformation, in the case of Eastern Europe, by bringing into being an inherently vulnerable order that would regularly tax Soviet control and, in the end, exceed it, and, in the case of China, by giving rise to another powerful, independent version of the revolution Russia and China now shared. The soil makes different wine from the same grape, and so the inevitable contrasts produced by these two very different societies soon transformed China from a triumph in Soviet eyes into a challenge.

Because the quarrel between China and the Soviet Union so long ago assumed the character of a bitter national conflict, fed by historic grievances and fears of aggression, we all but forgot its starting point. These two states fell out over ideas, not over the traditional grudges of nations. At the outset, true, the trouble began when the Chinese accused the Soviets of mismanaging their leadership of the socialist camp. In particular, Mao Zedong and his colleagues resented Nikita Khrushchev's failure to think through the consequences within Eastern Europe of his assault on the myth of Stalin and, more generally, his inability or reluctance to give the camp a severe and strong master.[4] But these misgivings simply anticipated far graver discord over deeply held values: over the nature of revolution in the nuclear era; over the requirements of the so-called national liberation struggle in the Third World; over the proper relationship with the "imperialist" adversary; and, indeed, over legitimate ways to build socialism itself.

By 1964 the conflict took on other qualities, when Mao re-opened the issue of territory seized by tsars and when increased troop levels along the border turned the petty skirmishes of the last several years into something potentially far deadlier. Yet even as the Sino-Soviet conflict evolved into a menacing, armed standoff, the alienating effect of ideology worked its deeper effects. Never did the conflict change entirely from an ideological contest into a political struggle, as so many outside observers argued by the late 1970s. Rather one dimension was added to the other and then fused with it. China and the Soviet Union did not become simply two antagonistic states, maneuvering to contain and diminish the other, but rivals whose whole identities were at stake. The heresy that each saw in the other's notions of the world and the legitimacy that each denied the other made it so.

When the two took up arms in March 1969, the conflict over fundamental values faded from our view, disappearing entirely two years later with China's turn toward the Americans. The triangle that now replaced the bilateral confrontation would be every bit as dynamic as the original conflict, with equally dramatic effect on Soviet foreign policy. It arrived as a revolution. The rapprochement of the Soviet Union's great socialist adversary with its primary capitalist adversary cannot be thought of as anything less. Over the eighteen years after Henry Kissinger's secret mission to Beijing in 1971, the triangle underwent profound transformations, with each new phase shuddering through the whole of the Soviet Union's Asian policy.

Initially, unnerving as it was to Soviet leaders to see their two major foes talking together, and much as the state of relations among the three favored the Americans, Brezhnev and his colleagues were not particularly glum. Indeed, in the early days of détente, they were convinced that they, not the Chinese, would suffer less in the new triangle. And the Americans, well positioned though they were, would not, it was assumed, feel free to do their worst. Soviet leaders took it for granted that the Americans regarded them as more important and cherished the prospects of détente too much to ally with the Chinese against them. In fact, judging from Soviet efforts to rally the Americans against the Chinese under the pretense of curtailing countries capable of instigating a nuclear war, the Brezhnev leadership even believed it could turn the triangle to its own advantage. At a minimum, there are signs that Soviet leaders took Nixon and Kissinger at their word when they promised not to tilt toward China.

In less than half a decade, everything had changed. By 1978 détente was slowly disintegrating; Carter's national security advisor, Zbigniew Brzezinski, was on his way to Beijing; and the Americans, it seemed, were choosing the Chinese over the Soviets. No longer was it a matter of the Americans maneuvering deftly between the two Communist powers so as to increase their leverage with both. They were tilting toward China. Worse, by 1978, they were even talking of security cooperation with China—against whom was obvious. The triangle took on its most menacing form.

The years between 1978 and 1981 were the nadir of postwar Soviet policy in Asia. It was the period of greatest threat to the Soviet Union, of the Soviet Union's greatest isolation in the region, and of its lowest influence. The three problems were connected. It was the period of greatest threat because the Soviet Union's two main adversaries were not merely in contact but in collusion, exploring strategic collaboration in the wake of the Vietnamese invasion of Cambodia and the Soviet invasion of Afghanistan. No Soviet leader could be sure how deep and elaborate the cooperation might grow and how many others would be drawn into it, including most notably the Japanese. It was the period of greatest isolation because the Soviet Union had only the Vietnamese to turn to (beyond their satraps in Mongolia). In every other quarter they faced a growing mistrust and hostility, with the partial exception of the North Koreans, whose churlishness had remained constant over time. And it was the period when the gap between military power and influence was greatest because the Soviet Union was without access to the politics in the region, without alternatives to its military power, and without significant allies to counter the alignments forming against it.

In the early 1980s the kaleidoscope turned again, and the dynamic within the Sino-Soviet-American triangle shifted radically. A slow renormalization of Sino-Soviet relations began in 1982, reversing the free fall of tensions from 1969 to 1979. A year earlier the specter of Sino-American collusion began dissolving into a more constrained and halting cooperation. By January 1982 the innovative voice of Alexander Bovin was predicting that "as long as the Americans scare themselves with the 'Soviet threat,' they are going to be haunted by the nightmare of normalized Soviet-Chinese relations."[5] "The expediency on which Chinese-American relations are based," he was now ready to argue, "will sooner or later be eroded." By then Soviet diplomacy had already quickened. In March 1982 Brezhnev traveled to Tashkent to give a speech intended primarily for a Chinese audience. China was again reminded of who had the friendlier position on Taiwan now with Ronald Reagan in office and urged to focus on opportunities to improve relations rather than on past discontents; it was invited to resume border negotiations and to consider confidence-building measures; and it was assured that Soviet leaders no longer questioned its commitment to socialism.

Brezhnev did not live to see the flowering of these early initiatives. (The first formal contacts occurred only two months before his death in November 1982.) But the process of normalizing Sino-Soviet relations, begun in 1981–82, would be one of his more important legacies to Gorbachev. It was one of the few areas of Soviet foreign policy that Gorbachev applauded and would build upon. More specifically, Brezhnev and his feeble transitional successors achieved four things. First, for the first time in more than two decades, the conflict crested and tensions eased. Second, Soviet grounds for fearing a strategic partnership between the United States and China disappeared. (By the Twelfth Chinese Communist Party Congress, in September 1982, Hu Yaobang, Mao's successor, was stressing China's foreign policy independence and again condemning both "hegemonism" and "imperialism.")[6] Third, from 1982 to 1985 various forms of cooperation were either reinstituted or reinvigorated. Trade, for example, although launched from low level, increased sevenfold over these years. And, forth, the ideological impulse weakened to the extent that the two sides ceased to repudiate the other's very claim to legitimacy. Moreover, as one acute Chinese observer noted at the time, on many of the issues over which the two sides had quarreled bitterly in the 1950s and 1960s, by the 1980s the Chinese had "largely accepted the Soviets' views."[7] This was true, he said, on matters of "war and peace, nuclear weapons and the nature of international politics, the possibility of a peaceful transformation to 'socialism,' the nature of Soviet society, and the possibility of peaceful coexistence between capitalist and communist states."

JAPAN: THE SECOND TRIANGLE

Normally triangles are not thought of as a stable form in social or political relationships, nor as a stabilizing influence within a larger setting. The great postwar exception was the Soviet-U.S.-Japan triangle. In its essence it remained unchanged over nearly half a century. Notwithstanding the fluctuations in U.S.-Soviet and Soviet-Japanese relations and, from time to time, the tensions in U.S.-Japanese relations, the relationship among the three countries scarcely changed. Its immobility may have been the single most stabilizing element in postwar Asian politics.

The Soviet-Japanese-American triangle mattered for a second reason: It, as Peggy Falkenheim was the first to note, drove Soviet policy toward Japan.[8] Only late—indeed, not until the Gorbachev era—did Soviet leaders recognize Japan as significant in its own right. For most of the postwar period, they judged and dealt with Japan largely as a function of the U.S.-Japan relationship. Thus, while Soviet leaders from Khrushchev to Chernenko cared about bilateral Soviet-Japanese economic ties and contended with Japan on the bilateral matter of the Northern Territories, neither issue determined policy. Policy instead remained the creature of the American engagement in Asia and Japan's part in it.

Through these many decades, Soviet diplomacy toward Japan became active, whether to intimidate or to cajole, when something of interest to Moscow was happening in the U.S.-Japanese pairing. The Soviet line hardened and grew mean when the U.S.-Japanese security treaty was upgraded (in 1960–61) or when Japan's flirtation with China complemented America's (in 1977–78) or when Japan's course too closely followed the Reagan administration's (in the early 1980s). It softened when U.S.-Soviet relations markedly

improved and Soviet leaders began to hope for a similar easing to
tensions in Asia and in Soviet-Japanese relations (in 1972–73).
Otherwise Soviet policy toward Japan was remarkably impassive
and motionless.

The steadiness of this Soviet policy over twenty-five years
doubtless reflected the underlying stability that Soviet observers attributed to the U.S.-Japan relationship. Nothing was more striking
than the unswerving reluctance of Soviet commentators to believe
in the possibility that things could fall apart between Washington
and Tokyo. In comparison with Soviet views of the potential for
trouble in U.S.–West European relations, the contrast was overwhelming. Specialists dutifully, and even with some interest, noted
moments of rising tension in the relationship. By the early 1980s
they paid attention to Japan's growing self-confidence and inclination to play a more assertive role in Asia and beyond. Always
in the end, however, they came back to the durability of the
U.S.-Japanese partnership.

Take, for example, Soviet treatment of the frictions in U.S.-
Japanese relations in the mid-1980s. Soviet writers missed no
chance to catalog the many signs of impatience and resentment
building within the two societies in particular over trade problems.
At the same time, while the Congress and parts of the administration bluster and fume, they said ultimately that American leaders
would refuse to act, first, for "fear of retaliatory trade and political measures," but, second and more important, because of an "unwillingness to weaken the military-political alliance of the two
countries, Japan playing a special part in American military-
political strategy."[9] Even Alexander Yakovlev, who before his
emergence as one of the architects of Gorbachev's new foreign policy had the reputation of believing in the cleavages within the "imperialist camp," laughed when asked whether U.S.-Japanese rivalry
would "inevitably rupture the common security interest."[10]

Inevitably the fact that the ultimate Soviet judgment changed
so little over a quarter century meant that neither did Soviet policy. In the end, Soviet leaders viewed Japanese orientation, particularly on East-West issues, as an adjunct of U.S. policy. Even when
the Japanese were acknowledged to have ambitions, it was not—
quite unlike Soviet hopes for the West Europeans—to steer a sep-

arate course or to exert influence on U.S. policy. Rather it was to do well by themselves by making themselves indispensable to the Americans; to expand Japanese influence and the Japanese role by operating within the American strategic design.

The other dimension of Japanese policy that mattered to the Soviet Union, of course, was Japan's relationship with China. Here too the Soviet approach remained fixed over a long period of time. Since Soviet leaders knew that Japan would not be drawn to the Soviet side in the Sino-Soviet conflict, they focused on second-order possibilities, such as doing what they could to keep the Japanese from leaning too far toward China. For a time in the mid-1970s, when the Sino-Japanese friendship treaty was under discussion, this became an overweening concern, and over two or three years Soviet diplomacy resorted to a host of appeals and threats to dissuade the Japanese from going ahead with the agreement, particularly one containing the so-called antihegemony clause, China's code word for Soviet expansionism. After summer 1978, when the treaty was concluded, Soviet leaders came to have few expectations and fewer fears. As there was no prospect of dramatic shifts in the Sino-Japanese relationship, for better or worse, Soviet leaders down to Gorbachev's day saw little incentive to reconsider their own calcified policy toward Japan.

THE MILITARY DIMENSION

There was another peculiar structural feature of the Soviet engagement in East Asia. Historically the Soviet Union was militarily, but not economically, a part of the region. As a result, the Soviet Union had only a security, not a foreign, policy in East Asia. Because this was the condition or, in truth, the plight of the Soviet Union in Asia, the region occupied a distinctly secondary place in overall postwar Soviet foreign policy.

Asia's comparative inferiority among Soviet preoccupations had two reasons: first, the mutual irrelevance of each for the other in the economic realm. Expressed more concretely, trade with Asia, was normally no more than 6 percent of all Soviet trade, and all trade was no more than 12 percent of Soviet gross national product. Of that 6 percent, nearly 50 percent was with Japan, and with Japan trade trends were downward after the late 1970s.

True, these negligible sums concealed a certain dynamism: From the mid-1960s through the 1970s, the Soviet Union broke out of the ghetto of socialist trade, where 85 percent of its economic activity in the Asia-Pacific and region had been—helped by the collapse of Sino-Soviet ties after 1960—and launched a promising economic engagement with Japan. Notwithstanding its insignificance in the overall scheme of things, Soviet trade with Japan grew nearly eightfold between 1965 and 1978 (from $326 million to $2.3 billion). Still, what counted most is the contribution to the whole, and, on that score, East Asia hardly mattered to Soviet leaders.

The second reason for the secondary importance of East Asia to the Soviet Union is less obvious. It had to do with the way Soviet military and political leaders thought about war in the postwar era. For them war was to be primarily, ultimately, and decisively a European matter. Europe, not Asia, inspired basic Soviet approaches to the acquisition, deployment, and planned use of military forces. When Asia intruded on this bias in the late 1960s as a consequence of armed clashes with the Chinese and the subsequent buildup of Soviet ground forces on the Sino-Soviet border, Soviet leaders simply added an Asian front to European war. Even that, at the outset, was basically a bilateral affair between the Soviet Union and China, not a regional one involving Japan and the United States.

Soon after the doubling of Soviet army divisions in East Asia from 1969 to 1972, another bilateral threat appeared: With the deployment of a new generation of U.S. and Soviet strategic nuclear submarines to the Pacific, Asia became part of the nuclear balance between the superpowers. The arrival of submarines bearing ballistic missiles with vastly greater ranges—ranges permitting them, in the American case, to roam entire oceans and, in the Soviet case, to fire on the United States from Soviet shores—led to an adjustment of Soviet strategy. This, in turn, created new requirements for Soviet forces in Asia. Briefly, the Soviet decision to deploy its new submarines in secure neighboring sea "bastions," such as the Sea of Okhotsk, compelled Soviet military planners to fashion forces, particularly naval forces, capable of keeping U.S. antisubmarine forces at arm's length. And this in turn put Soviet control of the Northern Territories, the islands claimed by Japan, in a new light. Notwithstanding Brezhnev's seeming flexibility during Japanese prime minister Tanaka's 1973 visit to Moscow on the Northern Territories issue, by then something fundamental had intervened: The Soviet military had acquired a direct stake in what happened to the islands.

Both the Soviet buildup of ground forces in Asia and the transformation of its nuclear posture in Asia had separate impulses, reflecting the geostrategic realities of the day. China inspired one development and the United States the other, but each represented a separate challenge, until the two came together in the 1970s. By the late 1970s, in response, the Soviet Union had modernized its naval, air, ground, and theater nuclear forces in ways designed to cope with an integral Chinese and U.S.-Japanese threat, a threat enhanced by the post-1978 growth in U.S. and Japanese security cooperation. Then in 1978 the Soviet Union created an integrated Far Eastern command to manage such a war.

In the 1980s the Soviet military added still another dimension. Presented with the opportunity, they eagerly extended their air and naval forces into Southeast Asia. At one level, although hardly overwhelming, the creation of a semipermanent Soviet military presence in Indochina gave the Soviet Union a chance to outflank the Chinese, Americans, and Japanese. Even when understood as a fortified coaling station and reconnaissance base—not as infrastructure for threatening the West's control of the seas—Soviet aircraft, ships, and submarines at Danang and Camranh Bay further shifted the contours of a complicated military balance. Politics, geography, and military power were flowing together in ever more intricate and elaborate ways.

THE GORBACHEV FOREIGN POLICY REVOLUTION

The collapse of the Soviet Union has so radically altered the face of international politics in East Asia that we forget we reached this point in two giant steps. The first of these was a profound revolution in Soviet foreign policy carried out by Gorbachev, Eduard

Shevardnadze, Alexander Yakovlev, and others around them. Because of what they wrought, had the Soviet state remained intact and perestroika alive, the international setting in East Asia still would have undergone far-reaching change; indeed, it already had long before the August 1991 coup d'état ushered in the end of the Soviet Union.

In the six years he was in power, Gorbachev fundamentally revised the three central features of postwar Soviet policy in East Asia. First, he freed it from the albatross of the Sino-Soviet conflict. Second, by suppressing the dominating idea of the East-West contest, he shifted the foundation of Soviet policy toward Japan. And, third, he began the process of demilitarizing policy and broadening its base by featuring his country's economic stake in relations with East Asian states.

Gorbachev was the first Soviet leader to understand and acknowledge East Asia's emerging importance in the larger international setting. He was the first to recognize that the economic dynamism of this region made it no less important to the Soviet Union than Europe, historically the focal point of Soviet foreign policy. Any area accounting for nearly a quarter of the world's gross product (WGP), whose share of WGP had grown by 30 percent or more each of the last three decades, and whose volume of exports measured in dollars had increased by nearly 20 percent every year for the last twenty years was sure to matter. Gorbachev knew that if his country was to rectify the fundamental deformations in its foreign policy and to find sustenance for perestroika from other nations, the Soviet approach to East Asia would have to change.

What followed in the years after his rise to power may have been less spectacular than the revision in U.S.–Soviet relations or the stunning turn of events in Europe, but the implications for the region were no less portentous. Before the end came, he had largely removed the Soviet Union as a military behemoth, preoccupied with a narrowly conceived security agenda, increasingly isolated within the region, and increasingly irrelevant to the key processes under way. He substituted a country seeking equitable solutions to unresolved problems with Asian neighbors, ready to build national security on the basis of mutual security, and eager to be a part of the dynamism within the region.

The prerequisite for all of this was an end to the quarrel with China. Brezhnev had begun the movement toward a normalization of Sino-Soviet relations in 1982, but neither he nor his infirm successors could bring themselves to address squarely the three issues at the heart of Chinese discontent: the massing of Soviet military power on China's northern border, the Soviet invasion of Afghanistan, and, most important, Moscow's part in Vietnam's prosecution of the war in Cambodia. Between 1987 and his arrival in Beijing for the May 1989 summit, Gorbachev gave the Chinese satisfaction on all three.

Notwithstanding Chinese distress over the demise of socialism in Eastern Europe in 1989 and the role attributed by them to his reforms, Gorbachev succeeded in putting Sino-Soviet relations on a fundamentally different footing. As a consequence, no longer did China stand as a massively distorting focus of Soviet policy in East Asia. No longer was it the inspiration for the self-absorbed and counterproductive approach of the Brezhnev years, an approach contaminating all of Soviet policy in the region. No longer did China sustain Moscow's preoccupation with the quantity and quality of arms in the region.

On the way to ending the Sino-Soviet conflict, Gorbachev also largely did away with the significance of the Sino-Soviet-U.S. triangle. Here too a major adjustment in Soviet thinking was necessary. Until then Soviet leaders approached the issue only in zero-sum terms. Over the years they had assigned greater malevolence sometimes to the Chinese, sometimes to the Americans, but always the relationship between China and the United States was perceived as menacing Soviet interests. Even under Reagan, despite U.S.-Chinese frictions over Taiwan, Soviet analysts continued to worry about the determination of the Americans to conspire with the Chinese against their country. As late as the signing of the Intermediate Nuclear Forces (INF) treaty (1987) and the first substantial easing of East-West tension in Europe, the Soviet Union's leading specialist on U.S. China policy still insisted that Washington sought a "significant strengthening of confrontation" in Asia, that it had long ago passed from a policy of "passive 'containment'" to a "policy of actively confronting revolutionary forces, especially the Soviet Union."[11]

But by 1989 prominent voices were taking a entirely different line. As one wrote: "What is perhaps a most characteristic 'outward' feature of Sino-U.S. relations in the latter half of the 1980's is that their normal course is quite compatible with the general improvement of relations between the USSR, China, and the United States."[12] From this came a radically different appraisal of U.S.-Chinese relations. The Americans, according to a newfound Soviet equanimity, had no reason to fear the emerging Sino-Soviet détente. First, Washington knew that neither China nor the Soviet Union intended to revive the partnership of the 1950s.[13] Second, because the United States was so much stronger militarily, the Americans needed the Chinese less. Third, U.S. leaders, like Soviet leaders, now realized that a zero-sum approach to the triangle was a mistake. And, fourth, U.S. leaders understood that pressuring the Chinese in order to block an improvement in Sino-Soviet relations would only be counterproductive.

Gorbachev did much more than liberate Soviet policy from the impediments of the Sino-Soviet conflict. He also freed it from the crude requirements of the East-West conflict. In this instance, the change went to the core of Soviet foreign policy, for Gorbachev and his team were not simply seeking ways to ease existing tensions and to introduce a new period of East-West détente. They were determined to cut policy free from the dead weight of old and encrusted Soviet notions. By letting go of such concepts as class struggle and emphasizing instead the interdependence among nations, they meant not merely to soften the East-West conflict; they meant to end it. In the process they altered premises underpinning long-standing Soviet assessments of Japanese foreign policy and ties with the United States.

This, in turn, opened the way to a basically different dynamic in international relations in East Asia. Most in the West were slow to realize it, but by 1988 or 1989 the Gorbachev leadership, having begun to shed traditional Soviet notions of threat and consciously to rethink what Soviet writers called the "enemy image," had set about to reverse the military dynamic in Northeast Asia. The conversations that Shevardnadze launched with the Chinese and eventually the Japanese over security in the region were genuine. His government was prepared to build a different security "regime" in the area, based on restructured and scaled-down forces. It was prepared to yield to the concerns of Japan and the United States, provided they reciprocated in some fashion.

In seeking to escape the lingering hold of the Cold War, Gorbachev and his colleagues were moved by more than a desire to discard burdens that they could no longer bear, although this was reason enough. They also wanted to engage their country in the economic life of the most dynamic region in the world. Weighed down by the prejudices and approaches of the past, their country, they knew, would remain on the sidelines.

Doubtless they were naive in their expectations. The obstacles to integrating the Soviet Union into East Asia's economy stemmed from more than wrong-headed past political actions; they were ultimately economic and could be overcome only by reforming the Soviet economy. Trade and direct foreign investment might be enhanced marginally in the meantime, but, in the end, the transformation of ineffective domestic economic structure was a prerequisite for elaborate economic relations with Asia's most vibrant economies, not the other way around.

The odds against a swift and sizable Soviet entry into the economy of the region were enormous, far larger than Gorbachev understood. His initial sally, a formal government statement published in *Pravda* and *Izvestiya,* on April 24, 1986, high-handedly dismissed talk of a Pacific Basin Community focused on Japan, the United States, and the other thriving market economies of the region and bravely presented the Soviet Union as a crucial part of the region's economic future.[14]

Three years later his bold claims already seemed a fantasy. The Soviet Far East, whose rapid development was to lead the country's entry into the Asian market, lagged behind the rest of the Soviet economy, as it had for the previous two decades. Worse, the entire Soviet economy was sliding helplessly into a deep economic crisis. Despite a handful of Japanese joint ventures and the opening wedge of trade with South Korea, almost nothing had happened to justify the bravado of 1986. The Soviet Union continued to run a trade deficit with Japan. (It grew from 234 million rubles in 1971–75 to 3.6 billion rubles in 1976–80, to 7.5 billion rubles in 1981–85, climbing still higher in the first two years under

Gorbachev.)[15] Moreover, Soviet observers were all too aware that, as Japanese industry introduced energy- and resource-conserving measures and Soviet exports to Japan continued to drop, prospects in Soviet-Japanese trade were not bright. Moreover, to make matters worse, in the 1980s the structure of the Japanese economy had shifted from "hard" goods production to "soft" activities, such as services and information processing, leading to an increasing share of finished goods among Japanese imports, a market Soviet exporters would find tougher yet to master.[16]

By 1989 Soviets talked of their country's role in Asian economic development in somber and restrained terms.[17] They openly admitted that the long-term development plan for the Far Eastern Economic Region had largely gone the way of the 1967 and 1972 commitments.[18] They acknowledged that it would "be rather difficult to get a foothold in Asia Pacific Region markets with our fuel and raw materials, and even with semi-finished goods (let alone finished, high-tech products), since there are in the region major highly competitive suppliers of such commodities."[19] They noted sensibly that direct investment had become the core of economic activity in the Asia-Pacific region, replacing simple export-import trade and ensuring that "no nation" could be "a full-fledged member of the new Pacific structure by merely boosting its exports quantitatively," more reason to think small if you were the Soviet Union.[20] Some, in what would seem to be a counsel of despair, argued that priority should be given to developing economic ties with Asia's socialist countries. In particular, they urged that these countries be thought of as an alternative source of consumer manufactures, created from Soviet raw materials and substituted for the deficient production of enterprises from the European parts of the Soviet Union.

Had this been the end of the story, had the Gorbachev era continued, East Asia would have been forever changed. The Strategic Quadrangle would have assumed a fundamentally different character. The challenges facing U.S. policy would have shifted no less. Viewed at the most basic level, Gorbachev's foreign policy revolution produced four vastly important effects. First, by altering Soviet priorities and by changing with whom and for what reason the Soviet Union would compete, Gorbachev brought to an end the pernicious geometry of the previous three decades. Triangles, by definition, are inherently tension-filled; they are tripolarity with built-in antagonism. Until Gorbachev, the Strategic Quadrangle was, in fact, two—perhaps three—triangles. He ended that—at least he terminated the two triangles in which the Soviet Union had a part.

Second, by walking away from traditional Soviet biases that ultimately left East and West unbridgeably divided, Gorbachev introduced an entirely different range of possibilities into Soviet relations with the United States and Japan. Nothing, after his innovations, said that these three countries must at the end of the day compete, that they could not in fact undertake a radically different range of collaborations—whether to quell ongoing regional conflicts and preclude new ones, or to fashion multilateral institutions addressed to the needs of the area, or to conspire in impeding nuclear proliferation and the traffic in high-tech weaponry.

Third, by rethinking the place of military power in Soviet foreign policy and beginning to revamp his country's prevailing defense posture, Gorbachev thoroughly reordered—at a minimum, thoroughly challenged—a critical guide of postwar Japanese, American, and Chinese policy in East Asia. Although full acceptance of the fact arrived slowly for understandably prudent reasons, with each new concession, Gorbachev removed bricks from the understructure of the U.S.-Japanese security partnership, the ramified outline of the U.S. military presence in Asia, and the reasons for the United States and China to set aside natural differences. The inertia of prior Soviet defense decisions and of entrenched U.S. and Japanese views delayed the effect, but, in truth, the entire military-strategic edifice in Asia was about to undergo wholesale change.

And, fourth, Gorbachev presented Japan, the United States, and other Asian states, such as South Korea, with the need to engage the Soviet Union. Initially the problem emerged as a question of how soon and how far these erstwhile adversaries should go in underwriting the process of perestroika. Given the very different state of the *bilateral* stakes in U.S.-Soviet versus Japanese-Soviet relations, the issue always threatened to distance Tokyo from Washington and the other capitals of the West. Beyond it, however, loomed the larger but concealed issue of how an economically backward and struggling state was to be integrated into the diplomatic and economic life of East Asia. Were the Japanese, Americans, and others to wait for the successful conclusion of perestroika or the revitalization of the Soviet economy before addressing the issue of a new role for the Soviet Union in the region, they would lose their chance to help influence the process of change. For these four reasons, the Gorbachev era deserves to be thought of as a separate historic stage in the evolution of the postwar East Asia order.

RUSSIA, CENTRAL ASIA, AND A POST-SOVIET EAST ASIA

The second giant step in the radical reordering of Asian international politics began when Gorbachev's time ran out. In December 1991 a single, cohesive state—indeed, a once-mighty superpower—disintegrated into an amorphous, potentially turbulent cluster of would-be states. The physical core of Eurasia, which after all is what the Russian empire was, dissolved into fifteen fragments, each of them left to struggle with the ruins of the old order, with the task of creating stable new political and economic systems, and with the wholly unanticipated need to manage relations among themselves as sovereign, independent states.

To most of the states of East Asia except China, this will seem an unusually dramatic way to put the issue. For them, particularly Japan, the change seems more modest, primarily because their focus remains Russia. The Soviet Union's large physical presence was for them always Russian. Russia still possesses nearly all of the resources of interest to them. Russia holds the key to solving large left-over issues, such as the Northern Territories dispute and the military competition in Northeast Asia. Hence, for them, unlike the Europeans, the collapse of the Soviet Union has not given rise to an entirely new landscape.

While Russia, in fact, is the centerpiece for these East Asian states—even more so than for the Europeans—to reduce the issue to it alone gravely miscalculates the post-Soviet challenge in the region. Within the Strategic Quadrangle Russia has replaced the Soviet Union, but it comes as a country vastly different on the inside and no less so on the outside. This radical revision of Russia's surroundings not only profoundly affects Russian foreign policy and, therefore, indirectly affects East Asia, but it directly affects East Asia because of the new, intervening reality of Central Asia. Thus, to understand Russia's part in the Strategic Quadrangle, Russia's place and preoccupations amid the shards of a shattered Soviet empire must be factored in.

Had Russia followed the course that its liberal foreign minister and perhaps its president initially had in mind, the consequences from the collapse of the Soviet Union would have been even greater. Long before the collapse of the Soviet Union, Andrei Kozyrev, Yeltsin's pick as the Russian Republic's foreign minister in 1990, began moving in a radically new direction. Soon after the abortive putsch of August 1991 and four months before Russian independence, he made plain his determination to deliver his country squarely into the Western world. Apparently with Yeltsin's blessing, he meant to make Russia not merely a country on good terms with the major powers of the West, but literally their ally.

In his day Gorbachev sought a dramatically improved relationship with the United States and its Western partners. He worked to end the crude hostility of the past and to substitute more cooperation, reflecting a less Manichean notion of international politics; and he even spoke of partnership with the major industrialized powers of the West in attacking a variety of global problems affecting all societies. But he never embraced the West. He spoke of common human values and of the great contribution made to civilization by other countries' histories, contributions such as the French and American revolutions. But he always thought of the Soviet contribution—including the Bolshevik revolution—as unique and large, and, because of it, he saw his own country as distinct from and, at some level, in peaceful competition with the capitalist states of the West.

Yeltsin and Kozyrev began by wanting their country to be of the West. They, unlike Gorbachev, had turned their back on Soviet values and, as thoroughly as their understanding permitted, embraced those of the West. They fully intended their country to be a part of the industrialized democratic world as much as Germany or Japan was. Thus, when Yeltsin and Kozyrev spoke of returning

Russia to the universe of "civilized nations," as they so often did in the early months, they were doing more than pledging in general terms to emulate the political and economic institutions of the West; they were announcing their intention to be accepted by these countries as one of them, as a working partner in the international arena, even as a fit member of their organizations.

Had this come to pass, all of world politics, including the dynamic within East Asia, would have been deeply affected. First, talk of a strategic alliance from Vancouver to Tokyo might have turned out to be less empty. As early as November 1991 in a presentation to the International Institute Strategic Studies in London, Kozyrev called for the states of the "northern hemisphere" to form a political and military union. Yeltsin himself spoke of a "democratic zone of trust, cooperation, and security," forming "across the northern hemisphere."[21] Mere talk, of course, would not have brought this about, but tangible movement forward would have put several of East Asia's major strategic issues in a rather different light. Balancing the rise of Chinese power, for example, would been easier, or, at least, the prospects would have seemed better for those who worried about a day when this might be necessary. Containing nationalist pressures within Russia itself and the threat they raise to stability in the region of the former Soviet Union would have been less difficult. And mobilizing decisive weight to cope with local Asian conflicts and fractious regional powers would have been more feasible.

Second, had the initial Yeltsin/Kozyrev inspiration endured, the Russo-Chinese relationship might well have followed a decidedly different path. By choosing the West so emphatically, Kozyrev clearly meant to choose against socialism. The Chinese had been angered and frustrated by Gorbachev because perestroika allowed socialism to perish in Eastern Europe and, in the end, destroyed socialism in the Soviet Union, but Gorbachev was not seen as an enemy of Chinese values.[22] He may have been inept—by Beijing's light, disastrously so—but he was not antisocialist. Ironically, considering the long years over which Mao taunted Gorbachev's predecessors for ideological heresy, at last in Yeltsin and Kozyrev Russia had leaders who were truly antisocialist, who truly wished to be part of a world abhorred by the current leaders of China.

Had Yeltsin and Kozyrev been able to complete what they started, Russo-Chinese relations would have been different because Russian priorities would have been different. Not that the two men wanted anything other than calm and civil relations with Beijing, but their Euro-Atlantic preoccupation caused them to look beyond the Chinese. More than that, it led them to emphases troubling to the Chinese. China's leaders found it difficult to swallow U.S. criticism on human rights abuse within their country. When the Russian foreign minister lectured them on the same theme, as he did on his March 1992 visit to Beijing, the instruction was nearly unbearable.[23] But Kozyrev lectured them, because he believed his own country's democratic choice was at stake and because his priority was to act like the state he aspired for Russia to be.

Third, Russia's initial quest held profound implications for relations with Japan. To be aligned with the West meant alignment with Japan, and that could scarcely have happened had the relationship continued as it was.[24] Important changes in Soviet policy toward Japan had been in the works in the Gorbachev era, changes pointing in the direction of a productive détente. But the Soviet Union of Gorbachev and Shevardnadze, while no longer preoccupied with the U.S.-Japanese security partnership and no longer interested in bullying the Japanese with its military power, nonetheless was scarcely ready to make common cause with Japan or to treat the U.S.-Japanese security tie as a necessary and constructive feature of East Asian politics.[25]

The Russia of Yeltsin and Kozyrev was. To move ahead, however, Russian leaders knew that the problem of the disputed islands would have to be put behind them. Initially in the weeks after the failed August coup d'état, the Russians seemed to be moving rapidly to achieve a breakthrough—one largely on Japanese terms. In a flurry of diplomatic activity and public statements they signaled a readiness to make the necessary concessions.[26] They expressly repudiated the Soviet notion that the islands belonged to the Soviet Union as the spoils of war. From the moment of Ruslan Khasbulatov's visit to Japan two weeks after the putsch—Khasbulatov at the time was a loyal representative of Yeltsin—they stressed that the issue must be dealt with in a way respecting international law and justice. They reinstalled the validity of the 1956 Joint Declaration offering to return Shikotan and the Habomais, two of the islands, on the conclusion of a peace treaty. Some even blurted out that all four islands should be simply handed over.[27]

The general impulse, however, did not last. By March and April 1992, scarcely three months after Russian independence, the ground began to crumble under Kozyrev and, by extension, his president. With the rise of a domestic opposition, focused first and primarily on the radical economic program of the Yeltsin government, foreign policy soon became a target as well. The roots doubtless lay in the delayed shock and anger over the collapse of Soviet power and Russian pride, but the frustration manifested itself in a growing assault on Yeltsin and Kozyrev's priorities (seen as wrongly reversed, with the world coming first and Russia's maddening new neighbors second) and on their predilections (seen as an undignified and even counterproductive kowtowing to the West).

Already by the time Kozyrev had his second meeting with Japan's foreign minister, Michio Watanabe, in March 1992, he was backpedaling from his earlier concessions on the territorial issue.[28] This was happening as part of a slow reorientation of Russian foreign policy overall. By late spring talk of Russia's role in a strategic alliance from Vancouver to Tokyo disappeared entirely. While the Russians, under Kozyrev's influence, continued to cooperate with the United States and Western Europe on most matters, they stopped describing their country as an aspiring member of the Western club and shifted their focus from the broader setting to the new states on their borders. Adding to the effect of Yeltsin and Kozyrev's own evolution, many other players began to get into the act, particularly parliamentarians, inevitably making some of these shifts appear sharper still. How much had changed became evident when Yeltsin arrived in India in January 1993. "We need to maintain a balance in our foreign policy relations with the West and the East," he proclaimed to the Indian Parliament.[29] His visits to South Korea, China, and India, he said, "are indicative of the fact that we are moving away from a Western emphasis."[30]

One specific and one basic consequence followed. As for the former, Kozyrev's initial inchoate but dramatically revised set of priorities simply went out the window. Had Russia continued as it began in fall 1991, Japan would have emerged as the first priority of policy. China, historically the centerpiece of Soviet policy in post-war East Asia, would have fallen to a lesser rank. Given its size and proximity, Russian leaders could scarcely have disregarded China or failed to pursue the normalization of relations advanced by Gorbachev. But Japan would have been the focus of Russia's political energy, the primary source of its hopes, its critical partner in effecting a new role for Russia in the region, and the key East Asian piece in its reconceptualization of international politics. For much the same reason, Russia's choice of South Korea over North Korea would have had the deeper context of a pro-Western and Japan-centric East Asian policy, rather than simple economic expediency.

Instead Russia's priorities in East Asia have turned out to be very different. Ironically China is back where it was for much of the last half century, at the top of the list. Far from the afterthought China was originally scheduled to be, the lion's share of Russia's diplomacy in Asia is directed toward it. China has become its most important economic partner in East Asia. The $7.7 billion in bilateral trade in 1993 is nearly 30 percent larger than in 1992, which was, in turn, more than 50 percent greater than the entire Soviet Union's trade with China in 1991, that at a time when overall Russian trade had fallen 17 percent from 1992.[31] It is, among a dwindling set of prospects, the most promising market for Russian arms exports. Russia's most important negotiations (on arms and borders) are with China. And it looms ever larger in Russia's strategic calculations, a point to which I will return. Meanwhile, the ongoing stalemate in relations between Moscow and Tokyo has left this potentially vital relationship loitering at the edges of each country's foreign policy. In the process, Russian relations with South Korea have lost a good deal of their larger political rationale and stutter on, largely according to the ups and downs (mostly downs) of their economic potential.

Second, and more basic, when Russia's uncritical pro-Western option evaporated, the deep contradictions in the country's circumstance stood starkly exposed, contradictions that are especially important to Russia's position in East Asia. Indeed, at the core of Russia's relationship with East Asia reside three sets of contradictions: first, in terms of Russia's basic identity; second, in its fundamental interests; and, third, in its strategic choices.

As Sergei Karaganov stated so well, "While making Russia less European geographically and economically, the disintegration of the USSR made it more European culturally and politically.[32] Karaganov refers, of course, to the physical barrier now separating Russia from Europe, save for Kaliningrad, the pencil point on the Polish border, and the narrow, far-northern reaches where Russia touches Norway, and yet, at the same time, the diminished Asian-ness of the Russian empire since losing Central Asia. Kozyrev's original commitment to the West, at some level, was meant to cir-cumvent this altered reality by rushing past it. He failed, however, as perhaps he had to, and, as a consequence, left the country to struggle with its confused identity. At once both European and Asian, yet in many respects neither, the country is more than ever divided between those who cling to a vision of Russia with and of the West—albeit by a path more uniquely Russian than imagined by Kozyrev and other liberals—and those who doubt that Russia's destiny can be anything other than apart from both Europe and Asia. The moderate version of the second view proposes Russia as a bridge between the two continents, but separate from both. The less moderate, conservative, and nationalist version is consumed with the uniqueness of Russia and usually also with the need to re-pudiate the influence of the West and to find a great power, even imperial, vocation of its own.[33]

In its basic interests, too, Russia is far more torn than its pre-decessor. For the first time in nearly three hundred years, the sole region of the world in which Russia has a physical presence is East Asia. No longer does it border South Asia, the Balkans, or Europe. Added to this, for the first time in many years—perhaps since 1917, certainly since the start of the Cold War—Russia has a chance to participate in East Asian affairs as an acceptable, unestranged member of the community. And Russia has substantial interests in the region, indeed, arguably greater interests than the Soviet Union had. Its economic stakes are higher. And so are its strategic stakes, considering the needs, the vulnerabilities, and the pressures on and from the Russian Far East. Yet on most days Russian attention never reaches East Asia, never reaches beyond Central Asia.

For Moscow Asia is overwhelmingly Central Asia. At the moment, to care about what is happening in the greater region would seem to most Russian politicians and policymakers a luxury alongside the immediate, preoccupying concerns raised by the new states to the south. The *Soviet Union*'s Asian security agenda, whose focus divided entirely between China and the U.S.-Japan connection, while not wholly abandoned, has for the new Russia shifted dramatically toward Central Asia. This increases China's importance to Russia among the East Asian states, for only China figures in the uncertainties and challenges of this area. This recasting of Russian interests, however, also draws Russian eyes away from East Asia and still farther south to the volatile regions directly below Central Asia. Nothing makes the point more sharply than to say, as several Russian commentators have, that for now Russia's most important ally in Asia is Kazakhstan. Not only is it formally allied with this country by a 1992 treaty, having taken on the role of Kazakhstan's nuclear protector—not unlike the United States with Japan—but Russia also cares more about internal developments within Kazakhstan and the evolution of its international relations (particularly with China) than about those of any other Asia state, including China.[34]

The third interlinked set of contradictions arises among Russia's strategic choices. Logic suggests—and knowledgeable Russians see—that Russia must find its security in East Asia as part of a larger security regime. Unlike the Soviet Union, it is not strong enough to guarantee by itself its long-term security against either the hazards of instability in the region or the potential threat inherent in the rise of other major Asian powers. Russia, as most Russian policymakers understand, needs to work with others in controlling crises and balancing the growing power of both China and Japan. Yet the only existing security regime in the region is dominated by the United States, and joining it means becoming a junior partner of the Americans. While many among the policy elites grudgingly—and a few, not so grudgingly—accept this fact of life, they are bound to cast about for various alternative schemes at least superficially less dominated by the United States. Within this contradiction resides another: For all but a hopelessly unreconstructed nationalist fringe, the U.S. presence in East Asia has become not merely acceptable but essential. Like other nations in Asia, the Russians view the U.S. role in the region as an indispensable source of stability, a constraint on Japanese militarization, and a further counterbalance to Chinese military power. Yet, at the same time, the Russian military in particular continues to construe U.S. military resources in the region as part of the threat.

These three conflicted dimensions form the backdrop to the new Russian part in the Strategic Quadrangle. Seen from the outside, however—that is, from the vantage point of the other three states in the quadrangle—the Russian part is different for other equally profound reasons. They bring us back to where we started, back to a vision of the future where the threat is not of (general) war but of diminished national and international welfare, not to peace but to prosperity.

Instead of worrying about what the Soviet Union might do to its neighbors, Washington, Tokyo, and the other capitals of the West, even before the Soviet Union collapsed, began to contemplate the dangers for them should Gorbachev's perestroika fail, particularly if its demise produced great internal instability or a retreat to authoritarianism. A fundamental shift from traditional security concerns, therefore, predated the end of the Soviet Union, but when the end came, the shift accelerated, speeding across an important threshold. Nations, including those in East Asia, crossed into a world in which they had more to fear from dangers than enemies—the dangers of political, economic, and ecological disorder. The primary stakes ceased to be security and became welfare—no longer war and peace, but the vitality of societies and the dynamism of economies. Commentators often speak of the changing nature of security, pointing to the new perils raised by trade conflicts, global warming, population pressures, and the like. Threats these are, but they menace the well-being of nations rather than their territorial integrity or political independence.

If this world begins to seem no less threatening, the reason is the former Soviet Union. Freed from the menace of general war, whatever its other forms of pain and trouble, the world should be a less perilous place, but the scale of malign influence possible in the post-Soviet region may not make it so. The problem starts from the fact that the former republics of the Soviet Union constitute, as said earlier, the physical core of Eurasia. These fifteen new states are potentially either a bridge between East Asia and Europe or a vortex, generating powerful forms of instability that could threaten the tranquility and prosperity of neighboring regions. This is particularly so because the core is surrounded by a collar of states, from North Korea to Poland, that are themselves potentially unstable and, therefore, more likely to transmit turmoil and crises within the former Soviet Union to the world beyond than to contain them. And between this collar of states and Russia is a new inner rimland—Central Asia, Transcaucasia, and Moldova—plagued with violent conflicts capable of creating friction points all along the outer rimland.

Second, the breakup of the Soviet Union has given particular force to Robert Scalapino's perceptive formulation: "The competition among localism, nationalism, regionalism, and globalism will be the epic drama of the coming decades."[35] It is the new states of the former Soviet Union that provide the most immediate and deadly illustrations of the most destructive of these "isms." Localism refers to ethnic and religious rivalry within the state, to which Russia and several other post-Soviet states add economic fragmentation, both of which contribute to the disintegration of the nation-state and bring intense instability. Nationalism, an essential and inevitable part of nation-building, which is one of the key tasks facing the new post-Soviet states—including Russia—has its dark and pathological side, and this other form already lurks in each state. Regionalism gone awry becomes exclusionary and discriminatory, adding to tensions in international relations; again, in the variety of incipient collaborations within the former Soviet Union, the threat is present. The successor states are scarcely the only place where the drama Scalapino describes applies, but they are its most concrete and comprehensive reflection.

Or, to borrow another more dramatic translation of Scalapino's list, Pierre Hassner describes a world with impotent nation-states, bypassed by the force of tribal passions, a world without effective arbiters, national or international, an environment tying everyone's fate closer together yet tolerating ever more selfish and self-centered behavior.[36] If the coming international order takes on many of the properties of the Middle Ages, a possibility Hassner raises, it will be because malignant parts impinge on other parts, such as the European Union, where cooperation and

; social and cultural ties until now have held the forces of
l, disorder, and animosity in check. Few parts of the world
appear to have such a powerful negative potential, but
suici, the states of the former Soviet Union are one.

RUSSIA AND CHINA

None of the other states in the Strategic Quadrangle finds itself
more under the shadow of this reality than China. Indeed, China
more than the others faces potentially the worst of two worlds.
Russia remains a military colossus to the north, still sharing a
lengthy border. Chinese foreign minister Qian Qichen, soon after
the failed coup d'état of August 1991, reportedly characterized
Yeltsin as a nationalist, capable of reviving "Great Russian chau-
vinism" and even of turning the country into "Tsarist Russia."[37]
Yet at the same time, China also has quite visibly worried about
the impact of developments in the new Central Asian states on its
own unsettled borderlands. In his April 1992 review of Chinese
foreign policy, Nicholas Kristof writes of Chinese nervousness over
the danger of rising nationalist movements in Xinjiang and Inner
Mongolia and the fear that they may be aided by Uygurs, Mongols,
and other kinsmen across the border.[38] News in July 1992 that a
party named "For a Free Uygurstan" had been founded at a congress held near the capital of Kyrgyzstan with the aim of fighting
for an independent state in Xinjiang province could not have been
welcome. And the Hong Kong press has carried stories that in the
last months of 1991, Beijing began moving large numbers of Han
Chinese farmers and forestry workers to areas along the border
with Kazakhstan and Kyrgyzstan.[39]

For the moment, Chinese misgivings and Russian fears bring
the two countries together. Neither wants trouble in the Central
Asian rimland. Each recognizes this desire in the other. Each, either
unilaterally or conceivably in cooperation, is prepared to do what
it can to prevent turbulence in the region, particularly involving
Kazakhstan, Kyrgyzstan, or Tajikistan, the three Central Asia
states with a China border.[40] Equally significant, China obviously
worries about instability in Russia itself. Leaders in Beijing appear

to be little concerned about who governs in Moscow as long as they are able to maintain peace and order within the country. True, China, like other nations, should have reason to hope against the rise of a nationalist and authoritarian regime in Russia, first, because Russia's military might would then seem more dangerous and, second, because Russia would likely become a source of trouble in the rimland. Whether the Chinese, however, actually think in these terms is less clear.

For Moscow, China's benign—and, in all likelihood, helpful—approach to conflict in Russia and Central Asia enhances a relationship that for other reasons has grown increasingly important to the Russians. With the collapse of prospects for large economic inputs from Japan, South Korea, and Taiwan, trade ties with China have emerged as particularly significant. China is the only major market for Russian nuclear energy facilities and arms, and certainly the only large market that the Russians can enter on barter terms. Of the rising trade between the two countries, more than 60 percent is in kind: mango juice for passenger aircraft, consumer goods for nuclear power plants.[41] They also push on with the only process of formally agreed arms reductions in Asia (and, for that matter, in all of Russian and Chinese foreign relations).[42] Thus, with China Russia has an opportunity to make a very long border free from the military pressures that mounted steadily for the Soviet Union from 1969 until the late 1980s, when the Chinese began cutting their forces.

By the time of Kozyrev's January 1994 visit to China, the Russians were devising fancy formulas to do justice to this increasingly important relationship. "We must," he said, "move from a full normalization of relations to constructive partnership."[43] Constructive partnership seemed to encompass not only accelerated economic cooperation, including Russian arms sales to China, but an overt meeting-of-the-minds on Central Asia. "Beijing," Kozyrev told reporters, "has a better understanding than certain Western capitals of the danger that Central Asia faces from religious extremism."[44] When Premier Li Peng toured Central Asia a few months later, encouraging his hosts with talk of a "New Silk Road," Russia was carefully counted in.[45] From there the diplomacy between the two countries intensified. Viktor Chernomyrdin, the Russian prime minister, spent four days in China at the end of

May; Qian Qichen, the Chinese foreign minister, returned to Moscow the following month, on the same day that Aleksandr Shokhin, the Russian deputy prime minister, was arriving in Beijing. In early September 1994, Jiang Zemin traveled to Moscow, the first Chinese president to do so in thirty-seven years. The two national leaders emerged from their talks pledging that cooperation between the two countries "will without doubt be a top priority," and declaring that the "constructive partnership" Kozyrev had set as a goal earlier in the year was now a reality.[46] They also signed a joint declaration committing each to stop training nuclear missiles on the other, and—of considerably greater significance—announced that the western portion of their border was now agreed upon for the first time in history.

In the longer run, however, the picture takes on darker hues. If there are for the Russians two radically new features in East Asia, it is these: First, for one of the few times in history, Russia is the weakest of the major powers in East Asia. China, Japan, and the United States all have vastly greater capacities for influencing events in Asia than Russia. Their bilateral relations with one another, particularly the Sino-Japanese relationship, have an importance far greater than Russia's relationship with any of them. Once more, as seventy years ago, Russia is the vulnerable object, not the architect of events in Asia.

Second, for the first time China's ascendant power in Asia is becoming more than a specter, more than a distant prospect used by a far stronger Soviet Union to galvanize its own military effort. Unless something goes terribly wrong within this giant neighbor, Russians know that, to quote one, "China's geopolitical status has altered to the extent that it could even be seen as the potential dominating power in continental Asia."[47] The currently sound, peaceful relations between the two countries, they nervously acknowledge, could sour were China to dissolve in chaos or, worse, veer toward more aggressive aims abroad. For this reason, they say, Russia "cannot afford to be indifferent" to the longer run when China's influence "within and outside the region may exceed the balancing capabilities of any neighboring state."[48]

All of this gives substance to Robert Scalapino's broader warning: "The low level of tension between Russia and China likely to persist in the near term rests not upon any fundamental geopolitical, cultural, or even economic compatibilities but upon the dominance of domestic priorities."[49] When and if these priorities are overcome in one or both countries, the "present 'equilibrium' of limited power or the capacity to use such power as exists will shift to a disequilibrium." Then, he writes, "tensions will again rise, especially since Sino-Russian competition for influence in the buffer states of inner Asia that are now emerging will be permanent. . . . We have not seen the end of their rivalry."

RUSSIA AND JAPAN

In another striking irony of the new East Asian environment, the rise of China affects Japan, the other strong state, more than Russia. The potential competition and mutual distrust between China and Japan, were it to grow into something large, would replace the postwar contest between the United States and the Soviet Union as the dominant feature of international politics in Asia. Then Russia and Japan's postwar roles would be reversed. Japan would become the decisive power and Russia, a secondary player, buffeted by the happenings in Sino-Japanese relations, caught between the two, and, to a far greater extent than was true of Japan, forced to make unhappy choices. Should the Sino-Japanese-Russian triangle revive, it will be much more dramatic than the late-nineteenth-century and Cold War versions.

For now, however, the Russo-Japanese part of the quadrangle remains utterly undeveloped. In the Soviet era, Moscow's policy toward Japan suffered, first, because foreign policy in East Asia was essentially only a national security policy and, second, because policy toward Japan had no independent content, absorbed as it was by the U.S.-Japanese relationship. Both of these disabilities have been shed, but the Russians still are unable to devise a policy engaging the Japanese. In turn, during the Soviet period, Tokyo's policy toward the Soviet Union also suffered shortcomings. Japan, in fact, did not have a Soviet policy, only a Northern Territories policy. This hole in the doughnut has survived into the post-Soviet era, albeit in a considerably mitigated form.

The problem is straightforward, but not the escape from it. Russia, despite the diplomatese of Yeltsin and Kozyrev following the visit-that-finally-took-place in October 1993, has not found—and in all likelihood cannot find—a route skirting the territorial issue.[50] Japan may be cutting off its own nose by suppressing any real effort to develop a comprehensive policy for dealing with the post-Soviet challenge until the Russians budge on the islands dispute, but such is the reality. For the moment, both sides understand that Yeltsin's hands are tied by the Russian public's unhappiness at the thought of yielding the islands, and each is doing what it can to prevent further deterioration in relations. They have taken small steps to move the relationship out of deadlock and to give a modest dialogue a chance.[51] Similarly, despite a skeptical eye, Japan did not break ranks with the other G-7 nations when in Tokyo in July 1993 a large aid package was put together for Russia.[52]

Still, until the Russians feel disposed to get the Northern Territories issue out of the way, the Japanese are not likely to break out of their own constricted frame of mind. Each time a Russian bureaucrat visits the islands and emphasizes Russia's ownership ("We cannot afford to lose such beauty"), the Japanese mood scarcely improves.[53]

When a monstrous earthquake decimated the infrastructure in the disputed islands on October 4, 1994, the sad condition of Russo-Japanese relations stood out in sharp relief. This would have been the time for Russia to free itself from the joint burdens of a vast reconstruction effort and a malingering relationship with Japan. Instead, Oleg Soskovets, the Russian deputy prime minister, audaciously proposed that Japan join Russia in turning the Northern Territories into a zone of joint economic exploitation. Japan's polite refusal was fully predictable. To complete the story, the morning of the earthquake Russian border guards sank a Japanese fishing boat, seized its three-man crew, and protested to the Japanese government.[54]

By 1994 no one, including the most optimistic observers of Russo-Japanese relations, held hope for a way out. Instead, Japan's own unsettled domestic picture added to the dismal prospects. At best this environment might be seen as a "transitional period," during which both countries must sort out their domestic problems and decide on new foreign policy identifies.[55] If two countries followed a modest, constructive course toward one another, some commentators wistfully observed, they might emerge poised to free their bilateral relationship from the past.

As long as things remain as they are, two important consequences follow. First, the Japanese public will continue to react to every bumbling slight on the part of a wayward Russian bureaucrat as proof for their dim view of the Russians, and the Japanese government will continue to view the Russian scene with a more wary eye than most Western governments.

One sees this in the official Japanese assessment of Russian military power in East Asia. Long after Western governments had discounted the Russian military threat, Japan remained worried about the deployment of new, more modern Russian weapons in the Far East and characterized Russian forces "as a factor of instability" for the security of others.[56] Russia had cut its troops in its Far Eastern region to a level half of what they were a few years ago, reduced its Pacific Fleet, cut the number of MiG-23 fighters on Etorofu from forty to ten, sharply reduced naval operations, and promised to stop constructing submarines for military purposes in the next two to three years.[57] Symptomatic of Russo-Japanese relations, however, Russia got little credit for these moves. For much of the first two years after the collapse of the Soviet Union, the Japanese emphasized Russia's ongoing military efforts—specifically the diversion of men and materiel from vacated bases in Eastern Europe to the east, the buildup of the strategic nuclear naval base on Kamchatka, and the continued routine of military activity.

Some of this may simply have been the concern of Japanese defense officials worried about maintaining resources and a coherent purpose with the end of the Cold War. By late 1993, the Japanese Self-Defense Agency was reported to be planning sizable cuts in authorized land forces, a partial redeployment of troops off of Hokkaido, and the renaming of the large exercise, "Special Assault Northward," explicitly in response to what was now treated as a lessening threat from Russia. In turn, the Russians took careful note of Japan's softening assessment.[58]

No sooner had this element of the relationship improved, however, when the December 1993 elections kindled new concerns in Tokyo. Even before his surprisingly successful showing in the elections, Vladimir Zhirinovsky's insulting language on the Northern Territories' issue and crude threats to use nuclear weapons against Japan had generated a stir in the Japanese press. The triumph of the right in the elections, the subsequent exit of reformers from government, and the general surge of nationalist sentiment in the country instantly shook Japanese confidence. So clear and inescapable were the collapsing prospects of even the slowest movement forward on the territorial dispute that Tokyo instantly drew back. Within days of Clinton's January 1994 trip to Moscow, the Japanese let it be known that they, in contrast, questioned the wisdom of sending their foreign minister there as a preliminary to a visit by Prime Minister Hosokawa.

Second, and more important, Japan remains only half open to Russian ideas for building security cooperation in Northeast Asia, moving on to new areas of arms control, and strengthening regional institutions. No longer does Japan work to keep Russia out of Asia's international organizations, but that restraint hardly substitutes for a genuine interest in working together to prevent or manage instability in Northeast Asia, including what might arise within the former Soviet Union. Unlike the Americans, the Japanese have not presented many proposals for new partnerships with the Russians to create the post–Cold War order.

On the Russian side, too, there are deeper sources of misgiving. In the end Japan represents still one more contradiction in Russia's strategic options, even were Tokyo ready to reach out to the Russians. Among many of those who adamantly reject the notion of Russia joining the West, there is nonetheless a widespread recognition that Russia needs to seek some level of strategic partnership with it, particularly to guard against threats arising on the southern rim of Central Asia.[59] Strategic partnership with the West means strategic partnership with Japan. Yet one of Russia's lurking fears is of Japan's growing economic and "politico-military weight," a phenomenon that these same people believe must somehow be offset. The Russian military meanwhile fights cutbacks in its Far Eastern forces by raising the bogey of a Japan eager to fill the military vacuum in East Asia.[60]

RUSSIA AND THE UNITED STATES

It may be, as some Russian policymakers have suggested, that for Russia to turn over some or all of the Northern Territories to Japan, a thorough recrafting of the security environment in Northeast Asia will first have to be launched.[61] In the end, a sense of safety may be more important in guiding Russian decisions, particularly from the side of the military, than Japanese economic largesse or U.S. good offices. Any hope of seeing the distribution and character of military power in Northeast Asia made less menacing, however, would involve a still-greater U.S. role, because without U.S. initiative little is likely to happen.

In this, one begins to see the chain that makes the U.S. role in East Asia vital, and for no country more than Russia. Russia, the weakest member of the Strategic Quadrangle, has most to fear from (1) the rise of an unfriendly, militarily strengthened China jousting with it along the inner rimland and (2) a collision between Japanese and Chinese power. To avoid both, the United States' might and active involvement remain critical.

Second, as the weakest member of the quadrangle, Russia to a degree risks assuming China's historic role in Asia: From the late nineteenth century through the first half of the twentieth, chaos within the country generated instability outside. Asia's incipient multilateralism, focused on the ASEAN postministerial, seems to be preoccupied with the South China Sea, Southeast Asia, the Korean peninsula, and the threatening Asian arms race, but not with the former Soviet Union. To change that, again, the United States must show the way, not the least because coping with potential instability in the former Soviet Union is a global problem. The full array of international institutions, from the United Nations to NATO, is needed to provide any hope of fashioning machinery at all proportionate to the tasks of crisis prevention and crisis management in this vast region.

Here two critical issues arise. First, effective multilateralism—which is simply to say collective action capable of containing the new sources of instability in East Asia, including its northernmost sphere—appears unthinkable unless the Strategic Quadrangle becomes its foundation. For that to happen Japan and Russia will have to find some way to constitute a normal and full relationship. Russia will also have to sort out its long-term relationship with the West. It need not integrate itself into the West, but unless Russia commits itself to a working partnership with the West—its disposition today, but who knows about tomorrow?—a new multilateralism will not emerge in Asia built from the Strategic Quadrangle up. And, finally, the United States will have to recover the wit (an appropriate set of concepts) and the will (public and congressional support) to bring this level of multilateralism into being. Alas, one does not get far into the list before realizing how high the odds are against it happening.

Moreover, this last requirement is linked to a second critical issue. For the most part, Russia, China, and Japan deal with one another, as they always have, in the Asian context. Russia and the United States do not. Their relationship plays out on a global scale, although the meaning of "global" has changed fundamentally since Soviet days. No longer does it refer to their competition in the far quarters of the world. The meaning is narrower and focused on the former Soviet Union itself. In the past the condition of the U.S.-Soviet relationship depended on their direct interaction (in an arms race, Third World trouble spots, and the Sino-Soviet-U.S. triangle). Henceforth, the condition of the U.S.-Russian relationship is more likely to depend on an *indirect* interaction. Far more important than bilateral frictions (over the sale of submarines to Iran, the transfer of missile technology to India, dissent on Bosnia, and the like) will be Russian behavior within the former Soviet Union, that is, toward its new neighbors. If Russia becomes a bully within its own neighborhood, U.S.-Russian cooperation cannot endure. The United States seems prepared to tolerate a dominant Russian role in countering instability in the former Soviet Union, particularly in the Caucasus and Central Asia, but not a license to intimidate or subvert its neighbors. Parenthetically, this is also the way Russia again becomes a military threat to the West: not by restoring capabilities and a posture menacing NATO or other U.S. allies, something beyond the ken of any Russian leadership, but by committing aggression against Ukraine, Kazakhstan, or another of the new states.

In the end, however, the very notion of a Strategic Quadrangle in East Asia appears to have lost meaning. Not only is Russia's influence in the region a fraction of the influence of the other three, even its problems fail to be treated as a serious part of the Asian agenda. China and the United States continue to develop their relationship with Russia, but quite separately. Little in the interplay between the two countries involves Russia, and the same could be said of their respective relationships with Japan.

When, at the July 1994 Naples meeting of the G-7, Russia was invited to a political G-8, the tokenism served as an apt symbol for Russia's place among the great powers of Asia: Russia came along as a self-invited guest, humored by the others, who worried more about needlessly offending bruised Russian pride than about engaging Russia on issues central to their concern. Even the political topics reserved for the sessions with Russia's leader were more perfunctory than substantive, not the least, because none of the G-7 nations felt any great desire to confront problems where Russia was key, that is, those within and among the post-Soviet states. North Korea's nuclear challenge came in for a moment's discussion, but again not because Washington and Tokyo considered Russia crucial to the outcome. Its influence over Pyongyang had largely disappeared, and anyway China seemed far better placed to coax the North Koreans toward a compromise. Rather, Russia figured in the conversation because its leaders used the issue to assert their independence, and this they did to satisfy nationalist pressures at home more than to protect a national interest in Asia. (Indeed, Russia's national interest, in the face of potential nuclear proliferation in Ukraine, was to shore up any possible erosion of the nonproliferation regime by forming the strongest possible common front with the United States and its allies.)

One senses ultimately, however, that these trends scarcely do justice to the future. Eventually Russia will re-emerge as a major power in international politics, including East Asia. But what kind of power? What most matters is how the Russians choose in coming years: With which states they choose to align; what role they choose to assign themselves in international politics; and what kind of international environment they seek to promote. These choices, in turn, seem sure to be dominated by the course of events within Russia and, no less importantly, by the outcome in and among the other post-Soviet states. They are choices over which the great powers, including China, Japan, and the United States could have some influence if they were determined to exercise it. Viewed with an eye to history, the last thing one would want is to replace the preoccupation once reserved for Russia by the other three with a new benign, or perhaps malign, neglect. But, more than ever, that is where the pressures of their own problems appeared to be carrying them.

Notes

1. Robert Scalapino has much to say about the core-periphery relationship in "The United States and Asia: Future Prospects,"*Foreign Affairs* (Winter 1991–92): 19–40.
2. A. Doak Barnett, *China and the Major Powers in East Asia* (Washington D.C.: The Brookings Institution, 1977), esp. pp. 288–333.
3. See Donald Zagoria, *The Vietnam Triangle* (New York: Pegasus, 1967).
4. The best account of this is still Zbigniew Brzezinski,*The Soviet Bloc* (Cambridge, MA: Harvard University Press, 1967, rev. ed.), pp. 271–308.
5. A. Bovin, *Izvestiya,* January 31, 1982, p. 5.
6. Later Soviet commentators would argue that China's shift in course during this period was still sharper. The Soviet Union was suddenly seen as weak, embroiled in disputes with many states, and no longer capable of its earlier "aggressiveness." The United States, with whom the Chinese had increasing disagreements, was in contrast viewed as on the counteroffensive. Hence, the Chinese made a conscious choice to exploit Soviet weakness to secure concessions from its leadership, while reducing their ties with the Americans, ties, moreover, that had weakened the Chinese standing in the Third World and within the socialist world. For this argument, see E. Bazhanov, "Konets bolshoi razmolvki,"*Aziya i Afrika segodnya,* no. 8 (1989): 9.
7. Huan Guo-cang, "Sino-Soviet Relations to the Year 2000: Implications for U.S. Interests," paper prepared for the Atlantic Council of the United States, mimeo, December 20, 1985, pp. 5–6.
8. See Peggy L. Falkenheim, "Evolving Regional Ties in Northeast Asia: Japan, the U.S. and the U.S.S.R,"*Asian Survey,* no. 12 (December 1988): 1229–1244.
9. Elina Kirichenko, "The USA and Japan: Rivalry and Cooperation," *International Affairs,* no. 3 (March 1987): 47.
10. Interview with Alexander Yakovlev, *New Perspectives Quarterly* 4, no. 2 (Spring 1987): 34.
11. B. N. Zanegin, "Tikhookeanskii aspekt vneshnepoliticheskoi strategii SShA,"*SShA,* no. 5 (May 1988): 11.
12. A.Z. Larin, "Kitaisko-Amerikanskie otnosheniya v menyayushchemsya mire," *Problemy dalnego vostoka,* no. 2 (February 1989): 49. Larin notes that others, such as Andrei Nagorny and Vladimir Lukin, have already made the same point.
13. This is drawn from ibid., but it had become a fairly common theme by 1989–90. See also, for example, Vladimir P. Lukin, "The USSR and the Asia-

Pacific Region,"*Adelphi Papers,* no. 248 (Winter 1989/90): 17–32; and Alexei Bogaturov and Mikhail Nosov, "The Asia-Pacific Region and Soviet-American Relations," *International Affairs,* no. 2 (February 1990): 109–117.

14. See *Pravda* 24 (1986): 1 and 4.

15. See Susan L. Clark, "Japan's Role in Gorbachev's Agenda," ms., Institute for Defense Analyses, May 31, 1988, p. 11.

16. See Kimio Uno, "An Overview of Soviet Exports to Japan: A Japanese Perspective," Research Institute on Peace and Security, Occasional Paper No. 18 (1989), pp. 1–32.

17. See, for example, the round-table discussion, "Sovetskii Dalnii vostok i ATR," *Problemy dalnego vostoka,* no. 3 (March 1989): 16–34.

18. See B. Slavinsky's comments in ibid., pp. 16, 20. (Slavinsky was deputy editor of *Problemy dalnego vostoka.*)

19. S. Diikov in ibid., p. 18. (Diikov was from the State Foreign Economic Commission.)

20. Y. Kovrigin in ibid., p. 19. (Kovrigin was from the Institute of Economic Studies of the Far Eastern branch of the Academy of Sciences.)

21. See Yeltsin's address to the Russian Supreme Soviet as broadcast live on the Russian Television Network, February 13, 1992.

22. I would not want to put too fine a point on the argument. According to the Hong Kong press, by November 1991 some Chinese officials had a pretty rotten view of the man. Bo Yibo, the chairman of the CCP Central Advisory Commission, in a secret speech had called Gorbachev a "traitor to Marxism-Leninism, a source of disaster to the Soviet people, the biggest traitor in the history of the international communist movement, an agent of imperialism and capitalism, and an international super beggar." *Cheng Ming,* no. 170 (December 1991), in Foreign Broadcast Information Service *Daily Report: China* (hereafter *FBIS)* 91/233, December 4, 1991, p. 6.

23. On the point see Yuri Savenkov, "A. Kozyrev's Thirty Hours in Beijing," *Izvestiya,* March 19, 1992, p. 4.

24. Kyoji Komachi, an official in the Japanese Foreign Ministry, notes in an unpublished paper that in February 1992, Yeltsin sent Prime Minister Miyazawa a letter in which he referred to Japan as "a potential alliance partner." (See Kyoji Komachi, "Concept of Russian Diplomacy: Struggle for Identity," unpublished manuscript, November, 5, 1993, p. 3.)

25. Gorbachev's most generous formulation on the issue was offered during his April 1991 visit to Japan, when, in the course of a speech to the Diet, he assured his listeners that his country did "not have any destructive intention against military and political structures existing in the region."

26. There is an element of exaggeration in this sentence. Those most eager for the breakthrough were the professional Japanologists, including the senior figure within the Ministry of Foreign Affairs, Georgy Kunadze. Yeltsin's own position, as revealed in the course of the last two years of the Soviet Union's existence, was more convoluted and hesitant. On balance, however, what mattered more is that Yeltsin, at this stage, left the foreign ministry free to shape Russia's Japan policy as it chose, that Kunadze and like-minded people had the full sympathy and support of Kozyrev, and that Yeltsin and most within the leadership sincerely expected to put Russian-Japanese relations on a different footing even if they had not thought through the process.

27. In September 1991 Grigory Yavlinsky, at the time the vice-chairman of the Soviet State Council's economic management committee, created a stir by saying that the territorial dispute should be resolved by simply "confirming" the border established in the 1855 Russo-Japanese Treaty of Commerce, Navigation, and Delimitation, an agreement placing these and the other islands under Japanese authority. He added that, if "correctly and candidly" explained to the Soviet and Russian peoples, "they will understand." See *The New York Times,* September 11, 1991, p. 11.

28. For the details see Tsuyoshi Hasegawa, "Russo-Japanese Relations in the New Environment—Implications of Continuing Stalemate," in Hasegawa, Jonathan Haslam, and Andrew C. Kuchins, *Russia and Japan* (Berkeley: University of California Press, 1993), pp. 428–429. As Hasegawa's account shows, Kunadze and others had become the object of nationalist scorn long before March-April 1992. But it was not until then that Kozyrev (and Yeltsin) began to yield to the opposition, including on issues involving Japan.

29. *Christian Science Monitor,* February 5, 1993, pp. 1, 4.

30. Even before Yeltsin's comments in India, the newspaper of the Russian parliament, *Rossiskaya gazeta,* had hailed Yeltsin's belated realization that "there was never any real basis to the slogan 'the West will help us,'" and new turn toward "the Orient." Said the paper, "This marks the end of the one-sided orientation of Russia's foreign policy toward the West alone." Then, in a malicious aside, the article concluded, "There is no longer any place for the current foreign minister in this different approach." see *Rossiskaya gazeta,* December 23, 1992, p. 1.

31. Taken from Xinhua, February 23, 1993 FBIS China, 93/35, February 24, 1993, p. 10, Interfax, January 10, 1993 FBIS Soviet, 93/7, January 12, 1993, p. 16, and the *Beijing Review*, September 5–11, 1994, p. 19.

32. Sergei A. Karaganov, "Russia and Other Independent Republics in Asia," in *Adelphi Paper,* no. 276 (April 1993): 29.

33. As a sample, Gennady Zyuganov, leader of the Communist Party of the Russian Federation, wrote in *Pravda,* December 24, 1993, of Russia "as a specific cultural and historical world . . . not just a state, but one-sixth of the earth, neither Europe nor Asia, but a special heartland continent—Eurasia—with its own cultural and historical destiny." Normally this destiny includes the "re-establishment of Russia within her [Mother Russia's] historical boundaries."

34. Alexei D. Bogaturov, a Russian academic expert on East Asia, makes both points in "The Yeltsin Administration's Policy in the Far East: In search of a Concept," *The Harriman Institute Forum* 6, no. 12 (August 1993): 5.

35. Robert A. Scalapino, "A Framework for Regional Security Cooperation in Asia," paper prepared for the Japan-U.S. Symposium entitled "The Prospects of Security Cooperation in Asia," Tokyo, June 19–20, 1992, p. 20.

36. Pierre Hassner, "Beyond Nationalism and Internationalism: Ethnicity and World Order," *Survival 35,* no. 2 (Summer 1993): 50, 52–53.

37. This was in a Reuters dispatch from Beijing, carried in *Straits Times,* October 2, 1991, p. 2, and summarized in *Supar,* Report no. 12 (January 1992), p. 33. Qian was supposedly speaking at a closed meeting of senior Communist officials. The suspicion is evidently rather durable. Two years after this alleged remark by Qian, Helmut Sonnenfeldt, a former U.S. policymaker on a visit to China, reported that Chinese leaders still believed that Yeltsin "is a 'hegemonist,' who for now does not have ambitions outside former Soviet ter-

ritory." See Patrick E. Tyler, "Russia and China Plan Pact to Avoid Conflict," *The New York Times,* December 5, 1993, p. 8.

38. See his article in *The New York Times,* April 21, 1992, pp. 1, 10.

39. See *South China Morning Post,* December 12, 1991, p. 1.

40. When Kozyrev returned to China in November 1992, he spent his time talking about the risks of instability in Central Asia and the need for Russia to stand as a barrier to the penetration of Islamic fundamentalism into the area (not, as on his first visit, about human rights). His counterpart, Qian Qichen, echoed their two countries' "common interests in preserving stability" in the region and acknowledged Russia's special relationship with the Central Asian states. See Rajan Menon, "Russia, America, and Northeast Asia After the Cold War," in George Ginsburgs, Alvin Z. Rubinstein, and Oles M. Smolansky (eds.), *Russia and America: From Rivalry to Reconciliation* (New York: M.E. Sharpe, 1993), p. 259.

41. Not that Sino-Russian trade is any freer from the disruptions suffered by others who would do business in Russia. Russian enterprises do no better in fulfilling contracts with their Chinese counterparts than with others. In the border trade, no more than 15 to 20 percent are reportedly met. See *Zhongguo xinwen she,* June 8, 1993 in FBIS China, 93/109, June 9, 1993, p. 6. As a result, in many quarters, Chinese traders are having second thoughts.

42. Again, the original credit goes to Gorbachev, who with Premier Li Peng in Moscow in 1990 agreed to principles to guide mutual arms reductions and confidence-building measures. Negotiations begun then continue today, although now they are transformed into multilateral talks among China, Russia, Kazakhstan, Kyrgyzstan, and Tajikistan. The tenth round was held in Beijing in May and June 1993, with the sides reporting continued progress.

43. Konstantin Eggert, *Izvestiya,* February 1, 1994, p. 5.

44. Ibid.

45. See "Premier's Tour Opens New 'Silk Road,'" *Beijing Review,* May 9–15, 1994, p. 5.

46. Moscow ITAR-TASS, September 1994.

47. Karaganov, "Russia and Other Independent Republics in Asia," p. 23.

48. Bogaturov, "The Yeltsin's Administration's Policy in the Far East," p. 6. Bogaturov, like Karaganov, is a foreign policy moderate, not at all an anti-Chinese nationalist.

49. Scalapino, "Russia's Role in Asia," p. 196.

50. In his October 15 press conference on his return to Moscow, Kozyrev distinguished between two ways of maintaining one's principles: In one case, stubbornly, as Russian reactionaries in domestic Russian politics, thereby impeding progress; in the other, as the Russian and Japanese governments had decided to do, constructively, allowing the two countries to "find ways of cooperating, living together, and tackling many outstanding issues" (FNS Service, SOVSET).

51. This has even included seminars between representatives of the Japanese Self-Defense Agency and the Russian Ministry of Defense, including one in Tokyo in February 1993 attended by first deputy chief of the General Staff, Major-General Gennady Ivanov.

52. Before the Tokyo G-7 summit of July 1993, Japan had already extended $177.5 million in bilateral grant assistance to Russia and $2.6 billion in loan

assistance; increased technical assistance from $1.6 million in 1991 to $6.7 in 1993; participated in the April 1992 $24 billion support package by the Western nations and the debt rescheduling of the Paris Club; and contributed $20 million to the creation of the International Science and Technology Center. (Information from the Japanese Ministry of Foreign Affairs, February 1993.)

In April, at the finance ministers' meeting preceding the Tokyo summit, Japan pledged an additional $1.8 billion as part of the $40 billion joint program of credits. (All but $350 million of this was in loans and trade insurance.)

53. ITAR-TASS Report, June 28, 1994, as taken from COMTEX wire services.

54. Sergei Agafonov, "Russia Shooting, Protesting, and Asking for Money," *Izvestiya*, October 7, 1994, p. 3.

55. I. Tselishchev, "Yaponiya kak politicheskii partner," *Mirovaya ekonomika i mezhdunarodnye otnosheniya*, no. 6 (June 1994), pp. 70–78.

56. Agence France Presse report, April 2, 1993, included in *RA Report*, Center for Russia in Asia, no. 15 (July 1993): 133–134.

57. Yeltsin made the last pledge himself on his visit to South Korea in November 1992. See Andrew Pollack, "Yeltsin Plans End to A-Sub Program," *The New York Times*, November 20, 1992, p. 20.

58. See Vladimir Kutakhov, ITAR-TASS, December 25, 1993, and *Komsomolskaya Pravda*, December 15, 1993.

59. See, for example, the foreign policy strategy developed by the Council on Defense and Foreign Policy published in *Nezavisimaya gazeta*, August 19, 1992.

60. See Major General Georgy Mekhov, "Military Aspect of the 'Territorial Problem,'" *Krasnaya Zvezda*, July 22, 1992, p. 3. Mekhov, in addition, provides a detailed account of the way the Northern Territories figure in the defense of Russia and, in the process, a clear image of the threat Russian military leaders continue to see in U.S.-Japanese forces in the region.

61. Lee Konstantin Sarkisor, "Russia and Japan," in Robert D. Blackwill and Sergei A. Karaganov, eds., *Damage Limitation or Crisis?* (Washington: Brassey's 1994), pp. 259–272. (This, it goes without saying, assumes a very different Russian domestic atmosphere, one in which Russian leaders are not frozen in terror of offending popular nationalist sentiment.)

CHAPTER TWO

China and the Strategic Quadrangle: Foreign Policy Continuity in an Age of Discontinuity

DAVID M. LAMPTON

INTRODUCTION: DOMESTIC NEEDS AND FOREIGN POLICY STRATEGY

President Clinton came to power determined that foreign policy would not distract him from the primary task of governing and changing the United States: "It's the economy, stupid!" The anxieties of internationalists were to be assuaged by the intuitively appealing proposition that an effective foreign policy in the future requires a strong domestic economy and society as a foundation. At the same time that the president wanted to minimize resources, particularly his time and political capital, devoted to concerns abroad, the administration expanded the ideological objectives of American policy through the strategy of "enlargement." In the September 21, 1993, words of the assistant to the president for national security affairs, Anthony Lake, "The successor to a doctrine of containment must be a strategy of enlargement—enlargement of the world's free community of market democracies."[1]

Whether an expansion of objectives and a simultaneous diminution of resources and attention devoted to their attainment is a workable combination remains to be seen. But, irrespective of its feasibility, Washington's modus operandi provides a fundamental contrast to Beijing's foreign policy and its approach to the strategic quadrangle, the topics of this chapter. Most fundamentally, Beijing sees its individual policies toward the United States,

Japan, and Russia as part of an interrelated strategy implemented with little ideological content. For Washington, great-power relations largely are seen as a set of bilateral relationships with high ideological content. The tensions between Washington's and Beijing's approaches to great-power relations will be a major force shaping the history of interstate relations in the next decade. If Washington is not careful, it could find itself pursuing a set of goals neither Beijing, Moscow, nor Tokyo will support and, in the process, isolating itself from the most dynamic growth center in the contemporary world economy.

It is fashionable to say that countries can no longer (if they ever could) pursue integrated foreign policy strategies given regional diversities, central-local conflicts, social pluralization, bureaucratic politics, and the globalization of economic relations and information. Policy is the accumulation of incremental reactions to essentially unpredictable circumstances in a global media fishbowl. This low expectation for foreign policy control and coherence has been given added force by the demonstrable uncertainties of the post–Cold War era and the explosion of long-suppressed forces of nationalism and ethnicity.

Although there certainly is a highly reactive component to Chinese foreign policy, these reactions occur within the framework of a clearly articulated and widely shared foreign policy framework. This framework specifies goals, the flexible roles of the major powers, and the means by which core Chinese objectives may be achieved. This framework has been articulated by Deng Xiaoping and his chief subordinates since late 1982 (the "independent foreign policy" enunciated by Hu Yaobang at the Twelfth Party Congress)[2] and it has been implemented effectively (with minor modifications) by Qian Qichen, foreign minister since 1988. In short, while the post–Cold War international and domestic political tumult has seen major reassessments of foreign policy in Tokyo (sending peacekeepers abroad and Morihiro Hosokawa's emphasis on a more penetrable Japanese economy), Moscow (the Yeltsin revolution), and Washington (Clinton's strategy of "enlargement"), there has been remarkable stability in Beijing's foreign policy behavior and rhetoric to date, though increasing American pressure and instabilities associated with the succession in China have given rise to some voices calling for reassessment.

The Tiananmen tragedy of June 1989 and the collapse of the European Communist world in the period from 1989 to 1991 presented Beijing's strategy with uncertainties, to be sure. But the strategy has not yet been modified significantly because the post-1982 approach has been successful and no competing or compelling alternative foreign policy vision has been advanced by any potent leadership group. It is in America's interest that the Chinese continue to adhere to this strategy. It would be a costly irony if Washington's policy of "enlargement" were to embolden currently inchoate domestic forces in China to adopt a different approach, as has been suggested by some, particularly in the Chinese military.[3] More significant for the long run, there is a diffuse but clearly rising nationalistic tide that resents continual American "pressure tactics."

China's more than decade-old foreign policy framework is based on the following four key assumptions/assertions: (1) global, great-power conflict is a remote possibility for several decades;[4] (2) economic strength is the basis of overall national power, and the economic arena will be the major domain of competition in the era ahead; (3) regional conflicts will occur, but East Asia is an area where there could well be comparative stability (with fears about strife on the Korean peninsula being a notable exception); and (4) because East Asia is an area of rapid economic growth, excess capital in search of higher rates of return than can be obtained in the United States, Japan, and Europe is available, and ethnic Chinese capital can be brought to the service of modernization in the People's Republic of China (PRC). China therefore has the best chance to modernize it has ever had; the United States is a country that has overextended itself since the end of World II, it goes through phases of ideological assertiveness, but its capital, willingness to transfer technology, and ability to restrain Japan all serve China's interests; the relationship with the United States is the key bilateral relationship for Beijing, and the effective management of this tie is the first external priority of the PRC's foreign policy; and Japan is the principal economic and security challenge looming in China's future. With the collapse of the Soviet

Union, its successor, Russia, poses a reduced military threat, but Russia is likely to generate ongoing uncertainties by virtue of the combination of weak political institutions, a failing economy, nationality conflicts, and rising popular frustration. In the short run, certain economic and technological gains can be made from Russia's distress, but, in the long run, Russia never can be counted out as a regional power or as a potential threat to Chinese interests.

These core assumptions give rise to predispositions and regularities in Beijing's foreign policy behavior: a disinclination to become involved in extraneous conflicts that divert energies from economic modernization; the pursuit of balance among the major actors (Russia, Japan, and the United States) in East Asia so as to make it unlikely that any dominant power could effectively challenge core Chinese interests at home or in the region; the use of appeals to economic opportunity, rather than ideology, to build international support for Chinese objectives and make each of the great powers in the region aware that moving against core PRC interests is likely to compromise each one's own economic stakes; and a reluctance to take global foreign policy initiatives—there is a strong preference to react to the initiatives of others. In short, China has an active and purposeful foreign policy that seeks to support domestic modernization. The goal is to make China a regional power first, exercise limited global influence, to be expanded as its economy and resources grow, and to finish the still incomplete agenda of national reunification.

There has been remarkable stability in these assumptions and patterns of behavior over the last decade plus, because China's foreign relations reflect their roots in the domestic reform process. As one Chinese foreign policy official recently told me, China has "no problem making our foreign and domestic tasks mesh." To sketch in only broad strokes, the key features of Chinese economic reform and foreign economic policy have been to:

1. Concentrate the bulk of investment and budgetary resources on domestic construction.[5]

2. Give a greater proportion of financial resources and managerial power to provinces, localities, and economic units.

3. Open up coastal areas to foreign investment first, taking advantage of these areas' comparative advantages in transport, educated workforces, and links to the international economy.

4. Seek trade and investment wherever it can be found without reference to the character of the regimes involved.

5. Improve the domestic environment for foreign participation in economic growth.

6. Move toward market pricing gradually.

7. Build institutions able to operate in, and regulate, a marketized system.

All the while, Beijing has sought to keep a tight grip on the levers of domestic political control, hoping (probably unrealistically) to avoid for at least several decades the pluralization of political power that China's leaders fear would bring instability and set back the economic growth on which the regime's survival depends.

Because the enclave strategy of special economic zones articulated by Deng Xiaoping in the late 1970s greatly advantaged coastal areas, the predictable resentments of interior provinces (and rising wage rates along the coast) have continually forced Beijing to extend similar advantages to other areas throughout the country. To buy internal peace, Beijing has permitted ever larger numbers of provinces and localities to develop economic ties to "natural" nearby trading partners—to form "natural economic territories" (NETs).[6] This has resulted in the explosion of international economic linkages between Chinese provinces and contiguous areas, linkages that have produced exponentially growing economic relations between Taiwan and China's Fujian Province; Shandong Province and South Korea; Heilongjiang and Jilin provinces with Russia (particularly Khabarovsk and Primorskyi kray); Inner Mongolia with "Outer Mongolia" and Russia; Yunnan and Guangxi provinces with Vietnam; Tibet Autonomous Region with India and Nepal; Xinjiang Autonomous Region with Central Asia; and, of course, Guangdong Province with Hong Kong, Taiwan, and the entire Pacific Basin. In turn, China's relations with these external areas has generally had to improve in order to facilitate and stabilize these spontaneously generated economic ties. It is no accident, therefore, that the 1980s and the early 1990s have seen improved relations between Beijing and Moscow, Hanoi, Seoul, New Delhi, Tokyo, and Taipei. It is, of course, also generally true that better political relations have fostered improved economic ties.

This proliferation of economic linkages with external areas and the decentralization of economic power domestically has meant that there is a powerful national constituency for an "omni-directional" foreign policy that emphasizes economic ties, and friendly relations and that minimizes resources going to central coffers—coffers that would have to be full if China were to embark on a confrontational foreign policy that required a strong military with great outward reach. Central government revenues currently constitute a smaller proportion of China's national economic output than at any previous time in the PRC's post-1949 history.[7] In short, the last decade's stability in Chinese foreign policy has been underpinned by the economic reform strategy in China itself.

All this could change, dramatically, of course, but it is unlikely to do so unless either a major power (or powers) renders the strategy unworkable or there is a fundamental reorientation of China's reform drive due to leadership changes, economic problems, and/or social instability resulting from inflation and corruption. The contingencies that could produce such changes in China's foreign policy strategy deserve some discussion.

With respect to succession in a leader-centered polity such as the PRC's, one can never be certain that the departure of the supreme leader will not occasion a reorientation of domestic and/or foreign policy. Nonetheless, I would rate dramatic departure from current policy as having a very low probability of occurring when Deng Xiaoping leaves the scene, if his demise occurs under anything like current circumstances. This is so for two principal reasons: First, whether one looks at either domestic or foreign policy, the period from 1978 to 1994 has been highly successful when compared to previous policy eras in modern Chinese history. No coherent leadership group in Beijing is arguing for fundamental policy departures or has a credible basket of policy alternatives. At most, some leaders are waiting in the wings to make adjustments to current policy—some desire somewhat slower and more sustainable economic growth; others prefer a harder crackdown on corruption; and others prefer a somewhat tougher line on the United States and are not averse to fostering power centers elsewhere (for example, the Middle East) that might prove troublesome to the United States and generate revenue for Beijing in the process. In short, the argument is over degrees, not the fundamental direction of policy. Also, turning to leaders at the county, provincial, and ministerial levels who are in the succession pipeline, we see technically competent individuals who, for the most part, seem to have economic performance objectives, not a radical ideological agenda.[8]

Beyond the concerns over the succession to Deng Xiaoping and the instabilities that could result from the ever-present inflationary potential and corruption (as well as growing unemployment), there are several important countervailing eddies in Chinese foreign policy itself, currents that are troubling to many in Washington and, to a lesser extent, Tokyo; Moscow has its own problems. Were these currents to be carried to extremes or result in policy failure, a sequence of events could develop that would produce a fundamental change in China's foreign policy strategy.

One trend concerns China's military and its growing expenditures since 1988.[9] During the decade from 1978 to 1987, China's military expenditures as a percentage of gross national product (GNP) fell; in the mid-1980s China undertook to reduce military manpower by 1 million persons. By 1988–1989, however, the combination of this prolonged budgetary diet, mounting inflation, and the army's role in the suppression at Tiananmen created a powerful incentive for budgetary increases for the military in the period from 1988 to 1993. This momentum was accelerated further by the startling ease with which Saddam Hussein's army was devastated (an army equipped with better Russian weaponry than China possessed) by America's high-tech arms in the 1991 Gulf War and by growing tensions in U.S.-PRC relations over human rights and arms sales. The People's Liberation Army (PLA) saw clearly just how antiquated its technology was and how vulnerable its forces had become.[10]

It remains to be seen how long substantial military spending increases will continue. Further, the distribution of these increases among competing needs to protect the livelihood of PLA troops in an increasingly marketized (and inflation-prone) economy and the desire to acquire new weapons merit careful observation. Even if new weapons are acquired, the actual force projection capacity achieved by the military as a result remains to be seen. If China's still-modest military modernization sets off a regional arms race, Beijing may have unleashed forces of reaction among neighbors that will compel changes in its own foreign policy strategy, to no one's benefit.

Another important foreign policy–related eddy has its origins in the decentralization of economic, political, and decision-making power in China itself. China is a nation in which men, not laws, rule. Localities, enterprises, and individuals throughout China are striving to make money as rapidly as possible, and the legal or regulatory systems are very inadequate to constrain this mad dash. The result is that there is a rapacious quality to some Chinese behavior at home and abroad, whether it is the frequently corrupt influence-peddling by relatives of leaders at all levels of Chinese society, the large-scale smuggling of stolen autos from Hong Kong and the illicit trade in cars from South Korea,[11] the mislabeling of products made in China to circumvent textile quotas based on product origin, the growing trade in narcotics,[12] the trafficking in the parts of endangered species, or piracy in the southern and northern waters off China's coast. In short, the very decentralization of power and rising entrepreneurship that we in the West applaud on ideological and economic efficiency grounds—in combination with official corruption—sometimes produce reprehensible and destabilizing behaviors at home and abroad that we deplore in terms of practical effect. If Beijing cannot regulate the external behaviors (and indeed some of the internal behaviors) of its citizens and subordinate entities, China's relations abroad will suffer, producing reactions that may render the country's own foreign policy strategy less effective or unworkable.

Two other dimensions of China's external relations are particularly important and subject to considerable uncertainty: Taiwan and Hong Kong. While Beijing sees these as domestic concerns, for the rest of the world these are areas with great importance to the international system and areas in which two members of the Strategic Quadrangle (the United States and Japan) have very large economic, security, and historical interests.

With respect to Hong Kong, a botched transition to China's scheduled resumption of sovereignty over the city on July 1, 1997, would have major consequences for China's relations with the United States, most of the Pacific Basin, and Western Europe. Such a botched transition could be manifested by an early reassertion of Chinese sovereignty over the city, a total breakdown of economic cooperation between London (Hong Kong) and the PRC, and/or intemperate Chinese threats to completely remake the institutions of governance in Hong Kong after July 1, 1997. Other nations would react strongly if such developments occurred and led to mass emigration from Hong Kong, a sustained and sharp drop in asset values in the city, or violence and human rights abuses.

I would rate such extreme results to be of low probability, despite the hyperbole associated with Beijing's rejection of Governor Christopher Patten's political reform proposals and the seeming December 1993 breakdown of negotiations over them. I do so because, in economic terms, Hong Kong already is substantially integrated into the Chinese economy, and the markets in the city already have discounted the political uncertainties. Further, many key people in the city already have secured rights of abode elsewhere, have returned to Hong Kong to work, and are able to stay in Hong Kong relatively secure in the knowledge that they can leave if they must. Also, the PRC is by far the largest external investor in Hong Kong, and the PRC investors include every Chinese province, ministry, and many of the sons and daughters of the elite itself. No significant domestic elite constituency in China wants destabilization of Hong Kong. Only policy error in Beijing or political turmoil in Hong Kong is likely to lead the PRC to adopt highly destabilizing policies.

Turning to Taiwan and its relations to China's mainland, there is potential for difficulty that could change both Chinese foreign policy behavior and the response of other members of the strategic quadrangle. Political liberalization on Taiwan is giving increasing voice to forces that desire to jettison what they view as the undesirable fiction of "one China" and traditional Kuomintang (KMT), Nationalist Party, aspirations for reunification (albeit in the distant and indefinite future). Local elections on Taiwan in November 1993 further revealed a fragmenting KMT and strong voices for independence. Moreover, the independence forces in Taiwan have been emboldened by the combination of what they see as a rising global tide supportive of rights of national self-determination, growing economic success on the island and increasing Taiwanese financial muscle in the PRC, and by a hope that the pro-human rights policies of the Clinton administration and the United States Congress might translate into support for Taiwan's de jure independence. Were Taiwan to embark on a course of such independence under current and foreseeable circumstances, a forceful and highly destabilizing response from Beijing is to be expected. This response, in turn, would produce dramatic changes in the West's relations with Beijing and thereby compel a broader change in China's foreign policy strategy.

Nonetheless, countervailing considerations suggest that the current situation can remain manageable: The Clinton administration, in its preparations for the mid-November 1993 forum for Asia-Pacific Economic Cooperation (APEC) in Seattle, reaffirmed the United States' commitment to "one China"; there are ongoing discussions between Beijing and Taipei (behind the fig leaf of nongovernmental entities); and there is the mounting economic interest of both parties in not upsetting the apple cart of mutual economic benefit. Nonetheless, mainland-Taiwan relations is an area of policy instability that warrants careful monitoring and attention by the United States.

With this as background, we can now turn to an assessment of how Beijing views its relations with each of the other three quadrangle players: the United States, Russia, and Japan. We shall conclude with an evaluation of the implications for American policy.

BEIJING VIEWS THE UNITED STATES WITH AMBIVALENCE

Using Barbarians to Fight Barbarians

The specter of isolation from the world's fastest-growing economic region, and abandoning this fertile field to our economic competitors in Europe, Japan, Korea, and Taiwan, is one of two principal levers the Chinese believe they have available to influence the United States, a lever they intend to employ in order eventually to compel a more accommodating set of policies from Washington. The other point of leverage is cooperation (or withholding it) in the United Nations Security Council and on global issues.

A Chinese official laid out the basic line with respect to economics and trade in April 1993 to a group of visiting Americans in the context of President Clinton's first reassessment of China policy prior to his May 28, 1993, Executive Order on Most Favored Nation (MFN) tariff treatment for Beijing.[13]

> CAAC [the Chinese state airline corporation] signed a contract for 20 Boeing aircraft worth $600 million . . . If U.S.-China relations keep good, China's civil aviation is growing 30 percent per year, so China may be one of the biggest buyers of aircraft. Also . . . the head of the natural gas corporation [in China] was in Texas to purchase oil equipment and talk about oil exploration inland in China. The Tarim Basin is rich in oil, so if we can cooperate in oil and energy, there are rich opportunities for cooperation. Also, the State Planning Commission Vice Chairman . . . is leading a delegation to the United States to purchase automobiles and the purchase will be quite big. The auto market in China is growing rapidly, so there will be more and more cars in China and it will be the biggest market [for U.S. exports]. Also, AT&T is very interested in the telecommunications market here. If you come into the market too late, it will be occupied by others. The Chinese market is a big cake. Come early and you get a big piece. I hope our two countries have good relations, but it takes two to tango![14]

Six months later, speaking through surrogate outlets in Hong Kong, Beijing put the same essential proposition more poetically.

> If Sino-U.S. relations are damaged, China will not be the only one to suffer losses. . . . It [China] has opened up to the world an attractive and extensive market. If American corporations do not move in, there will be other corporations from other countries . . . In the long term, "a bird of prey is poised to pounce on the mantis which is trying to catch the cicada." . . . Other countries have marched ahead in strides and become tough competitors for the United States. Is this lesson not profound enough?[15]

In August 1993, in the wake of Washington's decisions to condition future MFN extensions for Beijing (May 1993), to push for inspection of a Chinese ship bound for Iran alleged to be carrying precursor chemicals for weapons of mass destruction (the "Yin He Affair" of late July, August, and September), and to impose additional trade sanctions on Beijing for alleged missile technology transfers to Pakistan in violation of understandings with the United States (August 1993), China's military exerted substantial pressure on the central party leadership to adopt a much harder policy toward the United States.[16] On September 1, 1993, the Standing Committee of the Politburo met on this subject and, notably, decided to continue to pursue the foreign policy of the past. The policy is the "four nots": not to desire confrontation, not to provoke confrontation, not to dodge confrontation, and not to be afraid of sanctions and to resist them.[17] The analysis that undergirded this decision was leaked out through Hong Kong and is consistent with the foreign policy framework elaborated upon in the first section of this chapter:

- There are serious internal contradictions in the West, and this prevents the United States from making its relations with China completely acute.

- The changes in the Soviet Union and East Europe have not turned out to be what was expected by the United States, but have become a burden for the United States . . . : 1) The communist parties of the Soviet Union and East Europe still exist; 2) the process of privatization is too slow, and West Germany's effort to transform East Germany is not very smooth; and 3) although Russia relies on the United States, contradictions are upsurging.

- To handle international relations of a global and broad nature, the United States still needs China's cooperation.

- China is a big market.

- Clinton's domestic and foreign policies look weak, and a series of the measures he has taken to deal with China reflect the thought given to domestic contradictions.

- [The conclusion to which all this leads:] Consider the overall situation and stabilize relations.[18]

The other powerful lever the Chinese believe they have was mentioned earlier: "To handle international relations of a global and broad nature, the United States still needs China's coopera-tion." It is notable, and remarkable, that ever since the Gulf crisis of 1990–91, China either has abstained on or supported successive Security Council votes of high priority to the United States (e.g., resolutions on the use of force in the Gulf, the intervention in Somalia, and the crisis in the former Yugoslavia), despite the PRC's twin historic fears of great-power intervention in the Third World and infringement on sovereignty by international organizations.

However, the Chinese were (and are) tiring of supporting American positions and being repaid by additional unilateral trade sanctions imposed by Washington because of fictions in the trade, human rights, and proliferation areas. This weariness was mani-fested in early October 1993 (and again in June 1994), when the Chinese detonated a nuclear device underground. President Clin-ton had urged Beijing to halt the test so as to salvage his unilat-eral moratorium on American nuclear detonations, the continued observance of which he had made contingent on the cessation of nuclear testing by the other nuclear powers. Not only did people in China's high command believe the tests were necessary to improve the quality and safety of China's nuclear arsenal, its diplomats also wanted to send Washington a message: If Washington wants China's cooperation on global issues, the Clinton administration must be more cooperative in bilateral relations. As one Hong Kong outlet for Beijing's views put it, "China will put the Clinton ad-ministration in an embarrassing situation and, apart from that, it will tell the United States that China is not to be pushed around."[19]

Similarly, since early 1993 Washington has been trying to win Chinese cooperation in inducing North Korea to restore Inter-national Atomic Energy Agency (IAEA) verification of its nuclear status and to cooperate in applying sanctions to Pyongyang in the event Kim Il-sung does not permit IAEA inspection of his nuclear facilities. The Chinese have been willing to pursue quiet, behind-the-scenes diplomacy with Kim but have been unwilling to apply economic, much less military, pressure. This reluctance on Beijing's part has many origins, among which are: a fear that Kim is an un-predictable leader who, when cornered, is likely to start a conflict that would erupt on China's border and disgorge refugees into China; a recognition that South Korea and Japan also want to proceed cautiously against North Korea and that Washington must overcome fear and ambivalence in both Tokyo and Seoul; and a reluctance to join Washington in imposing sanctions against a Third World country, especially when the United States simultaneously is imposing sanctions on the PRC.

Beijing not only believes that it has some levers over Washington in terms of access to China's market and cooperation on global issues, it also reckons that Washington will, in the last analysis, be unwilling to isolate itself from its traditional allies in Europe and Asia by pursuing a policy that leads to breakdown with the PRC.

And finally, analysts in Beijing believe that Washington has greatly exaggerated the potency of its MFN card in extracting further concessions. In essence, the United States believes that Beijing simply cannot afford to ignore Washington's demands because the loss of such a huge market for Chinese exports would constitute a devastating setback to the regime's internal political and economic position. (The U.S. deficit with China was $18.2 billion in 1992 and almost $23 billion in 1993.) China argues, however, that much of its exports actually are the output of Taiwan, Hong Kong, and other foreign (export-processing) ventures on the mainland, with the bulk of profits from those enterprises going abroad. China, Beijing argues, makes only about $3 billion on this trade.[20] By way of contrast, were the PRC's access to the American market compromised, America's $8-plus billion in exports (plus many billion dollars in investment in China itself) is directly threatened by what undoubtedly could be effective retaliation by Beijing. If each $1 billion in American exports equals 20,000 jobs, as the U.S. Department of Commerce uses as a crude rule of thumb, at least 160,000 American jobs are at risk—the Chinese peg the number at 250,000.[21] Beijing doubts the Clinton administration has the stomach for such losses, particularly with the American economy finally climbing out of recession and the White House commitment to generating jobs. Parenthetically, this analysis was borne out by President Clinton's late-May 1994 decision to unconditionally extend MFN tariff treatment for China and to end the declared linkage between MFN and human rights conditions in China.

This analysis was given added force by two developments in the second half of 1993: First, in the summer of 1993, the Clinton administration initiated a second review of China policy (the first was undertaken prior to issuance of the May 28, 1993, executive order) that, by September, resulted in a strategy of "comprehensive engagement" and "dialogue" with Beijing. This strategy was to be operationalized through a series of high-level meetings, including secretary-level visits to China, a restoration of military-to-military exchanges, and a meeting between presidents Bill Clinton and Jiang Zemin on November 19 in the context of the APEC meetings in Seattle.

Second, the APEC meeting in Seattle and the flurry of Clinton administration statements about the shifting center of gravity of American foreign policy toward Asia further confirmed the Chinese in their line of thinking. In particular, the statements of Winston Lord, assistant secretary of state for East Asian and Pacific affairs, were given particular weight. Lord was reported to have said that President Clinton had made reviving the domestic economy his number-one priority and that "Asia and the Pacific now are the most lucrative terrain for American exports and American jobs, and therefore the most relevant region of the world for the President's domestic economic agenda."[22]

The Chinese, in short, believe that domestic economic concerns, the unwillingness of America's traditional partners to follow its lead in a tough policy against China, and the interest-group character of American politics in which business will push Congress and the administration to protect its economic stakes will all combine to produce a moderation in American policy—sooner or later. Sooner is better, but China can wait.

In late October 1993 it was clear to the Clinton administration that this was precisely the Chinese view. As one State Department official was quoted as saying: "It looks like the Chinese don't think we have the guts to withdraw MFN."[23]

The Softer Side of the Chinese Strategy: Accommodation and Reason

Earlier I emphasized the hard-edged dimensions of the Chinese approach to relations with the United States in the context of the Strategic Quadrangle. But Beijing also realizes that great gains are to be made from positive ties to the United States, gains in terms of trade, technology, and education, avoiding excessive dependence on Tokyo, and using Washington to restrain the growth of future Japanese military power. Beijing also knows, however, that since the bloodshed in and around Tiananmen Square of June 1989, there has been an interlocking set of American views about China, its internal and external behaviors, and its role in the world that provide the conceptual backdrop against which the U.S. Congress and the president have adopted policies Beijing finds contrary to its interests. These views and assumptions include the following:

- China's strategic importance to the United States has declined since the end of the Cold War.

- China is a neomercantilist state stacking up hard currency in its trade with the United States, a surplus that is achieved by a combination of unfair trade practices and denying American exports legitimate market access.

- China is a rising military power that lacks either the will or the capacity for responsible behavior, whether it is weapons sales or technology transfers.

- China's regime is shaky, because of the imminent succession, the lack of legitimacy stemming from repeated political repressions, and/or mounting inflationary pressures and corruption. In any event, the conclusion seems to be that the United States merely needs to wait for a more pliable regime.

A critical part of Beijing's strategy has been to assuage some of the grievances giving rise to these views and to counter these assumptions.[24]

The Chinese government and party apparatus has realized since 1990–91 during the Bush administration that three concerns are uppermost on the American agenda: trade (market access, intellectual property protection, and the mounting trade deficit), proliferation of weapons and technologies of mass destruction, and human rights. China has sought to reach agreements with the United States in the first two areas, after hard bargaining (and subsequently fitful implementation), while remaining unwilling to weaken its basic policy of maintaining tight political control at home as economic liberalization proceeds. China's elite believes that the lesson of the collapse of the East European and Soviet regimes, and the subsequent descent of many of these systems into political disorder, is that the Asian path of development (economic growth first, political liberalization later) is the only sensible road to take. As one Chinese Politburo member told a visiting American group in July 1993, "Collapse in China would be a hundred times worse than collapse in Yugoslavia."[25] In short, weapons and arms control policies are negotiable, but human rights concessions (except for tactical releases of political prisoners and other similar moves) that Beijing believes weaken either internal control or make it look supine in the face of American pressure are not. So, for example, in November 1993 Foreign Minister Qian Qichen indicated that Beijing would give favorable consideration to a request from the International Committee of the Red Cross for visits to Chinese prisons. Qian was careful not to make it appear that Beijing was buckling under Washington's pressure.

The general pattern of willingness to negotiate on trade and weapons issues is seen in the agreements that Washington has reached with Beijing in the post–Cold War era. In the economic and trade area, in January 1992 Beijing signed a landmark agreement to protect American intellectual property and subsequently joined the Berne Convention. By most accounts the Chinese have made fairly earnest efforts to implement this instrument, within the context of their poorly developed legal system, weak enforcement, and provinces and enterprises going their own way. A particularly severe problem has been the ongoing piracy of American software and compact discs in south China, sometimes in cooperation with offshore entrepreneurs elsewhere in "greater China."

At midyear Beijing signed a Memorandum of Understanding committing itself not to export to the United States goods made with prison labor. In the agreement China promised to provide Americans access to prisons believed to be involved in the export of such goods. Implementation of this agreement has been mixed and unsatisfactory to Washington, in part due to links to the human rights domain and the decentralized character of the Chinese economic system.

In October 1992 the United States signed a historic "market access" agreement that promised a gradual diminution of tariff and nontariff barriers to American exports over a five-year period. Implementation of this agreement has been satisfactory in some areas; in others it has not. Beijing rationalized the concessions it made with the twin thoughts that they promoted domestic economic reform and facilitated China's early entry into the General Agreement on Tariffs and Trade (GATT). Given the explosive growth of China's market, the mounting U.S. trade deficit with Beijing, and the desire of local officials in China to protect local industries from competition, we can expect issues of access for American firms to be an ongoing source of conflict.[26]

The weapons proliferation domain has proven to be an area where Sino-American agreement is possible, but subsequent implementation has been variable. In 1992 China overturned almost twenty-five years of steadfast refusal to join the Non-Proliferation Treaty and also agreed to observe the guidelines and parameters of the Missile Technology Control Regime (MTCR). In November 1991 China also gave then Secretary of State James Baker assurances that Beijing would not transfer M-11 missile technology or systems to Pakistan. Subsequently obtained American intelligence indicated a violation may well have occurred. As a result, in August of 1993 Washington unilaterally imposed two-year sanctions on the transfer of some high technology.

Overall, therefore, China has been willing to reach agreements in the trade and weapons areas, though implementation has been uneven; this very unevenness and the resulting American pressure for compliance, in turn, have become additional irritants in the relationship.

China not only has endeavored to demonstrate the utility of positive agreements, it also has sought to attack the idea of it as a "threat" to global and regional stability. Among the pieces of evidence cited by Americans and the PRC's somewhat anxious neighbors about growing Chinese military capabilities and feared ambitions are the already cited military budget increases since 1988 as well as consummated, planned, and rumored Chinese weapons purchases. In 1992 China bought about $1.8 billion in Russian-made weapons and agreed to have Russian experts help upgrade some of its own weapons manufacturing industry.[27] In early November 1993 Russia and China signed a five-year military cooperation agreement.[28] And, in early 1994, China's National People's Congress approved another hefty increase in the defense budget.

The thrust of the PRC's rebuttal is that: (1) China is a very small weapons seller and buyer, in comparative terms; (2) China's economic weakness requires the continued placement of priority on nondefense spending for a very long time; (3) proponents of the "China threat" theory are self-interested competitive arms sellers or international relations analysts looking to sell their alarming forecasts;[29] and (4), most of the budget increases are eaten up by inflation and go to support the livelihood needs of military personnel, not hardware modernization.

At this point, given the lack of transparency in the Chinese military, procurement, and budgetary systems, Beijing's protestations have not quieted concerns, whether in the United States or the nations on China's periphery, including Japan. The post-Tiananmen absence of high-level military-to-military contacts between Washington and Beijing (until the November 1993 trip to Beijing of Assistant Secretary of Defense Charles Freeman) further reduced the exchange of information that might help reduce some of these anxieties and moderate Chinese behavior.

Summing Up Sino-American Relations in the Context of the Strategic Quadrangle

China has had a remarkably stable approach to foreign policy and quadrilateral relations since 1982, despite the massive changes in both the world system and in the character of its three other partners in the quadrangle—a move away from the Reagan-Bush era in the United States, the collapse of the Soviet Union, and the loss of power by Japan's Liberal Democratic Party (LDP), just to mention a few of the more salient transformations. Beijing's foreign policy framework has been stable because it has its origins in China's domestic goals and needs rather than in the international system itself. Beijing needed good relations with each member of the quadrangle in 1982; and the same is true in 1994.

In essence, China's foreign policy framework has sought to induce the inflow of capital and technology into the country, to promote exports abroad, and to minimize external entanglements and defense expenditures. Foreigners are to be persuaded to cooperate through a mixture of holding out the promise of economic gain, reminding those from afar of the possibility of falling behind competitors, and using Beijing's leverage in the domain of global issues. Further, in dealing with those abroad, trade and arms control issues are negotiable; external demands for rapid political liberalization on the mainland are not. If the United States pushes the human rights agenda too hard, it will find that its traditional allies will not follow. The United States then will be isolated, with Japan, Moscow, and indeed the rest of the world refusing to follow Washington's lead. As the Chinese see it, the United States has a foreign policy problem at least as large as China's, perhaps larger.

DEALING WITH RUSSIA IN THE CONTEXT
OF THE STRATEGIC QUADRANGLE:
THE LIMITS TO COOPERATION

In late 1992, Gerald Segal could plausibly assert that "no single external event has had as much impact on the People's Republic of China as the disintegration of the Soviet Union."[30] This statement seems plausible until it is checked against empirical reality. Such a check reveals that the collapse of the Soviet Union absolutely convinced Chinese leaders to stay their previous course, a course in which economic reform would run far ahead of political liberalization and foreign policy was in the service of domestic modernization.

The collapse of the Soviet Union, in the Chinese view, occurred because of Gorbachev's failure to provide tangible economic benefits to the citizenry, benefits the weakened Communist Party could not provide because it could not enforce policy or impose discipline and because political pluralization gave vent to rising popular frustrations that resulted in snowballing instability. That instability, in turn, made economic growth impossible. In short, Beijing's analysis of the Soviet collapse was conceptually identical to the trap of development Samuel Huntington warned against in *Political Order in Changing Societies* twenty-five years ago—political demands exceed the capacities of political and social institutions; that situation feeds instability; and instability, in turn, makes it impossible to aggregate the wealth, human resources, and institutional capacity that could satisfy demands and restore social order and stability.[31]

As a result of this analysis, Beijing's commitment to its own "omnidirectional," economically oriented foreign policy was further strengthened. Consequently, Beijing's actual 1994 foreign policy behavior toward Russia differs little from what it had been toward the Soviet Union between 1982 and 1991. With the exception of a very brief period in August 1991, when Beijing's leaders seemingly supported the hard-line coup attempt against Gorbachev, the PRC has rather consistently (since 1982) sought gradually to improve bilateral relations, whether under Brezhnev in his last years, Gorbachev, or Yeltsin. This gradual and sustained improvement of Sino-Soviet relations began in the waning years of Leonid Brezhnev,[32] continued through the Gorbachev era, and endures into the current Yeltsin period, most recently manifested by the November 1993 five-year military agreement signed by Moscow and Beijing and by the May 1994 visit of Russia's premier to China.

Undergirding this continuity in policy in Beijing is an analysis of Russia and its future and where China's long-term interests lie. The truth of the matter is, in the words of Walter A. McDougall, "Russia and China will continue to dominate East Asia's mainland in an uneasy balance. A Russo-Chinese detente is not impossible, but except for the monetary savings to be gained from reducing frontier deployments, neither country has much the other needs. What Russia and China need is the capital, technology or markets of Japan and America."[33]

With the exception of Chinese incentives for border trade (to diversify exports to new markets and bring raw materials to China's industrial Northeast) and the Russian starvation for decent-quality consumer goods and the desire to sell high technology, including weapons, the primary incentive for Beijing is to place emphasis on developing economic relations with Japan and the

United States. Economics is the name of the game in East Asia, and Russia looks like a minor league player to the Chinese, though Beijing is too shrewd to say so publicly. As Robert Legvold tells us in Chapter 1 of this volume, Moscow views the economic gains to be made from the relationship as greater than Beijing does.

Beyond this modest level of common interest is the fact that a deep level of cultural suspicion still separates the two peoples. In my own 1993 travels to China's Northeast and the Russian Far East, I noted that Russians distrust the Chinese across the Amur and Ussuri rivers and view them as rapacious plunderers of resources. For example, the chairman of Primorskyi's Ecology and Natural Resource Agency asked another visitor, "You want to know about Chinese business?" He "pulls a Siberian leopard skin" out of a cupboard "and tosses it, claws clattering, onto the table. 'That's Chinese business.' "[34]

On the Chinese side, the view is that the Russians, at best, do not have a central government that exercises effective control locally, that officials change frequently, and that the combination makes a long-term relationship difficult. There also is the feeling that the Russians make promises cavalierly and rarely implement them effectively. In mirror-like fashion, the Russians feel the same way, as is evident from the paraphrased remarks made by a senior official in the Russian Far East in the fall of 1993. "As for the Chinese . . . all their promises even at the highest level do not work, they simply do not keep them. All his practice [as an official] is evidence of this."[35]

There is another concern in Beijing: Will Moscow be able to maintain sufficient central control and social order to keep tight control of nuclear weapons and military forces and ensure that there is no uncontrolled cross-border migration? Indeed, in the first half of 1994 the Russians and the Chinese tightened up border-crossing procedures. Beijing worries about these things but believes there is not much to be done other than monitor the situation carefully and be modestly helpful when opportunities arise. One example of modest helpfulness is the fact that "Russia's debt to China now stands at $1.07 billion."[36]

With respect to the other states of the former Soviet Union, particularly those along China's border, the interests include control of military forces and the prevention of migration as with Russia, plus assuring that each of these new states does not establish formal diplomatic relations with Taiwan and bolster Taipei's drive for enhanced international status.

In short, the Chinese will derive what benefit they can out of local border trade with the Russians (and other states of the former Soviet Union), what technology and weapons they can from a cash-strapped Moscow, hope for (and seek to modestly help ensure) stability in Russia and states of the former Soviet Union, and try to ensure that Moscow and the newly independent states of the former Soviet Union do not make unwelcome moves toward Taiwan. Beyond this, there are serious constraints on cooperation between Moscow and Beijing, unless both Tokyo and Washington force the two together. This is something the United States and Japan should avoid assiduously. As one Western diplomat in Beijing was quoted as saying, "The overall policy line is caution, caution over whether a Russia that is hostile to China might emerge."[37]

A CLOSER LOOK AT CHINESE INTERESTS
AND CONCERNS REGARDING RUSSIA

The Economic and Trade Dimensions

Beijing's interest in growing trade and economic relations with Russia has its origins in two factors, beyond the self-evident commercial and security objectives of China's overall policies. First, Beijing's strategy for economic reform initially brought benefits to China's coastal areas. In order to buy peace with heartland regions, over time Beijing has had to allow inland provinces and border areas to have similar advantages in dealing with their natural trading partners. For China's industrial Northeast, an area saddled with many marginally productive state enterprises desperately looking for external markets, Russia and central Asia were the natural trading partners and places where even rather shoddy products could find a ready market. Indeed, Beijing and Chinese cities in the Northeast are full of burly Russians with gray duffel-type bags buying up light industrial goods and flying back to Russia with the overweight baggage to sell the contents at considerable profit. These individuals are referred to in Russia as "*Kamazy,*" or "trucks" made at the Kama River vehicle works.

The second reason Beijing has been eager to augment economic ties with Russia has been to diversify its export markets so that it is not so dependent on Western markets, particularly America's, that could be closed off due to protectionist pressures or through the imposition of sanctions designed to extract concessions from China in any number of areas, from human rights to weapons and proliferation.

> A State Council leader said: In the first half of this year [1993], China's exports increased by 4 percent. Greater efforts should be made in the second half of the year in order to fulfill the export target laid down by the state. In the future, the strategy for developing foreign trade is:
>
> First, diversifying markets. At present, over 70 percent of China's commodities is exported to Hong Kong and 25 percent is exported to North America and Western Europe. Absolute trade liberalism and absolute trade protectionism are both absurd and will not appear. The less diverse the export market, the more the risks there will be. In the future, China's foreign trade should first be developed with Russia; second, with Southeast Asia; third, with the Middle East and Gulf countries; and fourth, with the African countries. Russia has a population of 180 million people, and has rich resources for exchange. . . . [38]

It is important to note that these figures understate the dependence of China on the American market—about two-thirds of China's exports to the United States pass through Hong Kong and, therefore, are considered by Beijing to be exports to the colony. The urgency of diversifying exports beyond the American market is far greater than suggested above.

Nonetheless, diversification of exports to Russia has its limits. In 1986 I observed that "despite the improvement in relations [between Moscow and Beijing], the scale of Sino-Soviet ties is comparatively small. In 1985, Sino-American trade was almost 3.5 times as large as Sino-Soviet trade."[39] By 1992 that ratio had jumped to approximately 6:1. The Sino-Japanese trade ratio also was about six times as large as China's two-way trade with Russia in 1992.[40] Even though trade volume between Russia and China "soared" to more than $5 billion in 1992, it still is modest in

China's overall trade picture, amounting to about 3 percent of China's total two-way world trade in 1992.[41] Further, nongovernmental border trade accounted for 60 to 80 percent of this Russo-Chinese volume, with much of "this trade carried on by freelance peddlers, 'business tourists' and 'exchange students' from the two countries."[42] The cooperation of local authorities, therefore, is more germane to development of this commerce than national policies, as long as central governments do not get in the way.

The flourishing border trade is a mixed blessing for local authorities on both sides of the Russo-Chinese border. There are frequent reports of brawling among Chinese traders in Russia, between Chinese and Russians, and "Highway robbery, extortion and racketeering are all on the rise . . . says Mayor Pavel Karaovin [of the border town of Pogornichnyi], with Chinese the main victims. It takes a bribe of US$500 or more just to get into the customs area, according to Chinese migrant workers milling in the ankle-deep slush in front of the Pogornichnyi depot."[43] It is these types of frictions, and the mounting number of Chinese in Russia, that accounts for the aforementioned tightening in border-crossing procedures in 1994.

On the other hand, Chinese, particularly in the PRC's northeast provinces of Jilin and Heilongjiang, are highly motivated to tap into rich Russian resources[44] and build cooperative transport arrangements with Primorskyi kray to gain access to the Pacific Ocean so that the region's growing cities (and indeed Mongolia) can greatly shorten transport lines to the world market and avoid dependence on a single North Korean port. If development of the Tumen Project among Russia, China, and North Korea proceeds, all these pressures and incentives will be intensified further.

In short, trade is growing and it is important to local authorities on both sides of the border. But this commerce also brings in its wake the kind of close contact that deepens the mutual stereotypes that produce conflict as well as the cooperation induced by interdependence. The Russians and Chinese may do business, but conflicts will provide barriers to intimate cooperation, unless pressures from elsewhere in the international system force them together. To Beijing, growing and stable economic relations with Russia will provide a modest hedge against the possibility that markets in Japan, Western Europe, and/or the United States decline or are closed off to it—but not much, at least for the next decade.

Foreign Policy and Military Relations

Looking at Russia's foreign policy options globally, the crux of the Chinese analysis is that there is an inherent conflict between Moscow and Washington that will act to govern the development of cooperative relations that could threaten Chinese interests, particularly if Beijing plays its cards right. Beijing believes that at least four major categories of friction (either latent or actual) between Washington and Moscow provide openings for its own diplomacy.[45]

1. The United States has promised substantial aid to Russia but in reality has provided only very limited aid. "Moscow feels more and more that the Clinton administration's willingness to help Russia is only a means to make Russia bow and scrape before the United States."[46]

2. The build down in strategic weapons between Moscow and Washington has not been proceeding as rapidly as both sides might have hoped.

3. "Public opinion in Russia has repeatedly censured the United States for its 'tendency to issue orders' with regard to some international issues, and also 'holds a negative attitude' toward the U.S. attempt to 'play the leading role' in the world."[47]

4. The core American policy "toward national and regional conflicts in the regions under the former Soviet Union" is to "resolutely reject the possession of privileges by Russia to adopt action to 'maintain peace' in the regions under the former Soviet Union and the establishment by Russia of 'new spheres of influence' in those regions."[48]

In short, it appears that Beijing is not particularly worried that a unified and strong Russia will collaborate in an unholy alliance with the United States against Chinese interests. On the contrary, Beijing believes there are inherent conflicts between America and

Russia and that they are likely to grow under what is perceived to be an assertive U.S. foreign policy. The December 1993 parliamentary elections in Russia in which the ultranationalists (led by Vladimir Zhirinovsky) won nearly one-quarter of the popular vote served further to strengthen Chinese confidence in their analysis.

Looking at its own security interests and military relationship with Russia, Beijing sees two important opportunities to enhance its own security: (1) reduce the number of troops along the border and reduce friction by resolving as much of the border dispute as possible; and (2) purchase as much advanced military technology (and some weapons) as possible at the bargain-basement prices the Russians are offering. As mentioned earlier, this provides a cost-effective way to modestly upgrade PLA capabilities while adhering to the primacy of domestic economic modernization.

In late 1992 Boris Yeltsin paid a visit to China, a trip that by all accounts produced modest but important accords on "basic principles" for bilateral relations, scientific and cultural exchange, commercial relations, nuclear power cooperation, and an unpublished agreement on the purchase of military equipment and technology.[49] In addition, in the runup to the visit, negotiators for both countries resolved most of the territorial issues along their disputed eastern border, except for Bear Island in the Amur River facing Khabarovsk. It was clear from Yeltsin's trip that Russia was not about to ignite dispute with China over human rights[50] and that cash-starved Moscow had no intention of strictly restraining weapons sales to Beijing, irrespective of Washington's desires. In November 1993 Russian defense minister General Pavel Grachev made a four-day visit to Beijing and signed a five-year military cooperation agreement that focused on China's acquiring Russian military know-how and technology.[51] For its part, since 1989 Washington has imposed a series of unilateral sanctions prohibiting American arms and technology transfers to China.

All this raises the question of what kind of pressure the United States may seek to apply to Moscow in its attempt to win a moderation in Russia's arms and technology transfer policies. The Chinese do not believe Moscow can be dissuaded by Washington. Any U.S. attempts to do so coercively would simply feed Russian nationalistic impulses and push Moscow further in Beijing's direction.

Turning to China's actual and contemplated weapons purchases it is important to note that the Soviet Union had agreed to sell arms to China *before* the USSR's demise.[52] Shambaugh asserts that

> Russian arms sales to China totalled $1.8 billion in 1992. In addition to selling China state-of-the-art weaponry, Russian experts have returned to upgrade production lines in PLA factories. To date, the most major deal concluded has been the purchase of 24 SU-27 fighters and six long-range military transports. . . . According to some reports, during Boris Yeltsin's December 1992 visit to Beijing deals were finalized for the purchase of 72 more SU-27s, four long-range fighter-bombers, 18 S-300 guided missile anti-aircraft systems with 100 AA missiles, 70 Type-72 battle tanks, and three conventional submarines. Still under active consideration are MiG-31 and MiG-29 interceptors, attack helicopters, VSTOL aircraft, more air transports, long-range refueling aircraft, IL-76 AWAC aircraft, AS-15 air-launched cruise missiles, and apparently T-22 medium-range Backfire bombers.[53]

Other reports assert that Beijing has purchased missile guidance technology, rocket engines, and technology for uranium enrichment.[54]

Considerable debate exists in the West and in the nations on China's periphery about the impact of these actual and possible purchases on PLA force projection capabilities, particularly when combined with the aforementioned budgetary increases and doctrinal changes in China's military. The doctrinal alterations place a new emphasis on outward, active defense rather than the earlier "luring deep" approach of Mao Zedong that was self-evidently defensive in character.

For their part, the Chinese are sufficiently alarmed at some of the foreign analyses of their motives and capabilities which they now refer to as the "China threat" genre of analysis that Beijing has launched a concerted propaganda barrage to seek to counter them.[55] In addition, Beijing has affirmed its willingness to engage in Asian security dialogues in order to calm anxieties.

As of mid-1994, it appears that China's force projection capabilities are modest and likely to remain so for the next decade, even when compared to the limited capabilities of its neighbors. Demands in the military for keeping standards of living up in the face of significant inflation will sap resources, and the strong competition of domestic priorities should restrain the growth of capabilities. Nonetheless, trends in China's military strength are worth monitoring carefully.

One other dimension to Chinese consideration of Russia (and the other states of the former Soviet Union) calls for attention: Beijing does not want either Moscow or the other states to establish formal diplomatic ties with Taiwan or be a source of weapons for a Taipei that is seeking to break out of its formal diplomatic isolation and acquire new generation weapons. In September 1992 Yeltsin issued a decree on Taipei-Moscow ties that reassured Beijing that Moscow would avoid formal political relations. Further, the Chinese have private assurances from Russia that Moscow will respect China's concerns relative to weapons sales to Taiwan.[56] The Chinese have been engaged in a continuous effort to forestall the establishment of formal diplomatic and military relations between other states of the former Soviet Union and Taipei. For example, Vice Premier and Foreign Minister Qian Qichen was in Ukraine in September 1993 and told Ukrainian foreign minister Anatoliy Zlenko, "We appreciate the Ukrainian Government's adherence to the principles of one China and the joint communiqué on the establishment of diplomatic relations between China and Ukraine. For some time, Taiwan has engaged in activities aimed at its so-called re-entry into the United Nations. We are absolutely against it."[57]

Summing Up

The principal factors shaping China's policies toward Moscow are: the expectation of Russia's prolonged economic weakness (particularly in Asia) and protracted political disorder; a desire to continue reducing bilateral tensions that would impede China's concentration of resources on economic modernization; and a fear that destabilization in Russia could spill over into China. In addition to the economic and trade objectives that China's state enterprises and entrepreneurs are pursuing, Beijing wants to keep Moscow from strengthening Taipei's search for support in achieving greater international status and modernized armed forces. Finally, Beijing seeks to prevent Moscow and Washington from cooperating in ways detrimental to its own interests and to avoid a situation in which the United States and Russia jointly seek to pressure China. Beijing believes it can accomplish this by emphasizing the divergent interests that separate Moscow from Washington.

Beyond this, a Chinese official, summarized for me his thinking about Russia's importance in the Strategic Quadrangle: "They have their problems."

CHINA VIEWS JAPAN IN THE CONTEXT OF THE STRATEGIC QUADRANGLE

The relationship with Japan is the most important bilateral relationship Beijing has, *after* that with Washington. PRC leaders see an intimate connection between their policies toward Washington and Tokyo. From Beijing's perspective, there is a "strategic triangle"[58] in Asia (the United States, Japan, and China), and it is Beijing's purpose to utilize that three-way relationship to its advantage.

Beijing has sought to use the prospect of improved political and economic relations with Japan to induce Washington to be more politically cooperative, to elicit more American investment in China, and to encourage Washington to relax a variety of post-Tiananmen sanctions. Conversely, until Tokyo fully and convincingly renounces its military history of the latter part of the nineteenth century and the first forty-five years of the twentieth, China will want the United States to act as a brake on any expanding Japanese military role in the region. Also, Beijing will use Tokyo's ceaseless quest for market share and the specter of American penetration of the Chinese market as a means to extract maximally favorable commercial, aid, investment, and technology terms from Japan.

Behind this somewhat antiseptic Chinese view of Japan, however, is a deeply ingrained set of attitudes (some of which find their analogues in Japanese views of China) that limit the warmth and intimacy of Sino-Japanese relations and introduce volatility into bilateral ties. Among those Chinese attitudes are feelings that the Japanese desire to dominate the PRC economically; that Tokyo's trade and commercial practices are unfair, unethical, and feed corruption; and that Japan is an arrogant, closed society that generally rides roughshod over neighbors when given a chance. In short, there may be occasional warmth in Beijing-Tokyo ties, when it serves the purposes of both nations; there will not be intimacy in any foreseeable future. Even though Washington is interventionist, ideological, and difficult to deal with in Beijing's view, it is to be preferred over Tokyo. In the end, Japan is near and the United States is far away.

Gerald Curtis admirably summarizes China's view of the intimate connections between its policies toward the United States and Japan.

> China is committed to a program of rapid economic modernization that requires Japanese aid, investment, and trade. It would be foolish to pick a fight with the country whose economic assistance is a critical factor in realizing China's economic goals. Of equal importance, China is deeply worried about the possibility of a hardening of U.S. policy toward China under the Clinton administration. They hope that Japanese influence with Washington can help keep Sino-American relations from deteriorating. The Chinese are trying to position themselves as best they can so that, should relations with the United States worsen, they will avoid a simultaneous deterioration in relations with Japan. Talking about good relations with Japan is at least in part a way for China to deal with its American problem.[59]

Among America's most important strategic purposes in Asia must be the avoidance of a simultaneous, dramatic worsening of relations with Tokyo and Beijing. For Tokyo's part, in Chapter 3 in this volume Mike Mochizuki argues that the recurrent nightmare of Japanese foreign policy leaders is that they face "exclusionary policies toward Japanese imports and investments" in the United States, that Washington weakens its security ties in East Asia, and that this combination could produce an isolated Japan that would have to devise its own means to deal with rising Chinese economic and military power.

Beijing's Views on the Importance of Ties with Japan

Japan is, by far, China's largest aid donor, with nearly 1 trillion yen extended between 1980 and 1991; aside from educating a huge number of Chinese students and scholars, the United States doesn't even have a regular government-to-government assistance program with the PRC. In addition, Japanese banks have more than 4 trillion yen in loans for China on their books, "25% more than is held by the rest of the world."[60] Sino-Japanese trade was $23 billion in 1991, rising to $29 billion in 1992, a growth rate of nearly 27 percent.[61] *China* had a surplus of $5.6 billion in its trade with Japan in 1991 and had another surplus in 1992 as well.[62] In 1991 Japan ranked number three in terms of new investment (after Hong Kong and Taiwan), a position it maintained in 1992. Japan is moving some of its labor-intensive, low-end consumer goods manufacturing capacity (e.g., textiles) to China and investing comparatively heavily in northeastern China, in infrastructure, and in Shanghai's new Pudong Development Area.

Japanese economic involvement in China not only has its own direct and obvious utility, it also has a foreign policy advantage for Beijing. Fear elsewhere in the West of possible Japanese domination of China's huge potential (and rapidly opening) domestic market spurs others to accelerate their own investment and discourages other countries (such as the United States) from linking political and trade issues together.

Equally important, the Chinese know that Tokyo habitually likes to keep economics and politics separate—something Beijing welcomes in the behavior of others, even if it occasionally links economics and politics in its own policies (e.g., in the dispute with London over Hong Kong). The Chinese further know from the G-7 Houston Economic Summit of mid-1990 that Japan was the driving force behind encouraging G-7 countries to resume normal economic and political relations with China after Tiananmen, and the Chinese believe that then Japanese prime minister Kiichi Miyazawa urged President Clinton to accord MFN status to China when they met in April 1993 in Washington.[63] When I met with former Japanese prime minister Noboru Takeshita in August 1992 in Tokyo, he delicately argued for a more restrained American policy that did not jeopardize economic and political relations in pursuit of rapid changes on the human rights front. In short, Beijing values highly the degree to which the Japanese have sought to moderate American behavior and have made it impossible for Washington to create anything like a unified Western policy on China.

Sino-Japanese Relations in the Wake of Emperor Akihito's Visit to China

Beijing's policies with respect to Tokyo must be understood as emerging from: the important economic stakes identified earlier; a fear of Japanese economic domination; a deep distrust of Japan (particularly among the older generation in the PRC) that stems from both history and the belief that economic strength begets political and military power[64]; and a desire to parlay good relations with Japan into more pliable policies from Washington. Two developments in 1992 and 1993 made the Chinese feel more confident that they could thread the tiny eye of this diplomatic and economic needle: the six-day October 1992 visit to the PRC of Emperor Akihito[65] and the August 1993 end of uninterrupted Liberal Democratic Party rule in Japan and what proved to be the temporary rise of Morihiro Hosokawa as prime minister.[66]

Emperor Akihito Visits.　Millions of Chinese perished in Japan's invasion and occupation of China in the 1930s and 1940s. To see the powerful grip this carnage still has over the collective Chinese psyche, one need only visit the Nanjing "holocaust" museum to see small groups of Chinese students going through the exhibits, mouths agape, and older Chinese citizens weeping. With these memories, the Chinese have attached monumental importance to receiving a clear and unambiguous apology from the Japanese throne and each successive Japanese cabinet, apologies that generally were either not forthcoming or were ambiguous.

The Chinese remain acutely sensitive to statements concerning Japanese responsibility (or lack thereof), even statements by low-ranking and inconsequential public and private figures. Indeed, for example, in May 1994, remarks by the Hata government's just-named minister of justice Shigeto Nagano (indicating that he believed that the 1937 massacre in Nanjing was a "fabrication") set off a firestorm of Chinese, and South Korean, criticism. Nagano was promptly forced to resign. Further, Beijing is hypersensitive to increases in levels and rates of Japan's spending for its Self Defense Forces. In the early 1970s, when syndicated columnist James Reston visited China, then-premier Zhou Enlai told him that his basic view of Japan was that economic power begets military power. Japan was a growing economic power that would acquire military strength; China would have to deal with this. There has been no change in this fundamental axiom of Chinese policy in the last two decades.

Against this backdrop and Beijing's post-Tiananmen desire that Western leaders meet with China's elite, the PRC attached enormous weight to the October 1992 visit of Japan's new emperor, Akihito. The Chinese wanted to believe the sentiments conveyed by the emperor in his toast to China's then-president Yang Shangkun. He said he "deplored" the "unfortunate period" in which Tokyo "inflicted great sufferings on the people of China."[67] On the other hand, the language was restrained and vague, and Beijing heard other voices in Japan that created uncertainties about what all this meant. Further, realism and practicality were not entirely absent from Beijing's calculations—perpetuating guilt was a useful lever to win periodic concessions from Tokyo. Another use for the emperor's trip was that it demonstrated that while Washington might choose to avoid high-level exchange with China's leaders, no American ally was going to follow suit.

The Japanese had their own calculus in going to China, beyond the obvious economic objectives and the desire to reassure Asian neighbors of Tokyo's maturity as its regional roles (including dispatching troops to Cambodia under the United Nations banner) grew.

> [T]he Japanese, increasingly uncertain about the future of the U.S. presence in Asia, believe they must adopt policies toward neighbors based on their own national objectives rather than the interests and politics of what they perceive to be a declining and perhaps less interested superpower. In this scenario, China looms all the more important for Japan as U.S. interest, presence, and influence in Asia seem to diminish.[68]

Japan's LDP Loses Power and the Rise and Fall of Morihiro Hosokawa. The August 1993 end of the LDP's long post–World War II rule in Japan and the rise of a coalition government led by Morihiro Hosokawa was basically welcomed by China, as it was by the Clinton administration. For Washington, it seemed that the corruption of former LDP party officials and the government's resistance to the domestic consumption desires of the Japanese people all aggravated the difficulty the United States had in getting a serious, sustained, and effective response to its economic grievances. For China, which wants even better penetration of Japan's market, hopes for more reticence in Tokyo about rising military budgets, and desires more international aid, the preliminary analysis of the Hosokawa government was promising, even though in late 1993 Beijing correctly assumed it to be a transitional government of uncertain duration, with an uncertain capability of fundamentally changing policy.[69] Indeed, in April 1994 Morihiro Hosokawa resigned over allegations of financial indiscretion and the first minority government in Japan's post–World War II history was formed under the leadership of Tsutomu Hata. Hata's eight-party coalition was assumed by the Chinese to, itself, be transitional, though Beijing expected Hata to maintain the principal contours of Hosokawa's policies.

The basic official Chinese government analysis of the Hosokawa changes is that "though an heir to conservatism, the Hosokawa non-LDP coalition administration in the post-1955 system climate is beating a somewhat different drum in certain respects of its policies."[70] Those respects are:

- "Hosokawa advocates for an [sic] reassessment of past policies in favor of turning Japan into a 'country with a high quality life' through home demand expansion, improved market access, amelioration of resentment against Japanese mercantilism both at home and abroad, upgraded domestic cultural attainments, enriched material comforts and enhanced natural environment."[71]

- Hosokawa said, "Japan will offer cooperation in solving global issues through providing official development aid in the form of capital and expertise, and support the reform process in the developing world and the socialist countries. . . ."[72]

- "Hosokawa has tentatively decided that the increase rate of [the] defense budget next year [1994] will be kept below 2%. This will be the lowest figure since 1961."[73]

- "He declared on August 15 that 'Japan will forever renounce war as a means of policy' and expressed his sincere 'feelings

for all war victims and their surviving families in the neighboring nations of Asia.' And in his first policy speech on
August 23, he made a deep introspection over and offered
public apologies for the miseries and sufferings inflicted upon
the Asian neighboring countries by Japan's war atrocities and
colonial rule. Such candid admission by a Japanese prime minister on his country's culpability for launching the Pacific War
is the first of its kind for postwar Japanese cabinets."[74]

In short, Beijing welcomed the Hosokawa coalition government on these scores, but simultaneously expected a bumpy road.
Beijing expected the Hosokawa government to be transitional for
several reasons, reasons that apply with even more force to the successor Hata government. Because Hosokawa led an eight-party
coalition, Beijing expected that Tokyo would become tied in knots,
unable to do much with respect to domestic political reform. Also,
the coalition had divergent tendencies within it, some of which
were sympathetic to strengthening ties with Taiwan and some of
which were more receptive to human rights considerations, impulses of which Beijing heartily disapproves.[75] Another fear was
that the Japanese cabinet would tackle the domestic political reform issue successfully and this success would, in turn, trigger another political realignment in Tokyo that the Chinese felt unable to
predict. Third, as of late 1993, revival of the Japanese economy appeared unlikely in the near term. The Chinese feared that this development, combined with the appreciation of the yen, could
further aggravate Tokyo's trade surplus with the United States,
which feeds protectionist and confrontational impulses in Washington. The Chinese hear voices in the U.S. Congress that draw a
parallel between Beijing's mounting trade surplus with the United
States and Japan's. A protectionist cannon aimed at Tokyo could
blast the PRC.

China's Analysis of Japan's Role in the Strategic Quadrangle in the New Era.

First, China does not believe that the Clinton administration will
long relax pressure on Japan to reduce its trade surplus with the

United States, despite Washington's mid-1994 decision to tone down its rhetoric aimed at Tokyo. This pressure, in turn, will limit the degree to which Washington and Tokyo can cooperate to China's detriment. Second, "[b]etter Japan-Russia relations are not in reach, either. Strong internal opposition renders it virtually impossible for Yeltsin to make any meaningful compromise with Japan on the territorial issue at this stage."[76] This analysis was not only borne out by Yeltsin's (twice-postponed) visit to Japan in October 1993,[77] but also by the demonstrated popular appeal of ultranationalism in the December 1993 parliamentary elections in Russia. Finally, Japan now is more dependent on trade with Asia than it is on its trade with the United States, China is the world's most rapidly growing major economy, and the PRC's domestic market is opening rapidly. In Beijing's view, Japan will become increasingly independent of the United States. On the one hand, this development worries Beijing, but, on the other hand, it makes China all the more important to Washington. Eventually Washington will face the choice of being isolated or moderating its demands and pressures on China.[78] Indeed, it was this combination of the prospect of being isolated in Asia and forgoing its share of the growing Chinese economy that led the Clinton administration to unconditionally extend MFN tariff treatment for Beijing in May 1994.

POLICY IMPLICATIONS OF THE STRATEGIC QUADRANGLE FOR AMERICAN POLICY IN EAST ASIA

The preceding analysis holds a number of significant implications for American policy; four should be underscored here. The most important is that while Washington may have heretofore thought (particularly in the wake of the Tiananmen tragedy of June 1989) that the job of U.S. policy was to avoid isolating China, thereby creating a potential rogue state, the real problem of U.S. policy may be how to pursue a values-driven policy without isolating ourselves from the economic dynamism of the region and without forgoing the Japanese, Chinese, and Russian cooperation we desire on global and regional issues. Put bluntly, not one of the other powers in the Strategic Quadrangle is going to sign on to a policy of vigorously pursuing the strategy of enlargement, particularly in its human rights dimensions. Russia has neither the will nor the capability. China is opposed. And Japan will not sacrifice its economic objectives to the attainment of those purposes.

Second, the Clinton administration's willingness to encourage, and be involved in, regional security dialogues is appropriate and useful, as is maintaining the current pattern of bilateral security alliances, particularly the security ties with Japan and South Korea. Each of the three other parties to the Strategic Quadrangle has suspicions about the other two, and the United States is the one distant power whose force in the region tends to foster stability and not ignite regional military competition.

A related policy implication is that the removal (or substantial and precipitous reduction) of the American forward military presence in the East Asian region would be highly destabilizing. China's military spending is growing, which ignites concerns in Japan. And the Chinese become absolutely preoccupied with the slightest increases in Japanese military spending and capability. Russia's need to move troops out of the European theater to areas east of the Urals creates the ever-present problem of other states in Asia becoming alarmed at those capabilities. Former President Nixon put it well in mid-1993 when he said, "Without the U.S., Asia's future rests on a three-legged stool which is very unstable. Anyone who believes a China, Russia, Japan balance of power is stable is crazy."[79]

Third, it is meaningless to talk about which of America's bilateral relationships—Japan, China, or Russia—is most central to our future and East Asian stability. The central reality is that there are four important powers that must maintain a stable and, it is hoped, mutually beneficial relationship with one another. In China, economic progress, political reform, and social stability all must be achieved—a single-minded pursuit by the United States of political reform may well impede the possibility of achieving the other objectives and produce a resentful, destabilizing response from Beijing in the process. In Russia, economic gains must be made if social and political stability is to be obtained. With respect to Japan, progress in addressing American economic concerns must be made without producing a rupture that would be catastrophic to our economic and strategic objectives. In short, the United States must have a differentiated policy with respect to each actor in the Strategic Quadrangle, but a policy that recognizes that our actions with respect to one member of the quadrangle affects the behavior of the other two. A one-size-fits-all strategic policy of "enlargement" will not work; it will foster instability in the region, and ultimately it will set back the realization of both American normative objectives and tangible interests.

And finally, China basically has become a status quo power while, in this post–Cold War era, the United States has become something of a revolutionary state. China has become the defender of an international system that operates on the premise of almost unbridled state sovereignty and, in so doing, seeks to reap the benefits of the sovereign state system that it rejected for so much of its long history. Beijing seeks to devote itself to internal transformation, thereby boosting national prosperity and strength. The United States, on the other hand, is seeking to transform the international economic and political systems, arguing that sovereignty confers immunity for an increasingly small range of state activity. China's national goals are to be achieved by defending the current international system—the future of the United States is to be achieved by change in that very system. America in its current incarnation feels more comfortable with a world organized along Wilsonian principles; the Chinese prefer those of Metternich and Morgenthau.

Notes

1. Anthony Lake, "From Containment to Enlargement," Address at Johns Hopkins University, School of Advanced International Studies, Washington, D.C., September 21, 1993, p. 5; see also Thomas L. Friedman, "U.S. Vision of Foreign Policy Reversed," *The New York Times,* September 22, 1993, p. A13.
2. See Hu Yaobang's speech to the Twelfth Party Congress, September 1, 1982, in *Beijing Review,* no. 37 (1982): 15 and 31.
3. Meng Lin, "Deng Xiaoping on Sino-U.S. Relations," Hong Kong, *Ching Pao* in Chinese, no. 6, September 5, 1993, p. 41, in Foreign Broadcast Information Service, *Daily Report: China* (hereafter *FBIS,*) no. 171 (1993): 14. "Deng Xiaoping said: Many people inside the Party, inside the Army, and among ordinary people criticize us for making too many concessions and compromises with U.S. hegemonism." See also Jen Hui-wen, "Background to China's 'Four Not's' Policy Toward the United States," Hong Kong *Hsin Pao* in Chinese, September 17, 1993, p. 24, in *FBIS,* no. 179 (1993): 1–3.

4. For instance, Liu Huaqing, member of the Standing Committee of the Politburo and vice chairman of the Party's Central Military Affairs Commission,
   delivered a speech in Guangzhou in September 1993 in which he urged troops
   to be diligent in training, even though the prospects for new equipment, or
   the need to use it, may only be in the distant future. See *Xinhua* Domestic
   Service in Chinese, September 22, 1993, in *FBIS*, no. 183 (1993): 36–37.
5. See Barber B. Conable, Jr., and David M. Lampton, "China: The Coming
   Power," *Foreign Affairs* (Winter 1992/1993): 133–149. Since 1990 there
   have been successive rounds of military budget increases that have led some
   to suggest that Beijing's strategy has changed. I believe it is premature to reach
   such a conclusion, but for the counterargument, see David Shambaugh,
   "Growing Strong: China's Challenge to Asian Security," ms. For a somewhat
   different view, see Paul H. B. Godwin, "China's Security: An Interpretation
   of the Next Decade," forthcoming manuscript for The Atlantic Council and
   the National Committee on United States-China Relations.
6. See, for example, Gerald Segal, "China and the Disintegration of the Soviet
   Union," *Asian Survey* (September 1992): 856.
7. This decline in the percentage of the economy embraced by the central budget reflects not only a policy decision, but also is a manifestation of a tax system that is unable to tap the proliferating sources of new income and the
   decline in the degree to which state enterprises can provide adequate central
   revenues. In 1993 Beijing's central government received only 28 percent of
   total revenues collected from taxes in China, according to a Shanghai official
   (November 1993). Indeed, the Third Plenum of the Fourteenth Party Congress of late 1993 announced the adoption of a new tax system that was
   designed to boost the center's share of the total national tax take.
8. One significant change that probably will occur sometime after the succession
   to Deng Xiaoping will be a regime reevaluation of the character of the
   Tiananmen demonstrations of mid-1989. Most likely constellations of post-
   Deng leadership will find it in their interest to adopt an at least somewhat
   more benign assessment of the basic character of the demonstrators and
   admit to some degree of regime misjudgment in handling those demonstrations. This, in turn, would lead to a further improvement in China's relations
   with Western nations.
9. Shambaugh, "Growing Strong," pp. 32–35; see also Godwin, "China's Security," p. 12. Official Chinese budgetary figures on military funding show
   the following increases: 1988, 8.2 percent; 1989, 14.9 percent; 1990, 14.6
   percent; 1991, 13.8 percent; 1992, 12.2 percent; and, 1993, 15.9 percent.
   Further, almost all outside analysts would agree that perhaps as little as 50
   percent of military spending is reflected in the officially released budgetary
   data of the Chinese government. The remainder is thought to come from hid-
   den budgetary appropriations, direct and indirect subsidies for procurement,
   and revenues from outside the budget process entirely.
10. See, for example, Zhou Tao and Ren Yanjun, "Rally Under the Banner of
    Modernization—Summary of Panel Discussion by Some PLA Experts and
    Scholars on Deng Xiaoping's Thoughts on Army Building in the New Period,"
    Beijing *Jiefangjun Bao* in Chinese, August 22, 1993, in *FBIS*, no. 168 (1993):
    25. This article revealed the military's assessment of its own capabilities in

light of modern conditions of warfare. "In light of the realities of the Gulf War . . . in military confrontations, the most crucial thing in determining which side wins and which loses is still the factor of men. This is particularly so in military confrontations under high-tech conditions. . . . There currently are three weaknesses in our Army's modernization drive: Our weaponry is inferior to that of developed countries, our technology lags behind our weaponry, and the quality of our personnel lags behind our technology."

11. See, for example, "Shandong Governor Zhao Zhihai, Suspected of 'Winking' at Car Smuggling, Is Being Investigated by the Central Commission for Discipline Inspection," Hong Kong *Lien Ho Pao* in Chinese, September 20, 1993, p. 8, in *FBIS*, no. 180 (1993): 23–24.

12. Tien Chen, "Mainland's Weapons Management in Confusion," Hong Kong *Cheng Ming* in Chinese, no. 191, September 1, 1993, pp. 27–29, in *FBIS*, no. 180 (1993): 35–38.

13. For a thorough discussion of the process by which the Clinton administration developed the president's May 28, 1993, executive order, see, David M. Lampton, "China Policy in Clinton's First Year" in James R. Lilley and Wendell L. Willkie II, eds., *Beyond MFN: Trade with China and American Interests* (Washington, D.C.: American Enterprise Institute Press, 1994), pp. 9–35. On May 28, 1993, the White House released an executive order entitled "Conditions for Renewal of Most Favored Nation Status for the People's Republic of China in 1994."

14. Conversation with Chinese official in Beijing, April 1993.

15. Bao Xin, "A Thorough Exposure of the Ugly Features of U.S. Hegemonism," Hong Kong *Liaowang Overseas* in Chinese, no. 37, September 13, 1993, p. 2, in *FBIS*, no. 178 (1993): 9.

16. China's military has been especially sensitive to American pressure for a number of reasons stemming from its own interests, its nationalistic heritage, and its organizational commitment to the reunification of China. First, the PLA tends to feel that Beijing's civilian political leadership failed in June 1989, and that it had to step in to salvage the situation, causing conflict within the military itself, and the loss of respect among the citizenry that had been suppressed, and that it has been the special object of foreign sanctions, particularly by the United States. Second, President Bush's November 1992 approval for sale of 150 F-16s to Taipei offended many in the military and made them question the utility of reaching agreements with Washington such as the August 17, 1982, Communiqué on weapons sales to Taiwan. And third, sanctions such as those imposed on China on August 24, 1993, for alleged violations of the M-11 agreement affect China's military. (See U.S.-China Business Council advisory dated August 26, 1993.) Two articles that indicate the degree to which the military was disenchanted with what it perceives as too soft a policy toward the United States are: Lo Ping and Li Tzuching, "One Hundred and Sixteen Generals Write to Deng Xiaoping on Policy Toward the United States," Hong Kong *Cheng Ming* in Chinese, no. 188, June 1, 1993, pp. 14–16, in *FBIS*, no. 104 (1993): 35; see also Jen Huiwen, "Background to China's 'Four Not's' Policy Toward the United States," Hong Kong *Hsin Pao* in Chinese, September 17, 1993, in *FBIS*, no. 179 (1993): 1–3.

17. Jen Hui-wen, "Background to China's 'Four Not's' Policy," p. 2.
18. Lu Yu-sha, "New 'Eight-Character Principle' of China's Policy Toward the United States," Hong Kong *Tangtai* in Chinese, no. 30, September 15, 1993, p. 9, in *FBIS,* no. 178 (1993): 10.
19. Juan Tzu-san, "China Has Twice as Many Chips as the United States—The United States Is Bound to Pay a Price for Constantly Infuriating China," Hong Kong *Hsin Pao* in Chinese, September 23, 1993, in *FBIS,* no. 183 (1993): 8.
20. Ibid.: 7–8.
21. Ibid.: 7.
22. Thomas L. Friedman, "Bright Sun of Trade Rising in the East," *The New York Times,* November 19, 1993, p. A6.
23. Daniel Williams and R. Jeffrey Smith, "U.S. to Renew Contact with Chinese Military," *The Washington Post,* pp. A1 and A6.
24. Harry Harding, "The Sino-American Relationship Today," prepared for *At a Crossroads in American Policy Toward China: Rebuilding a Consensus,* forthcoming volume by The Atlantic Council and the National Committee on United States-China Relations, p. 2.
25. Interview with senior Chinese official, July 1993, Beijing.
26. Laurence Zuckerman, "U.S. Hopes Seattle Summit with Jiang Will Ease Tone of China Trade Disputes," *Asian Wall Street Journal,* November 1, 1993, p. 2.
27. Shambaugh, "Growing Strong," p. 17; see also Godwin, "China's Security," p. 15.
28. Patrick E. Tyler, "Russia and China Sign a Military Agreement," *The New York Times,* November 10, 1993, p. A15.
29. Pei Li, "The 'China Threat Theory' Is Utterly Groundless," Hong Kong *Tzu Ching* in Chinese, no. 9, September 5, 1993, pp. 43–45, in *FBIS,* no. 178 (1993): 5–7.
30. Gerald Segal, "China and the Disintegration of the Soviet Union," *Asian Survey* (September 1992): 848.
31. Samuel P. Huntington, *Political Order in Changing Societies* (New Haven, CT: Yale University Press, 1968).
32. David M. Lampton, "China's Limited Accommodation with the U.S.S.R.: Coalition Politics," in David M. Lampton, ed., *AEI Foreign Policy and Defense Review,* vol. 6, no. 3 (1986), pp. 26–34.
33. Walter A. McDougall, "The U.S. and Japan: Partners or Else," *The New York Times,* August 29, 1993, p. 15.
34. Lincoln Kaye, "Creative Tensions," *Far Eastern Economic Review,* January 7, 1993, p. 17.
35. Personal communication from Russian Far East, Fall 1993.
36. David Shambaugh, "Growing Strong," p. 16.
37. Patrick E. Tyler, "Russia and China Sign a Military Agreement," *The New York Times,* November 10, 1993, p. A15.
38. Hong Kong *Ta Kung Pao* in Chinese, September 8, 1993, p. 4, in *FBIS,* no. 178 (1993): 27.
39. David M. Lampton, "China's Limited Accommodation with the U.S.S.R.," p. 30.

40. Gerald L. Curtis, "Sino-Japanese Relations Through Chinese Eyes," *Institute Reports,* East Asian Institute, Columbia University, Occasional Paper (June 1993): 1.

41. Peter Harrold and Rajiv Lall, *China: Reform and Development in 1992–93,* World Bank Discussion Papers, China and Mongolia Department, no. 215 (Washington, D.C.: World Bank, 1993), p. 12.

42. Lincoln Kaye, "Common Interests," *Far Eastern Economic Review,* January 7, 1993, p. 16.

43. Lincoln Kaye, "Creative Tensions," p. 16.

44. Lincoln Kaye, ibid., p. 17, notes, "There is a boundless appetite across the border [in China] for forest products, including exotic herbs and animal glands, as well as minerals and fertilizer."

45. Wang Chongjie, "Complex and Subtle U.S.-Russian Relations," Beijing *Xinhua* Domestic Service in Chinese, September 15, 1993, in *FBIS,* no. 184 (1993): 8–9.

46. Ibid., p. 8.

47. Ibid.

48. Ibid., p. 9.

49. Lincoln Kaye, "Common Interests," p. 10.

50. Banning Garrett and Bonnie Glaser, "Yeltsin's China Mission," *Far Eastern Economic Review,* December 17, 1992, p. 24.

51. Patrick E. Tyler, "Russia and China Sign a Military Agreement," *The New York Times,* November 10, 1993, p. A15.

52. Gerald Segal, "China and the Disintegration of the Soviet Union," pp. 855 and 864.

53. David Shambaugh, "Growing Strong," p. 17.

54. Jeff Lilley, "Russian Handicap: Moscow Looks East But the Picture Is Bleak," *Far Eastern Economic Review,* November 26, 1992, p. 24.

55. See, for example, Pei Li "The 'China Threat Theory' Is Utterly Groundless," Hong Kong *Tzu Ching* in Chinese, no. 9 (September 5, 1993), pp. 43–45, FBIS, no. 178 (1993), pp. 5–7.

56. Garrett and Glaser, "Yeltsin's China Mission," p. 24.

57. Shen Faliang and Fan Weiguo, "Qian Qichen Completes 3-Day Visit to Ukraine," Beijing *Xinhua* Domestic Service in Chinese, September 7, 1993, in *FBIS* no. 172 (1993): 11. No fragment of the former Soviet Union is too small to receive Beijing's attention when it comes to Taiwan. In September 1993 Vice Premier and Foreign Minister Qian Qichen met Estonian Foreign Minister Trivimi Velliste in Beijing and the Estonian was reported to have indicated that "its stance of not seeking official ties with Taiwan will remain intact," *Xinhua* in English, September 2, 1993, in *FBIS,* no. 170 (1993): 4.

58. Michel Oksenberg and Charles E. Morrison, "Japanese Emperor's Visit to China Sends Important Signals to the United States," in *Notes from the National Committee,* vol. 22, no. 1 (New York: National Committee on United States-China Relations, 1993), pp. 2, 6, and 7. See also Lincoln Kaye, "Saving Faces: Both Sides Gain from the Emperor's Visit," *Far Eastern Economic Review,* November 5, 1992, p. 14.

59. Gerald L. Curtis, "Sino-Japanese Relations Through Chinese Eyes," in *Institute Reports,* East Asian Institute, Columbia University (June 1993): 2.

60. Kaye, "Saving Faces," p. 13.
61. Curtis, "Sino-Japanese Relations Through Chinese Eyes," p. 1.
62. Kaye, "Saving Faces," p. 14.
63. Curtis, "Sino-Japanese Relations Through Chinese Eyes," p. 1.
64. Ibid., p. 3.
65. Kaye, "Saving Faces," p. 13.
66. Liu Jiangyong, "Historic Change in Japanese Politics," in *Contemporary International Relations,* vol. 3, no. 9 (Beijing: China Institute of Contemporary International Relations, September 1993), pp. 1–14.
67. Kaye, "Saving Faces," p. 13.
68. Oksenberg and Morrison, "Japanese Emperor's Visit to China," p. 2.
69. Liu Jiangyong, "Historic Change in Japanese Politics," pp. 1–10.
70. Ibid., p. 7.
71. Ibid.
72. Ibid., pp. 7–8.
73. Ibid., p. 8.
74. Ibid., pp. 8–9.
75. Ibid., p. 10.
76. Ibid., p. 11.
77. David E. Sanger, "With Expectations Low, Yeltsin Arrives in Japan," *The New York Times,* October 12, 1993, p. A7.
78. Chu Hsing-fu, "Why Does the United States Adjust Its Policy Toward China?—Acknowledging the Main Threat to the United States (Part 2)," Hong Kong *Wen Wei Po* in Chinese, November 18, 1993, p. 2, in *FBIS,* no. 221 (1993): 15–16.
79. Karen Elliott House, "Focus on Asia," *The Wall Street Journal,* June 1, 1993.

CHAPTER THREE

Japan and the Strategic Quadrangle

MIKE M. MOCHIZUKI

A number of external shocks have buffeted Japan in recent years. The Iraqi invasion of Kuwait in 1990 shocked the Japanese into realizing the international inadequacy of their brand of pacifism. To the last moment until American-led air forces struck Baghdad, most Japanese did not think a large-scale multinational war would really happen. The collapse of the Soviet Union also has been a shock of sorts. It brought the Cold War to a definitive end, and with it the bipolar system that had provided the international stability (albeit an uneasy one) and predictability essential to Japan's prosperity as a trading nation. Now the United States has been asking Japan to aid a former enemy—just when Japan had begun to take more seriously the Soviet threat. With the geopolitical glue that held the U.S.-Japanese relationship together gone, Japan has to search for new ways to revitalize the trans-Pacific alliance. It also faces tougher American policies for dealing with bilateral economic disputes. Finally, yen appreciation has shocked Japan's economic system. Earlier, the Japanese successfully weathered the yen appreciation in the wake of the 1985 Plaza Accord by shedding productive capabilities in uncompetitive areas, by investing abroad and at home, and by using their financial clout to open up new external markets. But the 1993–94 yen appreciation has been different. The bursting of the so-called bubble economy severely weakened the Japanese financial system and plunged the country into one of its worst recessions since World War II. Given the growing American hostility to imports from Japan and the economic slowdown in both Europe and North America, the option of exporting out of the recession, a strategy often used successfully in the past, is no longer available. Japan is now burdened with industrial overcapacity and unfavorable terms of trade.

While confronting these diplomatic and economic challenges, Japan has entered a political transition period that is likely to last for several years. Although the issue of political reform triggered the realignment that ended nearly four decades of Liberal Democratic Party (LDP) rule in August 1993, the end of the Cold War provided the context that made this change possible. The collapse of Soviet-style communism discredited the traditional leftist parties in Japan and neutralized the issue of supporting U.S. containment policy as a matter of intense conflict between government and opposition. As a result, a sizable group from the LDP could leave the ruling party, cross the left-right ideological divide, and join a coalition government that included the Socialists. After Morihiro Hosokawa, who headed this seven-party coalition, resigned the prime ministership in April 1994, a new round of political maneuvering yielded a short-lived minority cabinet headed by Tsutomu Hata, followed by what had been inconceivable during the Cold War era: a coalition government involving Liberal Democrats and Socialists led by a Socialist premier, Tomiichi Murayama. Further realignments are likely as Japan implements a new electoral system and its political class undergoes a generational change. But the ultimate outcome of this transition process remains unclear given the complex cross-cutting cleavages in terms of policy positions and personal relations among political elites.

This era of domestic political fluidity in the context of international uncertainties raises a number of basic questions about the future of Japanese foreign policy. Will Japan become more proactive in the international arena, or will it remain primarily a reactive state? Will the Japanese economy become more open to foreign goods, services, and investments; or will a relatively closed, neomercantilist perspective for foreign economic relations persist? Will Japan become more assertive in political-military matters commensurate with its economic capabilities, or will it build upon its pacifistic tradition and contribute to international society in nonmilitary ways as a "global civilian power"? Will Japan continue to defer to the United States on important international issues, or will it gradually develop a foreign policy more independent of Washington? How will China and Russia factor into Japan's strategic calculations? Will Japan try to stay in step with the United States on China and Russia policy, or will it develop its own approach toward these two countries?

The linkages between international and domestic developments are inordinately complex, making definitive answers to these questions impossible. Under such circumstances, the temptation is to believe that the future will look much like the past. Given the strategic logic behind Japan's foreign policies after World War II and the domestic institutional support for these policies, forecasting more continuity than change does seem justified. But these are not normal times. If the last five years is any indication, the international environment could change further in dramatic and unpredictable ways. And in Japan itself, what was virtually unthinkable has happened: the end of LDP dominance, the emergence of fluid coalition patterns that cut across traditional ideological cleavages, and the selection of a Socialist prime minister. Therefore, the analytical challenge is to discern the signs of substantive change and grasp their underlying dynamic, even while recognizing the power of inertia and continuity. Of the countless factors that could shape the future of Japanese foreign policy, the dynamics of the Strategic Quadrangle (i.e., the interaction among the United States, China, Russia, and Japan) will certainly have a decisive impact.

LOOKING BEYOND THE COLD WAR

Japanese initially welcomed the end of the Cold War just as much as Americans and Europeans did. The collapse of the Soviet Union basically eliminated the possibility of Japan becoming embroiled in a military conflict between two nuclear superpowers. The failure of communism and the global push for military retrenchment affirmed the validity of Japan's postwar policies—that of minimizing military expenditures while concentrating on economic growth.

But while sharing the initial Western euphoria over the breathtaking events in Eastern Europe and the Soviet Union, the Japanese were also concerned about the uncertainties that lay ahead.

Their anxiety was not surprising because of all the major countries in the world, Japan had benefited the most from the Soviet-American competition. As part of its grand strategy to contain the Soviet Union, Washington promoted Japan's recovery after World War II. The militarization of American containment policy led to a commitment to defend Japan in exchange for access to military bases in Japan. While the U.S. forward deployment posture in the Pacific brought Japan into the American security system, it also obviated the need for Japan to undertake major rearmament. American military procurements that resulted from involvement in the Korean and Vietnam wars contributed greatly to Japan's recovery.[1]

The diplomatic price that Japan paid for the U.S. security guarantee involved two things. First, it became party to what has been called a "partial" rather than a "total" peace settlement. Although Tokyo was able to resume diplomatic relations with the Soviet Union in 1956, it could not sign a formal peace treaty with Moscow. Second, Washington compelled Tokyo to recognize the Nationalist regime in Taipei, rather than the Communist regime in Beijing, as the legitimate government of China. But on balance, the benefits of incorporation into the Cold War system outweighed the costs.

Because the United States saw a prosperous and stable Japan to be in its strategic interest, it sponsored the latter's incorporation into international economic organizations such as the GATT (General Agreement on Tariffs and Trade) and the OECD (Organization for Economic Cooperation and Development) while tolerating asymmetries in the economic relationship. The American market was open to Japanese goods, while Japan placed restrictions on imports and foreign investments. Japan thus became a free rider on the liberal international economic order in two respects. It did not assume the burden of creating or maintaining this economic system, and it adopted economic policies that often contradicted the system's basic principles.[2] In short, the alliance with the United States permitted Japan to pursue a neomercantilist strategy for economic reconstruction and expansion.

Furthermore, Japan over time found ways to overcome the constraints of the Cold War system to pursue its economic interests. During the 1960s Japan worked around the pro-Taiwan policy imposed by the United States by separating politics from economics (*seikei bunri*). It promoted trade relations with mainland China while following Washington in its refusal to recognize the Beijing government. This became a moot issue after President Richard Nixon's opening to China in 1971. Regarding the Soviet Union, the dispute over the Northern Territories did not prevent progress in economic relations. In the context of Soviet-American détente during the 1970s, the Japanese invested heavily in Siberia to gain access to raw materials.

Identification with U.S. foreign policy did play a role in triggering a major economic crisis in Japan during the 1973 Yom Kippur War. The Arab countries shocked Japan by suspending oil shipments and demanding that Tokyo sever diplomatic relations with Israel and support the Arab cause. As Washington provided the Japanese with little help to deal with the crisis, Tokyo shifted decisively in a pro-Arab direction by supporting Palestinian self-determination and Israeli withdrawal from the territories occupied since the 1967 war.[3] This break with the United States on Middle East policy, however, entailed surprisingly few costs. The fact that European allies also had difficulties with America's pro-Israeli line made Japan's new orientation less of a problem for U.S.-Japanese relations.

Given the great benefits and the minimal costs, Japan has had little incentive to alter its basic policy of aligning with the United States. Indeed, managing relations with the United States has been the primary preoccupation of Japanese foreign policy elites. But while the United States has been pivotal to Japan's national interests, three sets of tensions regarding basic foreign policy issues have emerged in the course of postwar history. These tensions not only have profound implications for domestic politics, but also will affect the character of Japanese foreign policy in the post–Cold War era.

The first tension is that between *rearmament* and *pacifism*. It emerged with the beginnings of the Cold War and the outbreak of the Korean conflict. The United States reversed its occupation policy of demilitarization and began to pressure Japan to rearm. While refusing to engage in full-scale rearmament, the Japanese government did agree to the creation of a National Police Reserve, which developed into the Self-Defense Forces (SDF), and to sign a security treaty with the United States. An important constraint against a major military buildup was the overwhelming pacifist sentiment among citizens who did not want the tragedy of their country's militarist past repeated. Some conservative political leaders, however, favored a more active defense policy as a way of resurrecting "nationalist consciousness and traditional Japanese values."[4] Although the conflict between rearmament and pacifism was one of the most contentious issues during the 1950s and early 1960s, a delicate equilibrium emerged during the 1970s because of the imposition of strict parameters for defense policy. During the 1980s Japan relaxed some of these constraints, but the tension between rearmament and pacifism persisted in domestic discussions about foreign policy. It emerged with particular urgency when Japan awkwardly tried to design a credible response to the Persian Gulf crisis of 1990–91. Because of international criticisms that Japan did not contribute much more than money to Operations Desert Shield and Desert Storm, younger leaders such as then–LDP secretary-general Ichiro Ozawa called for a reinterpretation of the constitution and major structural changes in domestic politics so that Japan can "contribute to international society" in the security as well as economic realms.[5] Their security agenda involved moving beyond homeland defense toward full participation in not only United Nations peacekeeping activities but also multinational coalitions against aggressive states. Since support or resistance to this agenda currently cuts across the government-opposition divide, questions of security policy could cause a new round of political fragmentation and realignment during the next several years.

Second, there is the tension between *neomercantilism* and *economic liberalism*. The basic thrust of Japan's foreign economic policy has been neomercantilism, which involves the practice of state assistance, regulation, and protection of specific industrial sectors in order to enhance their international competitiveness and ultimately to achieve national preeminence over the "commanding heights" of the world economy.[6] Many factors have contributed to this policy orientation: Japan's status as a late developer, its sense of economic vulnerability, the need to export in order to pay for raw material imports, an elite and cohesive state agency for industrial development, the dominance of a pro-business political party coupled with a weak and divided left, a myriad of networks between state and business elites, and a concern about social order and harmony. As Japan's economy recovered miraculously from its wartime devastation, the United States became less tolerant of neomercantilism. Beginning with the Kennedy Round multilateral trade negotiations in the 1960s, Washington pressured Tokyo to liberalize its economic policies and practices. To preserve its access to American markets and technology, Japan responded to these pressures by slowly opening its economy to foreign products and investments and by streamlining state intervention in business activity. The Japanese government now officially embraces the tenets of economic liberalism, but protectionist policies and practices persist in a number of industrial sectors, and state agencies continue to cooperate with businesses to enhance the nation's international competitiveness. Despite frequent campaigns for deregulation, government regulations over the economy have increased. The effect has been to obstruct the entry of business outsiders (both foreign and domestic) into managed, even cartelized markets. The tension between neomercantilism and economic liberalism lacks the ideological stridency of the conflict between rearmament and pacifism. Nevertheless, this dimension of foreign policy does invoke intense interest-based conflicts among state agencies and social groups.

The final tension is that between *globalism* and *regionalism* and relates not only to Japan's national interest, but also to its sense of national identity. Although Japan has been more comfortable in East Asia for obvious cultural and geographic reasons, historical circumstances have forced Japan to look beyond this region. The pre-1945 version of this tension ended in tragedy. America's opening of Japan in the mid-nineteenth century compelled the Japanese to look toward the West for models for enhancing national wealth and power and to play the European game of balance-of-power politics. But with the deterioration of relations with the United States, Japan opted for a misguided pan-Asian policy.

After World War II the strategic linkage with the United States steered Japan toward "trilateralism," leading ultimately to its participation in the G-7 economic summits and its official declaration that Japan was a "member of the West." Moreover, as its economy grew in power and scope, Japan recognized its vital stakes in distant areas, especially the Middle East with its oil fields. A recent expression of the globalist perspective was Tokyo's interest in gaining observer status in the Conference on Security and Cooperation in Europe (CSCE) and the North Atlantic Treaty Organization (NATO).[7] At the same time, however, an undercurrent of regionalism persists. One reason for this is, of course, the intricate economic linkages that Japan has been developing in East Asia. Japanese direct investments in the East Asian economies have grown rapidly since the mid-1980s. Japan's two-way trade with East Asia now surpasses that with North America. Japanese also feel an affinity in terms of basic values and social customs toward their Asian neighbors—especially those similarly influenced by the Confucian cultural tradition. And the end of the Cold War and mounting economic tensions with the United States have encouraged greater Japanese diplomatic activity in East Asia in order to cultivate a more hospitable regional environment.

How these three sets of tensions in Japanese foreign policy play themselves out in the post–Cold War era will be determined to a large extent by the dynamics of the Strategic Quadrangle: by the foreign policies of the other three powers, by the strategic interaction among them, and by Japan's own bilateral relations with each of them.

In the post–Cold War era, Tokyo's greatest worry is that the United States might adopt exclusionary policies toward Japanese imports and investments while weakening its security ties in East Asia. The possibility of such a turn in American policy invokes much fear among Japanese officials because it could lead to international isolation.[8] Given its meager natural resources, limited territory, and dense population, Japan would be unable to survive in isolation without a dramatic decline in its living standards and a sharp increase in the costs and risks of maintaining national security.

A rupture in U.S.-Japanese relations would be disastrous because Japan has no attractive alternatives to the United States. The territorial dispute remains an obstacle to close relations with Russia. Even if this issue were resolved in Japan's favor, Russia would not be a suitable economic partner until its domestic political situation stabilizes and economic reforms become more institutionalized. The brutal crackdown of the democracy movement in June 1989 clearly demonstrated that China would not be a good substitute for the United States. The other countries of East Asia are too disparate, too small, and still too suspicious of Japan. They are culturally and politically diverse, making the creation of a Pacific Asian community supportive of Japan's interests and aspirations a daunting task. Western Europe has become an important market for Japan, and Japanese businesses moved quickly to invest in this region and to forge corporate alliances with European counterparts before the establishment of a unified European market in 1992. But Europe is still too psychologically and geographically distant to be a viable strategic option in place of the United States. More important, a European connection without the American connection would be not only flimsy but also unimaginable. Consequently, the primary challenge facing Japan beyond the Cold War will be to keep the United States diplomatically and militarily engaged in Asia while simultaneously committed to a liberal, international economic order.

To preserve the bilateral relationship, Japan will continue to respond—albeit begrudgingly—to American pressures to liberalize its economy and to shoulder more of the security burden. But it also is becoming more resentful of what it is considers to be the United States' unreasonable demands and impatience. Japan could be tempted to use either China or Russia to gain leverage vis-à-vis the United States, but such a strategy is unlikely to work because neither China nor Russia is a viable alternative to it. To moderate U.S. pressures, Japan is more likely to use economic power to reduce America's degrees of freedom, rather than to play an independent power-balancing game in the Strategic Quadrangle. Japan also faces the challenge of keeping its policies toward Russia and China in step with those of the United States. Tokyo wants to avoid having differences in policy toward Beijing and Moscow aggravate relations with Washington.

Given the geographic proximity of China and Russia, Japan wants these large neighbors to be nonthreatening and stable. Although these two powers may not serve as leverage over the United States, they can help to hedge against a worst-case scenario: American neo-isolationism and a breakdown in bilateral relations. In such a situation, China and Russia would emerge as important players in Japan's quest to create a hospitable environment in the Asia-Pacific region. Certainly these two countries will be critical factors in a fundamental reassessment of its security policies.

A closer examination of Japan's bilateral relations with each of the other three powers in the quadrangle will reveal the underpinnings of its strategic calculations and the way that quadrilateral relations might affect the three tensions in Japanese foreign policy.

RELATIONS WITH THE UNITED STATES

The dominant picture that emerges from the last forty years of U.S.-Japanese relations is that of Japan responding reluctantly and incrementally to a variety of U.S. pressures in order to keep the American economy open to Japanese goods and investments, to maintain the flow of basic technology from the United States, and to preserve America's security commitment.

On the economic front, the basic thrust of American pressures has been to move Japan away from neomercantilism toward economic liberalism while moderating Japanese inroads into the U.S. market. During the early postwar years the United States tolerated and even encouraged this neomercantilism because it wanted Japan to recover for strategic reasons. But by the 1960s Washington shifted gears and initiated its long campaign for trade liberalization. Tokyo obliged grudgingly and started to lower its tariffs and remove other trade barriers. Nevertheless, liberalization was implemented strategically and incrementally to minimize the disruptive impact on domestic business. As Japanese firms succeeded in penetrating foreign markets (especially the United States) and their international competitiveness improved, both government and big business became more supportive of free trade—at least rhetorically.[9]

Japan resisted liberalization most stubbornly in the agricultural sector because of the importance of farmers for the ruling

Liberal Democratic Party's electoral base. Officials attempted to hold back U.S. pressures by raising food security arguments and referring to the large amount of farm products that Japan was already importing. When Washington's insistence made some kind of liberalization inevitable, Japan preferred to grant predetermined shares of the agricultural market to American producers rather than embrace the principle of free trade for farm products, as demonstrated in the 1977–78 negotiations on beef and citrus products.[10] Over a decade had to pass since the beginning of these negotiations before Japan would finally agree to eliminate import quotas for these commodities.

While the U.S. government was promoting trade liberalization, American industries that were losing market share to imports sought protectionist relief. In response, Japan agreed to "voluntary" export restraints and orderly marketing arrangements covering a variety of sectors including textiles, steel, automobiles, and most recently semiconductors. Furthermore, it encouraged firms to invest and produce abroad and to forge joint ventures with American companies so as to circumvent trade barriers, defuse protectionist sentiments in the United States, and preserve access to U.S. technology.

Japan also responded to U.S. pressures to liberalize and internationalize its financial system. The 1980 revision of the Foreign Exchange Law facilitated foreign access to domestic capital markets. After the Yen-Dollar Agreement of 1984, foreign commercial banks were permitted to begin trust banking operations, and it became easier for foreign financial institutions to participate in Japanese and European bond markets. In 1985 foreign security firms gained admission to the Tokyo Stock Exchange for the first time, and a year later the government opened an offshore banking facility in Tokyo. Although foreign pressure played an important role in stimulating these changes, just as critical was the lobbying from Japanese financial institutions that were seeking to become more involved in foreign transactions. Liberalization indeed increased the international role of the yen and Japan's presence in foreign capital markets.[11]

When Japan's trade surplus continued to soar during the early 1980s, the Reagan administration turned to macroeconomic solutions. It asked Tokyo to stimulate domestic demand to dampen the export drive, but Japan's Ministry of Finance refused. The ministry wanted to solve the nation's fiscal "crisis" by balancing the budget and blamed America's deficit spending under "Reaganomics" for the U.S. trade deficit. Then Washington opted for a realignment of exchange rates. In contrast to the early 1970s, when Japan stubbornly resisted yen appreciation and forced the Nixon administration to take unilateral action, Tokyo was more responsive this time around. In a dramatic display of policy coordination, Japan cooperated with the United States, Britain, France, and West Germany in the September 1985 Plaza Accord to devalue the dollar by intervening in foreign exchange markets and raising interest rates. The effect went beyond expectations. By February 1987 the dollar had plummeted to 154 yen from the 242-yen level before this agreement.

The sharp appreciation of the yen, however, did not reduce the U.S.-Japanese trade imbalance. In fact, Japan's trade surplus with the United States increased from $39.5 billion in 1985 to $47.6 billion in 1988. But without the exchange rate realignment, the trade imbalance may have worsened even more. Yen appreciation did have a major impact on Japanese business practices, trade patterns, and economic policy. Pressed by the deterioration in the terms of trade, firms relocated their production abroad in droves. Foreign direct investment soared from $12.2 billion in 1985 to $47 billion in 1988, with $21.7 billion going to the United States. Investment in Asia as a percentage of Japan's total direct overseas investment jumped from 11.7 percent in 1985 to 14.6 percent in 1987. At the same time, Japanese imports from Asian countries rose. In dollar terms, imports from the East Asian "newly industrializing economies" (South Korea, Taiwan, Hong Kong, and Singapore) more than doubled, from $9.8 billion in 1985 to $25 billion in 1988.[12]

Yen appreciation also accelerated the forces of industrial change within Japan. Many industries, including steel, shipbuilding, and consumer electronics, were forced to restructure rapidly; and the emergence of lower-cost foreign producers intensified efforts to move ahead in high-technology fields. But the social costs of this industrial transformation were not as great as many had predicted.[13]

The unemployment rate increased somewhat, but the nation's social cohesion was not undermined. One reason for this is that the government shifted from its austerity program of the early 1980s toward a looser monetary and expansionary fiscal policy.

The most dramatic effect of the 1985 Plaza Accord was to turn Japan into the leading creditor nation almost overnight. Japan's net external assets climbed from about $24.7 billion in 1982 to over $240 billion in 1987. The percentage of the world's foreign currency reserves held as yen increased from 4.3 to 7 between the years 1980 and 1987. Over the same period, international bond issues denominated in yen jumped from 1.5 to 14.1 percent, while those denominated in dollars fell from 66.5 to 35.8 percent. Japanese trade transactions, both imports and exports, became increasingly handled in yen rather than in dollars.[14]

In terms of security relations, the basic objective of U.S. policy has been to encourage moderate rearmament and to transform Japan from a reluctant to an active strategic ally of the United States. After the 1960 Security Treaty crisis, Washington soft-pedaled its military connection with Tokyo to avoid another flare-up of pacifist and even neutralist sentiment among Japanese. Also during the late 1960s and for much of the 1970s, the Japanese government worked to broaden public support for the U.S.-Japan Security Treaty and the Self-Defense Forces by placing limits on its own defense policies. These self-imposed constraints included the "three non-nuclear principles," the ban on arms exports, a 1 percent of gross national product (GNP) ceiling on military expenditures, and a codification of a strictly defensive military posture. The U.S. reversion of Okinawa back to Japan and the termination of American military involvement in Vietnam further contributed to the nascent public consensus on defense issues. Whereas only a minority of citizens endorsed the U.S.-Japan Security Treaty in 1960, by the second half of the 1970s, a large majority backed this treaty and even acknowledged the constitutionality of the SDF.

During the 1980s Soviet behavior as well as American pressure contributed to a more active security policy. The Soviet military buildup in Northeast Asia, the troop deployments on the Northern Territories, the invasion of Afghanistan, and the shooting down of the Korean airliner all began to convince the Japanese that there was indeed a Soviet military threat. In this context, Japan did begin to change from a reluctant to an active U.S. ally. Diplomatically, Tokyo abandoned previous statements about an omnidirectional foreign policy and stressed its firm commitment to the Western alliance. Japan, much more than the West European nations, supported U.S. economic sanctions against the Soviet Union after the Afghanistan invasion and the Polish military crackdown against Solidarity. Militarily, Japan began to participate in joint military exercises with American forces and discuss coordinated bilateral strategy and tactics in possible crisis scenarios. It increased its host-nation support for U.S. military forces in Japan from 43.5 billion yen in 1981 to 142.2 billion in 1989, which amounted to about 40 percent of the costs.[15]

Tokyo also weakened the earlier constraints on defense policy. Prime Minister Zenko Suzuki publicly announced the defense of sea lanes out to 1,000 nautical miles as a national objective. His successor, Yasuhiro Nakasone, rescinded the 1 percent of GNP spending limit on defense, agreed to transfer defense technology to the United States, and decided to participate in research for America's Strategic Defense Initiative. He expanded the concept of self-defense by arguing in the National Diet that it would not be unconstitutional if the SDF assisted U.S. forces operating to protect Japan *before* an actual attack on Japan took place.

Although defense spending as a percentage of GNP has remained about 1 percent, the absolute size of Japan's military budget in dollar terms is now among the largest in the world. More important, its military capability in terms of front-line equipment has become quite formidable. Japan will soon have three times as many destroyer-type surface ships and four times as many P-3C antisubmarine-warfare aircraft as the U.S. Seventh Fleet. Its tactical fighter planes will number 300 (including 200 of the advanced F-15s), which is comparable to the number of fighter aircraft defending the continental United States. To strengthen its ability to defend sea lanes from air threats, the SDF has been procuring the Aegis naval air defense system and has developed plans to acquire over-the-horizon radars and AWACS (airborne warning and control system) aircraft.[16] In short, Japan's status as a strong military power in Northeast Asia is beyond question.

Following U.S. suggestions to do so, Japan also increased substantially its foreign economic assistance as a nonmilitary means for promoting international security. By the early 1980s Tokyo embraced the concept of "strategic" aid and started to allocate more aid money to nations such as Turkey, Pakistan, and Egypt, which the United States viewed as critical from a security perspective.[17] Japanese official development assistance expanded from $2.22 billion in 1984 to $8.96 billion in 1989, surpassing the United States as the largest contributor.[18] Buying into the idea of a "global partnership" with the United States, Tokyo began to consider major aid initiatives to countries in Latin America and Eastern Europe.

This tendency to alter its economic and security policies in the face of American pressure has led some observers to characterize Japan as a reactive state. Despite its growing economic capabilities, Japan has eschewed proactive and independent initiatives while responding flexibly to external pressures. Compared to the middle-range powers of Western Europe such as Britain, France, and West Germany, Japan has been much more deferential to the United States.[19]

One explanation for this characteristic of Japanese foreign policy is that domestic political structures and processes have discouraged greater activism and independence. During the era of LDP dominance, the prime minister was unable to chart and implement a proactive policy because party factionalism circumscribed his executive authority. The fragmented nature of the national bureaucracy compounded the problem of policy coordination. Interest groups penetrated the state policy process directly and indirectly through LDP policy specialists, making it difficult to adopt foreign policy initiatives that would sacrifice these entrenched interests.[20] Despite the trend of ideological depolarization, government-opposition conflict constrained government policy on international issues. In addition to these internal factors, Japan's external environment also contributed to its deference to the United States. As noted earlier, Japan has lacked attractive and viable strategic alternatives to the United States.

This image of the reactive state does, however, raise the question of how responsive Japan really has been to American pressure. To what extent has Japan actually shifted from neomercantilism to economic liberalism and transformed itself from a reluctant to an active ally of the United States?

One can certainly marshal support for the claim that the Japanese political economy is becoming more liberal. Economists have shown that Japan's average tariff rate is lower than that of the United States and Western Europe, and its nontariff trade barriers may affect fewer markets than those of the United States.[21] The Ministry of International Trade and Industry (MITI), which had been the institutional bastion of neomercantilism, now has fewer policy instruments to shape industrial development. It can no longer direct large amounts of capital to targeted industries and use foreign exchange controls and allocations of raw materials to shape firm behavior. MITI has even proposed a tax-incentive scheme to promote imports.[22]

But there is also strong evidence that neomercantilist policies and practices persist. Japan continues to have huge trade surpluses not only with the United States (over $50 billion in 1993) but also with the world as a whole (over $120 billion in 1993). Japan's current account surplus also has soared, to over $131 billion in 1993. Although Japan has removed trade barriers for competitive sectors, there is still a "moving band of protectionism" to nurture emerging high-technology sectors (e.g., microelectronics, biotechnology, and new materials) and to ease the pain of adjustment in declining sectors (e.g., shipbuilding, aluminum refining, and paper and wood products).[23] Unlike other advanced industrial democracies, Japan engages in little intrasectoral trade. It does not import very much from sectors to which it exports a great deal. This means that Japanese export sectors have been able to insulate themselves from foreign import penetration.[24]

Neomercantilism is clearly evident in Japan's technology policies, which are designed to give Japanese firms the competitive edge in terms of innovation. To promote research and development in commercially risky fields, the government organizes collaborative projects among private firms and makes sure that all the participating firms will receive the patents based on the research. The government also has been known to delay foreign applications for patents so as to give Japanese corporations an opportunity to apply for patents on similar technology. While being reluctant to let foreigners tap into domestically generated technology, Japan has been very effective in absorbing foreign technology.[25] Quite apart from state policies, the organization of leading corporations into *keiretsu,* or business networks, still impedes foreign access to Japanese markets.[26]

In 1986–87, Prime Minister Nakasone's advisory panel, entitled "Economic Structural Adjustment for International Harmony" (the so-called Maekawa commission), recommended that Japan make sweeping changes to help revitalize the free-trade regime. The "Maekawa Reports," which became the manifestos of economic liberalism in Japan, advocated the promotion of domestic consumption, shorter working hours and adequate wage growth, deregulation and more effective competition policies, reform of the distribution system, changes in land use policies, tax breaks for homebuyers, and the introduction of market principles in the agricultural sector. The impact of this blue-ribbon commission on concrete policies, however, was meager; even big-business leaders expressed concerns about how the proposed measures would affect international competitiveness.[27]

Compared to the economic sphere, Japan appears to have been more cooperative with the United States on security matters. Most observers agree that bilateral security relations are better today than ever before and that there has been a clear strategic convergence across the Pacific. But there are still clear limits to Japan playing the role of an active ally. For example, during the Persian Gulf crisis of 1990–91, Japan's contribution was limited primarily to financial support (a total of $13 billion) to the anti-Iraqi multinational coalition. Constitutional and domestic political constraints prevented Japan from providing the United States with logistical support (e.g., air and sea lifts) for its military operations against Iraq.[28] Only after Kuwait was liberated did Japan send a modest flotilla for minesweeping operations in the Persian Gulf.

The greatest source of friction in bilateral security relations has concerned military procurement practices. Although Japan can acquire more defense equipment for much less money through off-the-shelf procurements from American suppliers, the Defense Agency since 1970 has favored indigenous development or coproduction arrangements with the United States. The controversy surrounding Japan's plans to acquire a new-generation support fighter, the FSX, to replace the aging F-1s illustrates Japanese priorities. Domestic industrial interests wanted to develop the FSX indigenously to give the aircraft sector a much-needed boost. When pressure from Washington eliminated this as a viable option, they reluctantly agreed to coproduction with U.S. contractors using the American F-16 fighter plane as the base. In short, economic calculations superseded the security interest of acquiring state-of-art-fighter aircraft at the lowest possible cost.[29]

The limits of responsiveness to American pressure pose a further question that turns the reactive state image of Japan on its head. Rather than asking why Japan's foreign policy has been so reactive, the more pertinent question seems to be why Japan has been so resistant to change when it has such a stake in good relations with the United States. At least three factors are important in answering this question. First, the same political characteristics that prevent Japan from having a proactive foreign policy also prevent Japan from being truly responsive to American pressures. The weak authority of the prime minister, bureaucratic sectionalism, sharp ideological conflicts between parties on security issues, and entrenched interest groups have all made it difficult for Japan to move decisively away from neomercantilism.[30]

Second, Japanese responsiveness has been limited because Japan does indeed have a perspective about economic policy and international affairs that is quite different from that of the United States. Although market forces are recognized as critical for encouraging productive efficiency and innovation, the Japanese, much more than the Americans, are willing to shape and check market mechanisms in order to promote national development, to compensate the weaker economic sectors, and to preserve social order. On security issues, the Japanese tend to oppose the use of force not only to settle international disputes, but also to intervene in civil wars. By contrast, the United States is willing to engage in foreign military intervention and sees military security in global terms. This persistent gap between Japan and the United States accounts for the many contradictions that riddle Japan's economic and security relations with the United States: (1) Japan's criticisms of U.S. protectionist tendencies in the face of its reluctance to take the lead in dismantling its own protectionist policies and practices; (2) its reliance on U.S. nuclear deterrence while it refuses to acknowledge openly the importance of port visits by nuclear-armed U.S. naval vessels; and (3) its willingness to let the United States use military force to maintain oil supplies from the Middle East while it adamantly resists the dispatch of Self-Defense Forces to support such missions.

Third, despite the fact that U.S. pressure has long been a feature of bilateral relations, in the end Washington has been restrained about its dealings with Tokyo. During the Cold War era, the U.S. government moderated its attempts to compel changes in Japanese economic policy because it did not want to damage the security relationship. Furthermore, Washington even exercised restraint on security matters for fear that Japan could go in one of two extreme directions: neutralism or major rearmament, whereby Japan would become threatening to other Asian countries and difficult for even the United States to manage.[31]

The passing of the Cold War, however, could fundamentally alter the dynamics of U.S.-Japanese relations that have prevailed until now. As a number of analysts have argued, the close strategic relationship between Japan and the United States helped to resolve economic conflicts in an amicable manner.[32] If the importance of Japan as a strategic ally, however, diminishes because of the end of the Cold War, then the United States is likely to feel less restrained about being tough in dealing with economic problems. And in turn, the Japanese may want to resist U.S. pressures more overtly.

There are clear indications that American perspectives of Japan are undergoing significant change. Numerous public opinion polls suggest that a growing number of Americans feel that Japanese economic power threatens long-term U.S. interests. Just as important as these negative public attitudes are the revisionist analyses by influential journalists and academic specialists.[33] The so-called revisionists argue that Japan is not a liberal economy like the United States and that Japanese ruling elites still have a neomercantilist strategy to achieve preeminence over the "commanding heights" of the world economy. While advocating a counterstrategy to revive America's traditional strengths, they also see the need to contain Japanese economic expansion.

In the context of these views about Japan, President George Bush became much more aggressive about promoting liberalism in Japan than his predecessor. In May 1989 the Bush administration responded to congressional pressure by citing Japan under section 301 of the new Trade Law for unfair trade practices regarding supercomputers, satellites, and forest products. It also asked Tokyo to commence talks to reduce dramatically the "structural impediments to trade" and began to demand liberalization of Japan's rice market. Tokyo responded to this aggressive liberalism in a measured fashion. While critical of Washington's heavy-handed style, Tokyo did not retaliate. Instead, the government earnestly tried to show that both countries, the United States as well as Japan, were to blame for the bilateral economic imbalances. During the 1989–90 "Structural Impediments Initiative" (SII) talks, Japanese negotiators insisted that *both* sides must undertake measures to mitigate the trade problem. In the end, the SII process did yield a two-way agreement. The major measures to which Japan committed itself included the allocation of 430 trillion yen (about $2.9 trillion) for public works spending during the period from 1991 to 2000, relaxation of regulatory measures against large-scale retailers, reform of land-use policies, and more effective antitrust law enforcement. U.S. commitments included reduction of the federal budget deficit, encouragement of long-term planning horizons among corporate executives, more spending for commercial and scientific research, the development of more effective workforce training programs, and the promotion of exports.[34]

President Bill Clinton has taken this aggressive approach a step further. While continuing to call for Japanese deregulation and transparency, the Clinton administration believes that "leveling the economic playing field" by focusing on rules and regulations is insufficient given the preferential trading practices of Japanese firms. Washington is now insisting on objective measurements to track progress on foreign access to the Japanese market at both the aggregate and sectoral levels. This approach builds on the various results-oriented agreements negotiated by Republican administrations for such sectors as semiconductors, automobiles, and auto parts.

Japan is adamantly resisting this Clinton strategy to correct the bilateral trade imbalance. The Ministry of Finance opposes a strong fiscal stimulus to increase domestic demand; and MITI is rejecting results-oriented agreements as antithetical to market economics. By charging the Clinton administration with embracing "managed trade," Japanese officials have ironically assumed the role of being the champions of free trade and economic liberalism. They argue that the setting of "numerical targets" for imports would go against domestic efforts at deregulation. The pervasive view in Japanese government circles now is that the United States is mostly to blame for the huge trade imbalance because of macroeconomic misman-agement and insufficient efforts to penetrate the Japanese market. Because Japan is experiencing a structural recession, business lead-ers have on the whole supported this resistance to U.S. demands. At a time of shrinking markets in North America and Western Europe, they want to lessen the pain of structural adjustment by hanging on to domestic market shares as much as possible. Given the wide gulf between Japanese and American negotiators, the bilateral relation-ship appears to be headed toward a real crisis.

With the geopolitical glue of a common Soviet threat gone, many Japanese strategists believe that the trans-Pacific alliance should be revitalized by expanding Japan's security role both re-gionally and globally. In their view, Japan should assume the human risks of maintaining international security and be willing to fight side by side with Americans to counter aggression and enforce peace. Japan should therefore embrace the notion of collective de-fense and cooperate with U.S. forces in military operations in the Asia-Pacific region beyond the defense of the Japanese archipelago. Japanese Self-Defense Forces should also participate in UN peace-making as well as peacekeeping operations. The ultimate aim would be to transform the U.S.-Japan relationship into something analogous to the U.S.-British alliance.[35] Ichiro Ozawa, who played a key role in toppling the LDP from power by leading his faction out of the party and forging the seven-party coalition, is generally supportive of this strategic vision. In his bestselling work, *Nihon kaizo keikaku* (Plan to Reform Japan), Ozawa writes that Japan should become a "normal country" by actively contributing to international security.[36]

The nuclearization of North Korea may become the first post–Cold War test in East Asia of the resiliency of the U.S.-Japan security relationship. While insisting that North Korea must cooperate fully with International Atomic Energy Agency (IAEA) inspectors to verify its adherence to the Nuclear Non-Proliferation Treaty, Tokyo has been more cautious than Washington about an open confrontation with Pyongyang. But if the United States were to press for economic sanctions against a recalcitrant North Korea, then Washington will expect Tokyo to back this effort by cutting off financial flows from Japan to North Korea. If the standoff with North Korea were to reach a crisis point, Washington will expect Tokyo to cooperate with U.S. and South Korean forces to counter possible aggression from North Korea. Any hesitancy on the part of Japan to support the United States in such a crisis will severely weaken, if not rupture, the bilateral alliance. In this sense, Japanese strategists may be right in focusing on security cooperation as the essential means for revitalizing U.S.-Japan relations.

But such an approach has two shortcomings. First, an effort to shed postwar pacifism and remake Japan into a "normal country" goes well beyond the existing public consensus and faces formidable opposition from within the government. Second, an expansion of Japan's military mission without a basic correction of the bilateral economic imbalances could backfire by provoking fears in the United States that Japan poses not only an economic but also a military challenge to the United States.

The best way to reestablish a stable equilibrium in U.S.-Japan relations would be for Japan to shift decisively away from its neomercantilist economic policies and business practices. The current process of political realignment ultimately could facilitate such a change by galvanizing social and political forces more supportive of consumer and worker interests over those of producers. The recent adoption of a hybrid electoral system combining single-seat constituencies and proportional representation will encourage further party realignments and greater aggregation of political forces. A two-party system, or something close to it, may emerge, and elections may become contested more on the basis of policy choices rather than distributive politics and the mobilization of well-organized interests. Greater weight would be given to urban middle-class voters who are more likely to support consumer over producer interests. Moreover, elections could produce clearer mandates, enhancing the power of political leaders over the bureaucracy and therefore their ability to effect major policy shifts. Such is the theory.

But there isn't much ground for optimism in the near future. Despite its stated commitment to promote the interests of consumers and average citizens "who are making a living," the Hosokawa government backtracked on agricultural liberalization, domestic demand stimulation, and deregulation. Its successor, the minority Hata government, could do little more than pass the national budget. Both of these cabinets deferred to the fiscally conservative Ministry of Finance which insisted on linking an income tax cut with a commitment to increase the consumption tax rate in the future. This linkage would weaken the stimulative economic effects of the proposed decrease in income taxes. Although the three-party coalition involving the LDP, the Socialists, and the Shinto Sakigake (New Party Harbinger) headed by Prime Minister Tomiichi Murayama enjoys a parliamentary majority and appears to be less deferential to the Finance Ministry, inter-party policy differences are likely to impede decisive efforts to transform Japan into a more open and liberal economy. Protracted political instability and weak governments will increase the ability of bureaucratic agencies and entrenched interests to resist deregulation. Key proponents of political reform such as Ichiro Ozawa and Masayoshi Takemura have failed thus far to articulate an effective strategy for mitigating problems in foreign economic relations and overcoming bureaucratic obstacles to economic liberalization. They still lack the power, if not the will, to promote the necessary changes. Public sentiment on behalf of deregulation, demand stimulation, and social investments remains muted.

Soon after taking office in August 1993, Prime Minister Hosokawa appointed a high-level commission chaired by Gaishi Hiraiwa, head of the powerful Japan Federation of Economic Organization (Keidanren). Like the famous Maekawa commission, the Hiraiwa commission was charged with developing a blueprint for domestic economic reform with an eye toward promoting international economic harmony. The group's report, released in December 1993, however, fell short on specifics.[37]

While domestic political constraints are preventing major economic policy changes in response to U.S. pressures, market forces in the context of yen appreciation and recession are pushing businesses to transfer production facilities to East Asian countries, to restructure *keiretsu* subcontracting relationships, and to move toward more flexible employment practices. As relations with the United States become more tense and the American economic recovery continues to be slow, the Japanese are turning their attention increasingly to East Asia—both as a region of economic opportunity and as a theater of major security uncertainties. It is in this context that one can best understand Japan's evolving relations with China.

RELATIONS WITH CHINA

The American factor loomed large in Japan's relations with China after World War II. Despite domestic pressures to change its policy, Tokyo loyally followed Washington's pro-Taiwan line until the latter's rapprochement with Beijing in 1971. Japan did work around this constraint by separating economics from politics to develop trade relations with mainland China, but only after the shift in U.S. policy did Japan normalize diplomatic relations. It was the Carter administration that nudged Japan in 1978 to move ahead with a Peace and Friendship Treaty with China despite Soviet protests and domestic concerns about maintaining an "equidistant" stance vis-à-vis the Sino-Soviet conflict.[38] In the post–Cold War era, however, Japan appears more interested in moving beyond the parameters of U.S. policy to strengthen its relations with China. Although this trend is clearly evident in the economic sphere, China also is becoming more important in Japan's thinking about international security and Asian regionalism.

Japan's economic interaction with China has fluctuated between periods of enthusiasm and of disappointment and caution. Immediately after normalization in 1972, the Japanese business community viewed the economic opportunities in China romantically. The basic complementarity of the Japanese and Chinese economies promised a mutually beneficial relationship. Initial trends in the postnormalization period clearly supported this rosy picture. In 1974 Japan and China signed a formal and legally binding trade agreement that granted China "Most Favored Nation" status as well as a civil aviation pact. Although Japan was already China's number-one trading partner in 1971, bilateral trade doubled in the first year after normalization. By 1975 trade between the two countries had grown to about $3.8 billion—well over triple the volume in 1972—and China had become the third largest importer of Japanese goods. In terms of investments, by 1973 Japan had concluded about $660 million worth of contracts for twelve major projects, such as for chemical and fire-power plants. This amount was over three times as large as similar Japanese investments undertaken during the 1960s. But after the deaths of Zhou En-lai and Mao Zedong in 1976, political uncertainties made China a less hospitable economic partner for Japan. In the context of a resurgence of autarkic ideological principles, China reduced its import contracts with Japan, and as a result the trade volume declined sharply in 1976.[39] All of this had a sobering effect on the Japanese.

Conclusion of the Long-Term Trade Agreement as well as the Peace and Friendship Treaty in 1978 initiated a new round of business enthusiasm for China. The return of Deng Xiao-ping to active political life and his consolidation of power set China firmly on a course of economic reform. Excited about linking trade with China's modernization program, Japanese firms quickly agreed to about $3.8 billion of contracts and orders. Two-way trade increased from $5.1 billion in 1978 to $18.9 billion in 1985. After declining somewhat during the next two years, trade volume reached a new peak of over $19.3 billion in 1988.[40] By the mid-1980s approximately one-third of China's imports came from Japan; and Japan purchased about a quarter of China's exports, mainly raw materials (especially oil and coal), agricultural products, and textiles. Industrial machinery, electrical equipment, and steel products comprised much of Japan's exports to China.[41] Japan also began to serve as the key supplier of capital to China in the form of official development assistance and private loans and

credit. By 1982 Japan had become China's largest official development assistance source. This aid contributed to trade expansion by
financing Chinese purchases of industrial equipment and facilities
from Japan and by funding infrastructure projects that facilitated
Chinese exports to Japan.[42]

As in the mid-1970s, euphoria again turned to disappointment. Unwilling and unable to provide the energy exports necessary to pay for the imports of capital goods, China unilaterally
suspended or canceled about $1.6 billion worth of contracts for
major industrial projects from 1980 to 1982. To cushion the losses,
the Japanese government had to put together soft loans and
deferred-payment plans.[43] Japan's growing trade surplus with
China during the mid-1980s also soured the economic relationship.
Although Chinese domestic developments, such as the rise in incomes, excessive investment, and the relaxation of foreign trade
controls, were largely responsible for the imbalance, the Chinese
echoed American complaints that Japan restricted the import of
foreign goods.[44] But after China devalued its currency and reim-
posed foreign trade and exchange controls, Japan had a bilateral
trade deficit by 1988. China also complained about Japan's low
level of direct investments. In response, the Japanese cited numerous unfavorable investment conditions in China, including poor infrastructure, the shortage of skilled labor and managerial support,
conflicts between foreign managers and Chinese Communist Party
members, tensions between central and local authorities, concerns
about legal safeguards for their investments, and general political
uncertainties.[45] Sino-Japanese economic relations reached a low
ebb after the June 1989 massacre of pro-democracy students in
Tiananmen. Japan fell in step with the Western nations by condemning the crackdown, by downgrading diplomatic contacts, and
by freezing economic aid.

By mid-1990, however, Japan's economic relations with
China were again on an upswing. At the June 1990 summit of the
major advanced industrial democracies held in Houston, Prime
Minister Toshiki Kaifu tried to get the other G-7 countries to agree
to a relaxation of economic sanctions against China. Although he
did not succeed in this, he did persuade President George Bush not
to block the resumption of Japanese lending to China.[46] Straight

economic interests were behind this decision to go ahead with the yen loan. The immediate concern was that without the $5.4 billion soft-loan package, bilateral trade would continue to decline and almost $2.5 billion worth of investments would be jeopardized. This third in a series of loan programs was designed to help China proceed with major infrastructure projects critical to its modernization.[47] But there was a long-term concern as well. Japan saw China's integration into the Asia-Pacific region as critical for creating a positive environment for Japan's future economic prospects.

By 1991 Japan had fully normalized its economic relations with China. It again permitted China to issue bonds in Japan. The Finance Ministry gave its official blessing for new direct investments into China, and the Japanese Export-Import Bank agreed to a special $4.6 billion loan program for Chinese resource development.[48] Japan's assessment of economic opportunities in China—especially southern China—became unmistakably bullish, resulting in a surge of new Japanese direct investments. They jumped dramatically, from $579 million in fiscal year 1991 to nearly $1.7 billion in fiscal year 1993. Many of the new investments have been in capital-intensive sectors such as automobiles, mining, and banking as well as the more traditional labor-intensive sectors such as textiles and consumer electronics.[49] On the trade front, the bilateral volume expanded from a little over $18 billion in 1990 to a historic high of nearly $38 billion in 1993—an increase of about 108 percent.

Although most business leaders recognize that China still suffers from severe economic bottlenecks, they are optimistic that Chinese economic reforms are now irreversible. This view is shared by many Japanese economists, who see China as a critical growth center for the region and envision a harmonious economic relationship based on a dynamic division of labor.[50] Some Japanese business sectors, however, are less positive about economic ties with China. For example, textile firms complain that Chinese producers sell their goods in Japan at unfairly low prices. But for most Japanese trade officials, the best way to curb Chinese dumping practices is to integrate China as soon as possible in various multilateral economic regimes such as the GATT so that it can be socialized into the rules of free trade and fair competition.

China's economic significance for Japan appears even greater if one thinks in terms of a "greater China." In 1993 two-way trade with Taiwan and Hong Kong was $31.8 billion and $24.7 billion respectively. After the United States, Taiwan and Hong Kong were Japan's largest export markets in 1993. Taiwan purchased about $22.1 billion worth of Japanese goods, while Hong Kong purchased about $22.7 billion. Given these trade ties, Japan has a keen interest in a smooth return of Hong Kong to the mainland and a peaceful management of the Taiwan question.

Given China's geographic proximity and mammoth population, the primary security concern in the near term is the danger of political instability. This explains why Japan's condemnation of the Tiananmen crackdown lacked the moral intensity of America's outrage. Protests from Tokyo were tempered by warnings against isolating China and fears that political chaos would bring a large influx of refugees.[51] Rather than focusing on Chinese human rights violations, Japanese officials have therefore noted the tension between economic modernization and political liberalization. Modernization may ultimately lead to democratization, but the process is unlikely to be smooth and may require periods of repression to preserve stability. As one senior Japanese diplomat explains, Japan's human rights policy involves a realistic approach that considers the specific circumstances (e.g., the existence of a strong middle class or civil society, the maintenance of economic stability and development, and the presence of political organizations to defend free speech and human rights) of the countries in question. Although human rights are indeed universal—not just Western—values, confrontational approaches to promoting them are not always effective.[52] International isolation would only exacerbate China's political problems and would end any influence—however limited—that external powers might exert to moderate Chinese behavior. A breakdown of order in China would undermine regional stability and pose an acute threat to Japanese security. This perspective has broad support not only among foreign policy elites but also among the major political parties and the public at large. Consequently Japan is generally at odds with ideologically oriented U.S. policymakers and citizens who wanted to use trade policy (e.g., the renewal of Most Favored Nation status) to compel

Chinese leaders to stop human rights violations and to liberalize the political system. Japanese views are more congruent with U.S. strategists who stress China's importance for dealing with a variety of international security issues.

In the longer term, the growth of Chinese power poses a security problem for Japan. During the late 1970s and early 1980s, Japanese leaders were already uncomfortable about American efforts to bring China into an anti-Soviet coalition in Asia. They were anxious that U.S. assistance for Chinese military modernization eventually would help China develop naval and air capabilities that could threaten Japan. There was even concern that a closer security relationship between the United States and China would diminish the strategic importance of Japan to the United States. After the collapse of the Soviet Union and the Tiananmen crackdown, such worries about Sino-American military cooperation have, of course, subsided. But the long-term geopolitical challenge remains. While acknowledging that China may experience a decline in growth rates and even some major economic setbacks, most Japanese analysts see China's evolution into a regional superpower as inevitable. Economic development will enable China to modernize its military and develop a power projection capability. Such a China is likely to be more assertive about its claims in territorial disputes. A worsening of tensions with Southeast Asian countries (especially Vietnam) about the Spratly and Paracel islands in the South China Sea could threaten sea lanes critical to Japanese commerce. A militarily more powerful China also may be less accommodating about its dispute with Japan regarding the Senkaku Islands in the East China Sea.[53] Moreover, as its hunger for energy sources increases with industrialization, China is likely to become more adamant about these territorial claims because the ocean beds around these islands may contain valuable petroleum reserves. At the same time, the sheer size of the Chinese economy will raise serious environmental and demographic concerns.

The mainstream Japanese view on dealing with this Chinese geopolitical challenge is to cultivate friendly relations with Beijing and to incorporate China into the regional economic system. By promoting Sino-Japanese economic interdependence and getting China to have a real stake in the economic dynamism of the Asia

Pacific, Japan could help encourage China to become a stabilizing force in the region. This perspective motivated the Miyazawa cabinet to accept China's invitation to have the Japanese emperor visit Beijing to commemorate the twentieth anniversary of bilateral normalization.[54] The imperial trip was announced in August 1992 and took place in October of the same year. The public debate that ensued revealed major disagreements within Japan about how to deal with China.

Proponents of the imperial mission alluded to how the cooperative relationship between France and Germany has been critical to European peace and stability after World War II. Similarly, close Sino-Japanese relations would be essential for East Asian peace and stability in the post–Cold War era. Toward this end, Japan should actively promote bilateral diplomatic exchanges such as the imperial visit and economic linkages. Moreover, Japan should work closely with China as well as other countries in the Asia Pacific on behalf of arms control and confidence-building measures. To the extent that Sino-American relations might become strained, Tokyo could play a mediating role between Washington and Beijing.[55] Supporters of this view, however, tend to be reluctant about going beyond verbal criticisms of Chinese behavior regarding the proliferation of arms and military technology. They also shy away from backing the growing sentiment in Taiwan for national independence and from actively seeking Chinese commitment to a peaceful resolution of the Taiwan question. Consequently, this accommodative perspective is so sensitive about provoking the Chinese that Tokyo forfeits its leverage vis-à-vis Beijing.

The opposition to the imperial mission raised a variety of arguments. Nationalistic voices expressed concerns that the emperor's honor might be compromised if the Chinese openly demanded an apology for Japan's imperialist past. This did not prove to be a problem. During his October 1992 visit to China, Emperor Akihito referred to the "great suffering" Japan inflicted on the people of China and stated that he "deeply deplore[d] this." In return, Chinese leaders welcomed the emperor and empress with warmth and courtesy. Some leftist critics questioned the constitutionality of using the emperor for such diplomatic missions, but this point did not have widespread resonance.

The most substantive criticism of the imperial visit rested on a general critique of the accommodative approach to China. Some argued that Japan should be less timid about criticizing China's human rights record and its behavior on arms proliferation. This view reflected more strategic concerns than a strong ideological commitment to democratic values. In the long run, Japan's ability to counter the geopolitical challenge from China depends on maintaining a robust alliance with the United States. Supporting the American agenda on human rights and proliferation with respect to China would be one way of doing this. Others have taken the geopolitical argument further. To increase its leverage over China, Japan should help construct a tacit maritime coalition by promoting good relations with Taiwan and the Southeast Asian countries as well as supporting U.S. criticisms of China.[56] Some even go so far as to recommend closer ties with India and the Central Asian republics to balance against China. Advocates of this view, however, are quick to note that their aim is not to isolate or contain China, but rather to constrain its behavior and compel it to be more cooperative on behalf of Japanese and Western interests.

Although the debate among intellectuals and journalistic commentators has been lively, the choice between an accommodative and a hard-line approach has yet to become a prominent public issue in party politics. In terms of concrete policy, differences on China still tend to be submerged in discussions within and across the powerful ministries. But a sharp turn in Sino-American relations (for better or for worse) or a crisis regarding the Taiwan question will certainly bring China policy to the forefront. In the meantime, the basic thrust of Japan's approach to China in the political-military realm will be more accommodative and integrative than confrontational. Such an approach reinforces Japan's growing economic stake in China's modernization and its concerns about Chinese political instability.

Prime Minister Hosokawa's visit to Beijing in March 1994 reflected a delicate balance between assertiveness and conciliation. In his meetings with Premier Li Peng, Hosokawa urged China to respect human rights, which are "universally accepted values in the international community." He also called upon China to make its military expenditures more transparent in an effort to promote regional security and trust. Regarding North Korea, the Japanese leader asked China to clearly communicate to Pyongyang the "international mood," which is critical of North Korea's procrastination in permitting unencumbered IAEA inspections of its nuclear facilities. Although indicative of Japan's general support of the U.S. policy agenda in Northeast Asia, these statements did not go beyond verbal persuasion. Tokyo remains reluctant to use its economic leverage over Beijing on human rights or security issues. And the Chinese are well aware that Hosokawa cautioned President Clinton against imposing a Western form of democracy on China.[57]

To the extent that Japan is interested in integrating China into an Asia-Pacific regional community, the way China views Japan is just as important as the way Japan views China. China continues to express concerns about Japanese remilitarization. Part of this anxiety stems from Japan's ongoing efforts to modernize its defense forces. Even if Japan embraces a strictly defensive military doctrine, the Chinese point out that Japan has the economic and technological capability to become a military giant quickly. They also note that although Japan may spend less than 1 percent of its GNP on defense forces, its military budget is one of the largest in the world in absolute terms, given its huge economy. From the Chinese perspective, the way in which Japan has dealt with its imperialist past is just as, if not more, problematic, than its military modernization programs. Chinese leaders refer to a number of negative indicators. One is the visits made by Japanese cabinet members to the Yasukuni Shrine—a shrine in Tokyo that honors several war criminals responsible for Japanese expansionism before 1945. When then Prime Minister Yasuhiro Nakasone visited the shrine in August 1985, Beijing issued sharp protests. The Chinese also have objected to the treatment of Japan's militarist past in school textbooks. For example, in 1986 China protested the Japanese Education Ministry's decision to substitute the word "advance" for "invasion" in a passage of a secondary school textbook describing Japan's actions against China in the 1930s. Masayuki Fujio, the education minister at the time, aggravated the situation by dismissing the notion that Japan had committed particularly atrocious acts against the Chinese.

Although many Japanese have resented this meddling in internal affairs, the government has accommodated Chinese sensitivities. Nakasone and his successors in the prime ministership have refrained from further official visits to the Yasukuni Shrine. During the textbook controversy, Prime Minister Nakasone fired Education Minister Fujio from his cabinet in September 1986. But these gestures have not satisfied or reassured the Chinese—many of whom doubt Japanese sincerity because they believe Japan was only responding to diplomatic pressure. In this context, Prime Minister Morihiro Hosokawa's statement during his first press conference after assuming office in August 1993 was a breath of fresh air. In response to a journalist's question, Hosokawa stated without ambiguity that Japan had engaged in a "war of aggression" and that he felt that it was wrong. But the positive impact of this candor quickly dissipated when several nationalistic politicians sharply criticized the prime minister in the Diet for giving such a one-sided interpretation of the Pacific war and for making Japan vulnerable to demands for compensation and increased aid packages from the East Asian countries. As a consequence, Hosokawa had to retreat somewhat from his earlier statement, despite the fact that it seemed so commonsensical to the rest of the world. Shigeto Nagano, Prime Minister Tsutomu Hata's initial appointee for justice minister, made matters worse with his careless remark in a press interview that the 1937 Nanking massacre was a "fabrication."

Until Japan openly can come to terms with its imperialist past, its relations with China, not to mention relations with the rest of the region, will remain uneasy. The problem of the past places Japan in a double bind. On the one hand, feelings of guilt restrain Japan from joining the West in forcefully criticizing China's human rights abuses.[58] This makes the Japanese appear to be apologists for the Chinese. On the other hand, persistent Chinese suspicions and animosity toward the Japanese prevent Japan from putting relations with China on a stable and healthy psychological footing. Consequently, recent discussions about the re-Asianization of Japanese foreign policy sound hollow.

RELATIONS WITH RUSSIA

As in the case of Sino-Japanese relations, Japan's relations with the Soviet Union during the Cold War were shaped largely by its relations with the United States and the dynamics of Soviet-American relations. In the post–Cold War era, however, Japan has begun to diverge from the United States on Russia policy. But whereas Tokyo has moved ahead of Washington on relations with Beijing, it clearly lags behind Washington on relations with Moscow.

The incorporation of Japan into the American security system caused Japan to accept a postwar settlement that excluded the Soviet Union. Tokyo and Moscow came extremely close to concluding a peace treaty during the mid-1950s during a brief thaw in the Cold War following Stalin's death. But at the last moment, domestic opposition in Japan prevented the government from accepting the Soviet compromise solution of returning the islands of Habomai and Shikotan to Japan (and not the larger Etorofu and Kunashiri islands) in exchange for a peace agreement. Then in 1960 the territorial dispute became explicitly intertwined with the issue of Japan's alliance with the United States. The Kremlin added the condition that all foreign troops (i.e., U.S. forces) would have to leave Japan prior to the reversion of the smaller islands. Meeting this condition would have amounted to abrogating the recently revised security treaty with the United States. Given the importance of the American alliance, however, such an exchange was unthinkable for Japan.[59] Moreover, a domestic consensus had emerged against a two-island compromise: All of the political parties (even the Socialists and Communists) advocated the return of all of the islands.

In the context of Soviet-American détente from the late 1960s to the late 1970s, Japan did expand its economic relations with the Soviet Union despite the lack of meaningful progress on the territorial and peace treaty issues. Acute concerns about stable supplies of energy and raw materials in the wake of the 1973 oil crisis prompted the government to encourage joint ventures in the Soviet Union through financial assistance. For example, in April 1974 the Japanese Export-Import Bank provided the Soviets with over $1 billion in long-term credit for resource development in the Soviet Far East. Major projects launched included the construction of new port facilities at Wrangel Bay and the development of Siberian timber resources, Sakhalin natural gas and oil, south Yakutian coal, and the Tyumen oil fields. In the end, the Tyumen oil development project collapsed, and many other ventures did not meet original expectations due to production and other problems. Nevertheless, bilateral trade increased substantially during the 1970s, with Japan selling primarily steel products and machinery and the Soviets exporting raw materials and energy sources.[60]

After concluding, with Washington's encouragement, a peace and friendship treaty with Beijing in 1978, Japan's relations with the Soviet Union deteriorated. Soon thereafter the Soviets deployed military forces on the northern islands claimed by Japan. When the Soviet Union invaded Afghanistan, Tokyo joined Washington in adopting a hard-line policy against the Kremlin. The Japanese tightened their credit to the Soviet Union, restricted exports of capital machinery, stalled their negotiations with the Soviets on economic cooperation, and boycotted the 1980 Moscow Olympic Games. Soviet-Japanese trade declined sharply as a result because the West European allies refused to participate fully in the economic sanctions. Japan fell from second to fifth place in terms of the percentage of total Soviet trade with non-Communist states. Nevertheless, important Soviet-Japanese ventures, such as the oil and natural gas project off Sakhalin Island, continued to move forward.[61]

Just as the growing Soviet military threat provided the Reagan administration the rationale to launch the largest peacetime defense buildup in U.S. history, Soviet military deployments in Northeast Asia also stimulated Japan to modernize its Self-Defense Forces. Military planners began to develop concrete scenarios under which the Soviets might invade Japanese territory. They concluded that the Soviet Union might want to seize northern Hokkaido in order to secure the Sea of Okhotsk as a bastion for its nuclear ballistic missile submarines (SSBNs) during a global conflict between the superpowers. Consequently, the Self-Defense Forces began to place greater emphasis on the defense of northern Japan.[62] The shooting down of the Korean airliner in 1983 demonstrated with tragic force the delicate military situation in the Northwest Pacific and reinforced the negative feelings that the Japanese already had toward the Soviet Union. Most opinion polls indicated that less than 2 percent of the Japanese had a positive image of this Communist power.

As this brief historical review demonstrates, the state of Soviet-Japanese relations fluctuated with the vicissitudes of Soviet-American relations. When Washington's relations with Moscow improved, so did Tokyo's relationship with Moscow. At first, Tokyo's cool response to Soviet perestroika appeared to depart from this dynamic. Despite the dramatic improvement in Soviet-American relations, Japan's relations with the Soviet Union lagged behind. One reason for this was the relatively low priority accorded to Japan policy by Mikhail Gorbachev himself during his first several years as Soviet leader. But Japanese leaders also were more skeptical than their American and West European counterparts about the revolutionary changes in Soviet foreign policy. Tokyo responded cynically to Gorbachev's outline of the Kremlin's new interest in Asia in a historic speech at Vladivostok in July 1986. The Japanese interpreted Moscow's primary objective to be a rapprochement with Beijing. While acknowledging that a reduction of Sino-Soviet tensions would promote regional stability, they did not see any immediate direct benefit of Soviet "new thinking" for Japan. They quickly dismissed Gorbachev's regional arms control initiatives as an attempt to drive a wedge between the United States and its Asian allies, and they greeted the Soviet interest in becoming integrated into the economic dynamism of the Asia-Pacific region with skepticism.

The Foreign Ministry—guardians of Japan's hard-line policy toward the Soviet Union—argued that the territorial dispute would have to be resolved before there could be closer economic relations between Japan and the Soviet Union. Although many Soviet intellectuals affiliated with influential policy research institutes floated numerous compromise solutions, Japanese officials adhered strictly to their position that Japan must regain sovereignty over *all* of the islands in question. They felt justified in taking such an inflexible stance because Japan was now in a stronger position vis-à-vis the Soviets. With its diversification of raw material sources, industrial restructuring, and the abundance of supplies in world energy markets, Japan was not as interested in Soviet natural resources as it was during the 1970s. Given the Soviet Union's economic weakness and its interest in Japanese technology and capital, officials calculated that sticking to their uncompromising line eventually would force Moscow to yield completely.

Soviet military deployments and activities in Northeast Asia also contributed to the cool response to perestroika. Tokyo, of course, welcomed the Kremlin's decision to dismantle the SS-20s in Asia as part of a Soviet-American agreement to eliminate intermediate-range nuclear missiles. But Japanese defense planners also noted that the Soviets were improving the qualitative strength of their conventional forces in Northeast Asia despite the announcement of unilateral arms reductions in Asia as well as Europe. Some Japanese strategists even argued that as long as the Soviet Union and the United States relied upon sea-based strategic nuclear forces as a strategic reserve, securing the Sea of Okhotsk as an ocean bastion would be a top priority for the Soviet military. The Soviets would, therefore, continue to deploy forces that could threaten Japan.

The tough stance of both the Foreign Ministry and the Defense Agency was politically sustainable because Japanese public opinion was slow to warm up to the Soviet Union despite Gorbachev and perestroika.[63] The ruling and opposition parties alike, the media, and the public at large vigorously supported the government's claims on the territorial question. Moreover, business interests did not clamor for a major improvement in political relations with Moscow. Japanese corporate leaders repeatedly stated that they were not that interested in close economic linkages with the Soviet Union. They referred to disincentives such as the lack of ruble convertibility, poor infrastructure, and the slow pace of economic liberalization. They stated that perestroika would have to progress much further before the Soviet Union could become an attractive partner for Japan and an integral player in the Pacific Basin economic system.[64]

After the revolutionary changes in Eastern Europe in 1989 and Gorbachev's historic meeting with South Korean president Roh Tae Woo in San Francisco in early June 1990, Japanese perspectives on the Soviet Union finally did begin to show signs of meaningful change. This was visible first in the area of defense policy, as arguments about an increasing Soviet military threat became less persuasive. Reflecting this new political mood, Prime Minister

Toshiki Kaifu in 1990 asked the Finance Ministry to slow the pace of defense spending increases. Before long, prominent politicians in the ruling LDP started to speak openly about the need for flexibility in dealing with the territorial dispute. One powerful conservative politician, Shin Kanemaru, even embarrassed the Foreign Ministry by raising the possibility of a two-island solution to the dispute. Kaifu himself went beyond the traditional Foreign Ministry position of having the resolution of the territorial question be the *precondition* for closer economic linkages. In a speech given at the end of July 1990, he stated that Japan will "use all its might" to help reconstruct and revitalize the Soviet Union. He also articulated the concept of "expanding equilibrium" (*kakudai kinko*) whereby the territorial dispute would be solved together with Japanese efforts at "intellectual cooperation and economic development."[65]

In an attempt to engineer a breakthrough in Soviet-Japanese relations just prior to Gorbachev's visit to Tokyo in April 1991, Ichiro Ozawa (then LDP secretary-general) reportedly worked with MITI and business leaders to put together a major aid package of $26 billion as a quid pro quo for meaningful Soviet concessions on the territorial question. Gorbachev, however, was in no position to make such concessions, given the intense domestic pressures that he faced; and the summit between him and Kaifu yielded little progress.[66] Although hopes for another breakthrough were raised after the failed Soviet coup and the collapse of the Soviet Union, they were again dashed when Russian president Boris Yeltsin abruptly canceled his scheduled visit to Tokyo in September 1992.

To keep from falling behind the Western nations, however, Japan has made some compromises in its policy of not separating politics and economics. Japan's Russia policy appeared to be headed toward a crisis when French president François Mitterrand suggested that the 1993 G-7 summit scheduled for the summer in Tokyo be moved to an earlier date at another place in order to support Yeltsin's reform efforts. Given the Clinton administration's keen interest in backing Yeltsin, there was a real danger of a split between Tokyo and Washington on this issue. In order to prevent a major embarrassment for Japan, senior diplomats quickly arranged an emergency G-7 foreign ministers' meeting in Tokyo to discuss the question of Russian aid before the Tokyo summit. At this meeting the Japanese government agreed to participate fully in a *multilateral* aid package to Russia. By "multilateralizing" the issue, the government wanted to deflect domestic criticism that it was weakening the nation's claims to the Northern Territories. What is remarkable about this episode is the flexibility of the traditionally hard-line Foreign Ministry when good relations with the United States and the West were at stake.[67] Moreover, except for some sharp attacks from a few nationalistic politicians and journalists, domestic opposition has been surprisingly mild. And certainly Yeltsin's decision to go ahead with his scheduled visit to Tokyo soon after the violent face-off between the Russian president and rebellious parliamentarians significantly improved the atmosphere of Russo-Japanese relations.

The long-awaited Russo-Japanese summit in October 1993 yielded a Tokyo Declaration in which President Yeltsin and Prime Minister Hosokawa agreed that the preconditions for bilateral normalization have been established. The two leaders stated that their countries shared the "universal values of freedom, democracy, and respect for basic human rights." They agreed that the promotion of market economics and free trade would lead not only to economic prosperity for their two nations, but also to a healthy development of the world economy as a whole. Hosokawa and Yeltsin also committed themselves to resolving the territorial issue in accordance with "law and justice" and to signing a peace treaty at an early date. An accompanying "Economic Declaration" embraced the principle of "expanding equilibrium" and identified specific areas for cooperation, including energy, transportation, telecommunications, conversion of military industries, and safety of nuclear power plants. The summit, however, did not lead to a dramatic increase in Japan's economic assistance to Russia.[68]

The lack of a major aid effort toward Russia reflects more than the obstacle of the territorial dispute. It also reflects the limited Japanese business interest in Russia. Without strong government backing, such as loan and investment guarantees, Japanese corporations are still reluctant to invest in Russia. Many business executives believe that given the present situation in Russia, making huge investments or providing large amounts of aid would be like pouring money down a black hole. Rather than wasting capital on Russia, they would rather focus on Southeast Asia and China. Nevertheless, new Russo-Japanese ventures backed by government guarantees for oil and natural gas development in Sakhalin are moving forward. Moreover, MITI officials have shown enough interest in Russian economic reform to present a report in May 1992 outlining their policy suggestions to the Russian government. In contrast to the free-market orthodoxy contained in the International Monetary Fund's blueprint for economic restructuring, the MITI report calls for policies similar to those pursued by Japan after World War II, including centrally guided "priority production programs" to ensure adequate supply of critical industrial goods, strategic allocation of capital through government and private financial institutions, and preferential tax policies to encourage capital accumulation.[69] Japanese also are watching with interest the efforts to create free economic zones in the maritime regions of the Russian Far East.[70]

Even Japanese strategists are beginning to look beyond the territorial issue in order to consider ways of engaging Russia on security issues. They support involving Russia in multilateral regional security dialogues, such as the recently established Association of Southeast Asian Nations (ASEAN) Regional Forum. They are deeply interested in getting Moscow to transfer its SSBNs from the Sea of Okhotsk to the Arctic Ocean so as to facilitate Russian military retrenchment from Northeast Asia. Japan has already committed $100 million in bilateral assistance to support the dismantling of Russian nuclear weapons. And it goes without saying that Japan would like to prevent Russia from disposing of nuclear waste from submarines into the Sea of Japan. As part of this effort, Tokyo recently agreed to establish an international fund to help pay for safer alternative ways of dealing with nuclear waste.[71]

All of this demonstrates that even without a resolution of the territorial dispute, Japan is both willing and able to modify its Russian policy in order to stay in step with the West and to pursue its own economic and security interests vis-à-vis Russia. This flexibility, however, does not mean that Japan will be able to play a Russian card against either the United States or China, although it might enhance Japan's ability to hedge against a deterioration of

relations with the United States. As the rise of conservative nationalist forces in Russia during the mid-December elections of
1993 demonstrated, Japan needs to remain vigilant about a
reemergence of a Russian external threat. While a democratic and
stable Russia would serve Japan's long-term security interests,
Japan does not want to embrace the American agenda of trying to
promote democratic stabilization in Russia. Most officials in
Tokyo doubt that external efforts will have much of an impact on
the complex political dynamics internal to Russia.

CONCLUSION

In the post–Cold War era, Japan seeks a reinvigorated U.S.-
Japanese relationship as part of a broader Western alliance including the European Union. To achieve this outcome, Japan must
move decisively away from its neomercantilist economic policies
and business practices. It also must transform itself from a reluctant to an active ally of the West in what some have called a "global
partnership." But a "global partnership" entails assuming diplomatic and military risks for the sake of international security and
the protection of vital Western interests. The danger is that
domestic political rigidities and the persistence of neomercantilist
and pacifistic perspectives will prevent Japan from responding
quickly and thoroughly enough to satisfy the United States. Persistent tensions in economic relations will increase resentment on
both sides of the Pacific and weaken domestic support in both
countries for a bilateral "global partnership." A crisis on the
Korean peninsula over Pyongyang's nuclear program will certainly
stretch the limits of Japan's fragile consensus on security policy. It
will also be a moment of truth for the U.S.-Japanese alliance.

Electoral reform and party realignments could make Japan
more effective in responding to the international challenges of the
post–Cold War era. A stronger political executive could emerge
that is capable of making hard foreign policy choices and mobilizing the domestic support for them. Consumer and worker interests
could have a greater voice in electoral politics and thereby steer
Japan away from narrow developmentalism and toward a greater

emphasis on the quality of life. Such a Japan would be economically more harmonious not only with the United States but also with other advanced industrial democracies. But the process of domestic political transformation has just begun. The next several years are likely to involve unstable governments, vacillating political leaders, and the resurgence of bureaucrats resistant to fundamental change. If so, relations with the United States will become increasingly strained and distant, and nationalistic voices for a foreign policy more independent of the United States will become stronger.

Over time, current differences over China and Russia policy could deepen and further complicate relations with the United States. Even while being concerned about the growth of Chinese power, Japan is likely to be more sensitive than the United States to the dilemmas China faces between economic growth and political stability. From the Japanese perspective, U.S. policy toward China lacks a steady realism and tends to be too easily swayed by ideological considerations. On Russia, Japan is less convinced than the United States that a monetarist "shock therapy" and a strict adherence to free market principles will put Russia on a clear course of economic revitalization and democratization. The Japanese find the American belief that they can decisively shape domestic developments in such large countries as China and Russia to be naive if not downright arrogant. On the other hand, Americans are likely to view Japanese "realism" as merely a cover for their pursuit of narrow economic interests.

The worst-case scenario for Japan would be the emergence of a neo-isolationist United States—one with weaker security links to East Asia and exclusionary policies toward Japanese imports and investments. To avert this from happening, Japan for the time being is more likely to use economic influence in the United States than to play a Chinese or Russian "card" against the United States. It will increase its financial contributions for maintaining U.S. forces in Japan. Its firms will forge corporate alliances with American counterparts to raise the stakes that the U.S. business community has in good bilateral relations. But as a hedge against a hostile United States, Japan will develop its diplomatic, economic, and cultural linkages with the Asian-Pacific countries (including

China and Russia) to foster a more congenial regional environment. This calculation motivates Japan's support for the Asia-Pacific Economic Cooperation (APEC) process and other multilateral dialogues and institutions. By embedding the U.S.-Japan relationship in a regional community, Japan will increase its international maneuverability and be better able to constrain American unilateral actions that could harm it.

A rupture in U.S.-Japanese relations will polarize current political alignments in Japan. Ultimately, Japan's external response will hinge on the character of the strategic environment that emerges in the region. A Russia that is continuing to retrench militarily and a China that does not pose an acute security challenge will encourage a more relaxed security perspective. Japan will then rely more on economic and diplomatic instruments to help construct a stable regional order and will eschew a prominent military role in the region because such a policy would only alarm other East Asian countries. It is likely to promote a cooperative security regime centered around confidence-building measures. But for this to work, Japan, China, and Russia will have to shed their historical geopolitical and cultural distrust of each other. A truly stable regional order would require at least a Sino-Japanese entente.

If a breakdown in U.S.-Japanese relations occurred in the context of a threatening China and/or Russia, then Japan will confront the severest dilemma. It will have to choose between two competing imperatives: countering this security threat through an expanded military role in the region versus forging ahead with economic regionalism by minimizing Asian fears about a revival of Japanese militarism. Emphasizing the former is likely to undermine its economic interests, while emphasizing the latter is likely to make it vulnerable to external security threats. The paramount challenge for Japanese foreign policy is to avoid ever having to make such a choice.

Notes

1. Michael Schaller, *The American Occupation of Japan: The Origins of the Cold War in Asia* (New York: Oxford University Press, 1985); William S. Borden, *The Pacific Alliance: United States Foreign Economic Policy and Japanese Trade Recovery, 1947–1955* (Madison: University of Wisconsin

Press, 1984); and Watanabe Akio (ed.), *Sengo Nihon no taigai seisaku* (Tokyo: Yuhikaku, 1985), pp. 2–85, 108–134.

2. Michael Mandelbaum, *The Fate of Nations* (Cambridge: Cambridge University Press, 1988), p. 358.

3. Yoshi Tsurumi, "Japan," in Raymond Vernon (ed.), *The Oil Crisis* (New York: Norton, 1976), pp. 113–127.

4. Hideo Otake, "Defense Controversies and One-Party Dominance: The Opposition in Japan and West Germany," in T. J. Pempel (ed.), *Uncommon Democracies: The One-Party Dominant Regimes* (Ithaca, NY: Cornell University Press, 1990), p. 145.

5. These ideas were initially articulated in a 1991 report drafted by the LDP Special Commission Regarding "Japan's Role in International Society," which Ozawa chaired.

6. Peter Gourevitch, *Politics in Hard Times* (Ithaca, NY: Cornell University Press, 1986), pp. 50–53; and Robert Gilpin, *The Political Economy of International Relations* (Princeton, NJ: Princeton University Press, 1987), pp. 31–34.

7. Yasuhiro Nakasone, "Japan Should Join in a Wider Europe," *The Los Angeles Times,* May 7, 1990; and Melissa Healy, "Japan Appears Interested in NATO, But Is NATO Interested in Japan?" *The Los Angeles Times,* July 31, 1990.

8. Yoshio Okawara, *To Avoid Isolation: An Ambassador's View of U.S.-Japanese Relations* (Columbia: University of South Carolina Press, 1990).

9. Ryutaro Komiya and Motoshige Itoh, "Japan's International Trade and Trade Policy, 1955–1984." in Takashi Inoguchi and Daniel I. Okimoto (eds.), *Political Economy of Japan,* vol. 2, (Stanford, CA: Stanford University Press, 1988) pp. 173–224.

10. Hideo Sato and Timothy J. Curran, "Agricultural Trade: The Case of Beef and Citrus," in I. M. Destler and Hideo Sato (eds.), *Coping with U.S.-Japanese Economic Conflicts* (Lexington, MA: Lexington Books, 1982), pp. 121–183.

11. Edward J. Lincoln, *Japan: Facing Economic Maturity* (Washington, D.C.: The Brookings Institution, 1988), pp. 234–266; and Frances McCall Rosenbluth, *Financial Politics in Contemporary Japan* (Ithaca, NY: Cornell University Press, 1989), pp. 50–95.

12. Japan Ministry of Finance, *Foreign Trade Statistics.* Reported in "Statistical Profile," *JEI Report No. 34A* (September 30, 1991), pp. 19–21.

13. See, for example, Peter F. Drucker, "Japan's Choices," *Foreign Affairs* 65, no. 5 (Summer 1987): 923–941.

14. Douglas Ostrom, "Internationalization of the Yen Advances," *Japan Economic Institute Report,* no. 41B (October 28, 1988), pp. 2–6.

15. Japan Defense Agency, *Defense of Japan,* 1989 (Tokyo: Japan Defense Agency, 1989).

16. James E. Auer, "Japan's Defense Policy," *Current History* 87, no. 528 (April 1988): 145–148, 180–182.

17. Dennis T. Yasutomo, *The Manner of Giving: Strategic Aid and Japanese Foreign Policy* (Lexington, MA: Lexington Books, 1986).

18. William L. Brooks and Robert M. Orr, Jr., "Japan's Foreign Economic Assistance," *Asian Survey,* vol. 25, no. 3 (March 1985): 327; and *Yomiuri Shimbun,* June 23, 1990.

19. Kent E. Calder, "Japanese Foreign Economic Policy Formation: Explaining the Reactive State," *World Politics* 40, no. 4 (July 1988): 517–541; and Michäle Schmiegelow (ed.), *Japan's Response to Crisis and Change in the World Economy* (New York: M.E. Sharpe, 1986).

20. Kent E. Calder, *Crisis and Compensation: Public Policy and Political Stability in Japan,1949–1986* (Princeton, NJ: Princeton University Press, 1988); and Takashi Inoguchi and Tomoaki Iwai, *"Zoku gi-in" no kenkyu* (Tokyo: Nihon keizai shimbunsha, 1987).

21. C. Fred Bergsten and William R. Cline, *The United States-Japan Economic Problem* (Washington,DC.: Institute for International Economics, 1987), pp. 53–60.

22. Charles Smith, "Bonus to Buy: Japan Ponders New Way to Cut Trade Surplus," *Far Eastern Economic Review,* October 5, 1989, p. 101.

23. Laura D'Andrea Tyson and John Zysman, "Developmental Strategy and Production Innovation in Japan," in Chalmers Johnson, Laura D'Andrea Tyson, and John Zysman (eds.), *Politics and Productivity* (Cambridge, MA: Ballinger Publishing Company, 1989), pp. 59–140.

24. Edward Lincoln, *Japan's Unequal Trade* (Washington, D.C.: The Brookings Institution, 1990).

25. Ezra F. Vogel, "Japanese Science Policy and International Economic Competitiveness," *Harvard International Review* 10, no. 4 (April/May 1988): 44–45; and Charles H. Ferguson, "America's High-Tech Decline," *Foreign Policy,* no. 74 (Spring 1989): 123–144.

26. Michael Gerlach, "*Keiretsu* Organization in the Japanese Economy: Analysis and Trade Implications," in Johnson, Tyson, and Zysman (eds.), *Politics and Productivity,* pp. 141–174.

27. Jon Choy, "The Maekawa Report: Reality or Rhetoric?" *Japan Economic Institute Report,* no. 39A, October 14, 1988: 1–17; and "Restructuring the Japanese Economy," *Japan Echo* 13, no. 3 (Autumn 1986): 22–46.

28. Yamaguchi Asao, *Nihon no kiki kanri* (Tokyo: Nisshin Hodo, 1991); and Asahi Shimbun "Wangan kiki" Shuzaihan, *Wangan senso to Nihon* (Tokyo: Asahi Shimbunsha, 1991).

29. Clyde V. Prestowitz, Jr., *Trading Places: How We Are Giving Our Future to Japan and How to Reclaim It* (New York: Basic Books, paperback edition, 1989), pp. 1–58; and Gregory W. Noble, *Flying Apart? Japanese-American Negotiations over the FSX Fighter Plane* (Berkeley: University of California Institute of International Studies, 1992).

30. Karel van Wolferen, *The Enigma of Japanese Power* (New York: Alfred A. Knopf, 1989).

31. Prestowitz, *Trading Places,* pp. 15–16, 373–417.

32. Hisahiko Okazaki, "The Restructuring of the U.S.-Japan Alliance," *Japan Review of International Affairs* 2, no. 2 (Fall/Winter 1988): 124.

33. Chalmers Johnson, "Their Behavior, Our Policy," *National Interest,* no. 17 (Fall 1989): 17–27; James Fallows, "Containing Japan," *Atlantic Monthly* 263, no. 5 (May 1989): 40–54; and Prestowitz, *Trading Places.*

34. NHK Shuzaihan, *Nichi-Bei no shototsu* (Tokyo: Nihon Hoso Shuppankai, 1990); and Leonard J. Schoppa, "Gaiatsu and Economic Bargaining Outcomes," *International Organization* 47, no. 3 (Summer 1993): 353–386.

35. Okazaki Hisahiko, *Atarashii Ajia e no dai senryaku* (Tokyo: Yomiuri Shimbunsha, 1993), pp. 130–144, 194–245.

36. Ozawa Ichiro, *Nihon kaizo keikaku* (Tokyo: Kodansha, 1993), pp. 102–137.

37. *Nihon Keizai Shimbun,* December 17, 1993.

38. Zbigniew Brzezinski, *Power and Principle: Memoirs of the National Security Adviser 1977–1981* (New York: Farrar, Straus, Giroux, 1983), p. 218; and Tanaka Akihiko, "Bei-Chu-So no aida de," in Watanabe Akio (ed.), *Sengo Nihon no taigai seisaku* (Tokyo: Yuhikaku, 1985), pp. 239–252.

39. Chae-Jin Lee, *China and Japan: New Economic Diplomacy* (Stanford, CA: Hoover Institution Press, 1984), pp. 13–20; and Akira Iriye, *China and Japan in the Global Setting* (Cambridge, MA: Harvard University Press, 1992), p. 127.

40. Japan Ministry of Finance, *Foreign Trade Statistics.*

41. Nicholas R. Lardy, *China's Entry into the World Economy: Implications for Northeast Asia and the United States* (Lanham, MD: University Press of America, 1987), p. 10; Harry Harding, *China and Northeast Asia: The Political Dimension* (Lanham, MD: University Press of America, 1988), p. 28; and Hong N. Kim, "Sino-Japanese Relations," *Current History* (April 1988): 179.

42. Lardy, *China's Entry into the World Economy,* pp. 10–11.

43. Walter Arnold, "Japan and China," in Robert S. Ozaki and Walter Arnold (eds.), *Japan's Foreign Relations: A Global Search for Economic Security* (Boulder, CO: Westview Press, 1985), pp. 102–109.

44. Harding, *China and Northeast Asia,* p. 31.

45. Jon Choy, "Sino-Japanese Economic Relations: Investing in the Future," *Japan Economic Institute Report,* no. 9A, March 6, 1987, pp. 6–7.

46. "The Houston Two-step: Japan to Resume Aid Programme to China," *Far Eastern Economic Review,* July 19, 1990, pp. 57–58; and "Japan Throws China a Lifeline," *The Economist,* July 14, 1990, p. 35.

47. "Why Aid to China Is a High-Stakes Gamble for Japan," *Business Week,* July 30, 1990, p. 39.

48. Edward J. Lincoln, *Japan's New Global Role* (Washington, D.C.: The Brookings Institution, 1993), pp. 189–190.

49. Qingxin Ken Wang, "Recent Japanese Economic Diplomacy in China," *Asian Survey* 33, no. 6 (June 1993): 630–631.

50. Watanabe Toshio, *Ajia shin choryu* (Tokyo: Chuo Koron, 1990), pp. 69–102; and Kobayashi Minoru and Wu Jing-Lian, *Chugoku: Koseicho keizai e no chosen* (Tokyo: Nihon Keizai Shimbunsha, 1993), pp. 259–336.

51. Akino Yutaka et al., "Posuto-Maruta no sekai o tenbo suru," *Chuo Koron* 105, no. 2 (February 1990): 181–182.

52. Ikeda Tadashi, "'Ajia-shugi' de nai Ajia gaiko o," *Gaiko Forum,* no. 65 (February 1994): 58–59.

53. Hiramatsu Shigeo, *Chukoku no kaiyo senryaku* (Tokyo: Keiso Shobo, 1993).

54. Tanino Sakutaro, "Tenno Kogo ryo heika no Chugoku gohomon," *Bungei Shunju* (October 1992): 128–132.

55. Kakizawa Koji, "Tenno ho-Chu-go no Nit-Chu kankei," *Chuo Koron* (December 1992): 202–210.

56. Okazaki, *Atarashii Ajia e no dai senryaku,* pp. 146–191.

57. *Yomiuri Shimbun,* March 21, 1994.
58. Yoichi Funabashi, "Japan and the New World Order," *Foreign Affairs,* no. 5 (Winter 1991/92): 66.
59. Toru Nakagawa, "Japan's Northern Territories in International Politics," *Japan Review of International Affairs* 2, no. 1 (Spring/Summer 1988): 18–19.
60. Kazuo Ogawa, "The USSR's External Economic Relations and Japan," *Japan Economic Studies* 12, no. 1 (Fall 1983): 26–53.
61. Peter Berton, "Soviet-Japanese Relations: Perceptions, Goals, Interactions," *Asian Survey* 26, no. 12 (December 1986): 1272–1273.
62. Nishimura Shigeki, "Nihon no bo'ei senryaku o kangaeru: gurobaru apurochi ni yoru hoppo zempo bo'ei ron," *Shin bo'ei ronshu* 12, no. 1 (July 1984): 50–79.
63. According to two surveys conducted in September 1989 and May 1990, the percentages of those polled who mentioned the Soviet Union as a trustworthy country were 2.8 and 3.5 respectively. These results are not much higher than those during the early 1980s. *Yomiuri Shimbun,* November 28, 1989, and June 20, 1990.
64. Barbara Wanner, "Japan's Relations with the 'Soviet Bloc,' " *Japan Economic Institute Report,* no. 3A, January 19, 1990, pp. 8–9.
65. *Yomiuri Shimbun,* July 29, 1990; and Charles Smith, "Time for Sweet Talk," *Far Eastern Economic Review,* August 9, 1990, pp. 18–19.
66. Harry Gelman, *Russo-Japanese Relations and the Future of the U.S.-Japanese Alliance* (Santa Monica, CA: RAND, 1993), pp. 20–26.
67. Owada Hisashi, "Kore ga Roshia shi'en no ronri da," *Chuo Koron* (July 1993): 30–38.
68. *Yomiuri Shimbun,* October 14, 1993.
69. Fusae Ota, Hiroya Tanikawa and Tasuke Otani, "Russia's Economic Reform and Japan's Industrial Policy," MITI Research Institute, 1992; and Yukitsugu Nakagawa, "Reflections on Restoring the Former Soviet Union: Can the Japanese Experience Help?" *IIGP Policy Paper #92E* (Tokyo: International Institute for Global Peace, June 1992).
70. Gilbert Rozman, "Japanese Images of the Soviet and Russian Role in the Asia-Pacific Region," in Tsuyoshi Hasegawa, Jonathan Haslam, and Andrew C. Kuchins (eds.), *Russia and Japan: An Unresolved Dilemma Between Distant Neighbors* (Berkeley: International and Area Studies, University of California at Berkeley, 1993), pp. 101–123.
71. *Yomiuri Shimbun,* October 25, 1993.

CHAPTER FOUR

The United States and the Strategic Quadrangle

MICHAEL MANDELBAUM

During the Cold War the policy of the United States toward the other three powers of the Strategic Quadrangle was coherent. In the wake of the Cold War it is complicated and confused.

From the 1940s to the 1990s American policy in East Asia was based on deterring and containing Soviet power. That was the common denominator of Washington's relations with the Soviet Union, China, and Japan—and indeed the entire world. It was the reason for deploying military forces in the region, the core of which was the Seventh Fleet with its fighter and bomber airplanes based on large oceangoing aircraft carriers supported by facilities in Japan and in the Philippines.[1]

The United States had other goals in addition to security; none, however, was more important. Where the requirements of deterring the Soviet Union came into conflict with other aims, all the others gave way. This is the normal practice when countries are at war. All else is subordinate to the requirements of waging the conflict. In the latter stages of the Cold War there were sources of friction with China and Japan, but they were largely suppressed for the sake of solidarity against the Soviet threat.

By the second half of the Cold War, that threat, although not vanquished, seemed far less pressing than the United States had taken it to be in the 1950s and 1960s. From the mid-1970s to the end of the 1980s, the United States enjoyed the best of both worlds in the Strategic Quadrangle: the coherence in foreign policy that war imposes without the costs and dangers that come with actual conflicts. In the second half of the Cold War, Washington's position was a comfortable, even a privileged one. Of the four major powers, only the United States played both a major military and a major economic role. Of the four, only the United States was indispensable both to the security arrangements and to the commercial life of the Pacific region.

Moreover, the United States had better relations with each of the other three powers than any two had with each other. In fact the other powers welcomed the American role in the region.[2] The American presence thus contributed to stability and prosperity in East Asia after the mid-1970s without imposing onerous costs on the United States.

The end of the Cold War has complicated American policy. The burden of an ongoing military confrontation with a powerful rival has been lifted. In that important sense the American position in East Asia, as elsewhere, is now easier. But the end of that conflict has brought to the task of conducting American policy in the Strategic Quadrangle a new agenda. The United States confronts choices—military, political, and economic—that are both unfamiliar and difficult to make.

The rationale for the American military presence has disappeared, but the demand for it within the region has not. East Asians continue to favor the deployment of American forces in their region in some form. The new military mission that they and American leaders envision for the United States, however, is a vague one. It is less intuitively plausible, and less likely to be attractive to the American public, than the Cold War goal of deterring the Soviet Union.

At the same time, issues that divide the United States from China and Japan, which had been kept manageable by the discipline of the Cold War, have now become more salient in the politics of the Strategic Quadrangle. With China the primary issue is the status of democracy and human rights. In the late 1980s congressional majorities began to demand that the United States exert pressure on the Chinese leadership to bring their domestic political practices into closer conformity with those of the democratic West, using continued Chinese access to the American market as leverage. With Japan the source of post–Cold War tension was the persistent Japanese trade surplus with the United States.[3]

Neither the putative new military mission for the United States in East Asia nor the contentious issues in Sino-American and Japanese-American relations emerged suddenly with the collapse of the Soviet Union. All three had germinated in the latter part of the Cold War period. But during the Cold War the American government—specifically the executive branch—was the effective champion of sustaining a military presence in East Asia and keeping China's violation of democratic norms and the Japanese trade imbalance from undercutting the anti-Soviet coalition to which Japan and China belonged.

In the wake of the Cold War, the opinions of the American public assumed greater political importance on all three issues. The continuation of the American military presence in the region depended on the kind of public support that the government had been able to obtain with ease when the conflict with the Soviet Union dominated American foreign policy, but that may prove difficult to sustain in the absence of the Soviet threat.

Similarly, American objections to Asian political and commercial practices stemmed from sentiments deeply held in the United States. It was the public that pressed the government to pressure Asian governments to change them. During the latter part of the Cold War, the president and the Congress were divided over the proper American response to Chinese political practices. They were divided as well over how to deal with Japanese economic policies that the American public deemed objectionable. With the advent of the Clinton administration in 1993, the executive branch became more sympathetic to the views expressed by the Congress and the public. This was not simply because the new president and the congressional majority were members of the same political party: in fact, the end of the Cold War had removed the principal incentive presidents of both parties had had to avoid the punitive policies that the Congress and the public increasingly favored.

American irritation with China and Japan was based on a commitment to democracy and a resentment of chronic trade imbalances that had deep roots in public opinion; but the practices that Americans found unacceptable had equally deep roots in the

Asian political and economic systems from which they sprang. Thus, while the disputes over these issues could be managed, and would certainly not lead to war, they were unlikely to be resolved quickly or easily—if they could be resolved at all.

In the aftermath of the victory in the Cold War, divisions among the victors began to appear. The result, in East Asia, will scarcely be as drastic as what happened in Europe after World War II. Neither Japan or China—nor the new Russian republic, for that matter—will take the place of the old Soviet Union as the global, mortal rival of the United States. The bitter ideological clash and the costly military competition of the forty-five years after World War II will not be repeated.

The American agenda in the Strategic Quadrangle in the first half of the Cold War was a grim and dangerous one; in the second half the rivalry with the Soviet Union still dominated that agenda, although in a less urgent way. The differences that mark the post–Cold War agenda are normal. Interests and preferences differ among sovereign states as they do among individuals. It is the task of a foreign policy to reconcile such differences where this is possible and manage them where it is not. For the United States, this task in East Asia is now less taxing in military terms than during the Cold War, but in another way it is more difficult.

After 1950 there was an American consensus on the task in East Asia: deterrence of the Soviet Union. American policymakers had to decide how to accomplish it. Now the United States confronts questions of ends as well as of means: What is the proper military role for the United States in the Asia-Pacific region? Is the promotion of democracy or of human rights in China an appropriate aim of American foreign policy? What kind of economic relationship with Japan is possible and desirable?

THE CHALLENGES TO SECURITY

The Cold War was a military confrontation. Its conclusion thus affected the forces deployed by the powers that had waged it. The changes in military deployments are not as dramatic in the Strategic Quadrangle as in Europe; but even without sweeping arms control accords such as the Conventional Forces in Europe Treaty of 1990 or the dissolution of a formal military alliance such as the Warsaw Pact, one result of the end of the Soviet-American conflict was that there were fewer and less capable military forces in East Asia.

In December 1988, three years before the Soviet Union itself disappeared into history, Mikhail Gorbachev announced the withdrawal of 200,000 troops from the Soviet Far East and of 6,000 more from Central Asia.[4] Russia inherited the Soviet Pacific fleet, which in 1993 still included 20 ballistic missile-carrying submarines, 90 attack submarines, 45 main surface warships, and 150 land-based strike aircraft. But the Russian economic collapse took a toll on its military forces. By one estimate, in 1992 only a third of the attack submarines, 40 percent of the warships, and half the aircraft were operational.[5]

As the Cold War waned, the United States also reduced its forces in the region. By the Cold War's end, only about 17 percent of all American military manpower was allocated to Asia.[6] The most important military bases in the southern Pacific—Clark Air Field and the Subic Bay naval facility, both in the Philippines— were closed in 1991–1992. In early 1990 Secretary of Defense Richard Cheney announced that 5,000 of the 43,000 American troops in Korea would be withdrawn. The Pentagon's 1992 plan for a global "base force" called for a 25 percent reduction from Cold War levels in overall military strength in East Asia.[7]

In September 1991 President Bush announced a global initiative on nuclear weapons that affected American nuclear deployments in the region; such weapons would be removed from South Korea and from surface ships in the Pacific, thus eliminating a source of friction with Japan and New Zealand, both of which had banned port calls for nuclear-armed vessels.

The reductions in the American military forces in East Asia and elsewhere were logical responses to the end of the Cold War. The forces' purpose, after all, had been to deter the Soviet Union. With the decay of Russian military forces in the Asia-Pacific region, the military threat to American interests had diminished. But the events that led to the decay of those forces had an even more decisive impact.

The withdrawal of Soviet forces from the heart of Europe, where their presence had triggered the Soviet-American rivalry in the first place, the collapse of communism in Europe, and the disintegration of the Soviet Union itself left no apparent adversary in East Asia for American forces to deter.

There are, to be sure, reasons for hedging a prediction that no great-power military confrontation will ever again take place in the region. In 1994 Moscow's policies toward its neighbors turned more assertive and its attitude toward cooperation with the industrial democracies less enthusiastic than in the preceding two years. Russia retained the foundations of a major military force in East Asia. Its control of the four southern islands of the Kurile chain, which Stalin had seized at the end of World War II, perpetuated a territorial dispute with Japan, which insisted on its own sovereignty over what it continued to call its "Northern Territories."

Still, Russia's internal disarray seemed likely to restrict its capacity to resume the kind of conflict with the other three powers of the Strategic Quadrangle that the Soviet Union had pursued during the Cold War, even if the Russian government wished to do so, at least through the 1990s and into the next century. Such energies as Russia had for international disputes were likely to be reserved for the "Near Abroad," the former Soviet republics turned independent states, several with large ethnic Russian populations. Russia may one day become a proper object of the kind of deterrence that dominated American policy in the Strategic Quadrangle from 1950 to 1990, but if it does, this will not occur soon.

It also is conceivable that China will qualify for Cold War–style deterrence. It is a power on the rise.[8] Its soaring economic growth rates portend a more powerful military establishment: The richer a country is, the more it can afford to spend on troops and weapons. Chinese forces are large but badly equipped. For most of the 1980s the military had a low priority in the government's budget. In the early 1990s, however, Chinese military spending as a proportion of national income rose modestly, and this at a time when defense spending was falling in most other countries. At the same time, as the enormous Soviet military-industrial complex broke apart, the Chinese government moved to acquire some of its weapons and technical expertise.[9]

In its long history, China has seldom tried to expand its sphere of direct control beyond its traditional borders. But the People's Republic of China has territorial claims in East Asia. The best known and potentially the most explosive of these concerns the island of Taiwan,[10] but there are others. Beijing's claim to the Spratly Islands in the South China Sea, the site of potentially valuable mineral deposits, has brought China into conflict with a number of Southeast Asian countries[11] and its claim to the Senkakus is a potential source of friction with Japan.

Like Russia, China has moved far from the orthodox communism under the auspices of which it had been at war with the United States in the 1950s. In the first half of the 1990s Beijing was firmly set on a foreign policy of détente in all directions and economic cooperation wherever possible. Like Russia if it were to become a military threat this would not occur until well into the next decade.[12]

Thus the first question for American military policy in East Asia in the wake of the Cold War was not how large a force to deploy but whether, in the absence of an adversary, the United States should deploy any forces at all. In fact, American forces did serve an important purpose, one that predated the end of the Cold War although it was neither emphasized by the United States nor always publicly acknowledged by those who benefited from it.

Both Japan and China saw the United States as a buffer against the other. As long as Washington accepted a measure of responsibility for Japanese security, the Chinese could assume Japan's military forces would remain limited; and as long as Japanese forces remained limited, they would pose no threat to China. For their part, in the absence of an American military role in the Strategic Quadrangle, the Japanese would have reason to be concerned not only about Russia but also about China, which was, after all, a nuclear power.

The countries of Southeast Asia—Thailand, the Philippines, Singapore, Indonesia, and Malaysia—also benefited from the presence of American forces. None had felt particularly threatened by the Soviet Union during the Cold War, but each was wary of China and Japan. Some had ethnic Chinese populations. All were sensitive to the power that China possessed by virtue of its size. And to the admiration with which they all regarded Japan's economic strength was added a touch of resentment, arising from their memories of Tokyo's imperial aspirations in the 1930s and 1940s, of which they had been the victims. For them an American military presence also was welcome.[13]

The American role of buffer offered deterrence at one remove. It gave other countries not so much protection against an existing threat as a measure of assurance that new threats were not likely to arise. The historian and strategist Michael Howard has drawn a distinction relevant to the American role as a buffer in East Asia, a distinction between deterrence and what he calls "reassurance." He defines reassurance as the task of instilling confidence in allies so that they can conduct their domestic affairs and foreign policies without feeling intimidated. Like reassurance as Howard defines it, the role of buffer that the United States came to play in East Asia in the 1980s spared others the need to make adjustments in their own policies that they preferred to avoid.[14]

With the end of the Cold War, the case for an American military presence to reassure the other three countries of the Strategic Quadrangle, as well as the lesser states of North- and Southeast Asia, became in some ways even more compelling. The withdrawal of the United States would leave a vacuum that would create pressure within each country to strengthen itself, if only out of fear that if it failed to do so, others would. Each country would be tempted to arm itself preemptively, as insurance against threats arising from others doing the same thing.

Each country feels the need for a hedge of some sort, some military assurance against the potentially aggressive designs of the others. Each is willing to rely on the United States to provide such assurance; American military forces are uniquely acceptable to all powers in the region. Without the United States, each would feel compelled to rely on itself, leading to higher force levels, greater political tensions, and perhaps eventually outright conflict.

An American withdrawal from East Asia could set in motion what political scientists call a "spiral model": One party takes measures for defensive reasons that appear aggressive to another, the other responds in kind—again for defensive purposes but in a way

the other interprets as offensive—and a spiral of measures, coun-
termeasures, and mounting distrust unfolds.

So it might be in the Strategic Quadrangle in the absence of
American military power; and as the Cold War ended, preventing
such a spiral became the official rationale for the continued American military presence. "In this era of shifting regional power balances," Defense Secretary Cheney said in 1990, "our forward
military presence supports our aim of maintaining the stability that
lets other nations flourish, by preventing the emergence of dangerous power vacuums or imbalances and by staving off regional arms
races."[15] Warren Christopher, secretary of state in the Clinton
administration, echoed this message in 1993: "While the tensions
of the Cold War have subsided, many Asian nations harbor
apprehensions about their closest neighbors. An American withdrawal would magnify those concerns. And so America must
stay engaged."[16]

Reassurance is plausible in theory. In practice, however, it pre-
sents several problems. The first stems from the perennial military
question, "How much is enough?" It is difficult enough to decide
what forces are needed to deter an armed force whose size is
known. It is all the more difficult to decide what is needed for reassurance, a mission that is vague, open-ended, and requires moving from "threat-based to uncertainty-based" military planning.[17]

The forces the United States would need to reassure the countries of East Asia must be roughly comparable to those that would-
be adversaries could field. This too raises a potential problem.
Local military forces could expand rapidly simply because of the
rates of economic growth in what is the fastest-growing part of the
world.[18] That would require the United States to expand its own
forces, which would impose costs the American public might not
be willing to pay.

Moreover, reassurance is a military mission that, unlike deterrence, may require the kind of multilateral organization that is
common in Europe but almost completely absent—for good reason—in East Asia.[19] To be reassured, all parties would have to be
satisfied that none of the others was behaving, or planning to be-
have, in a threatening manner. This in turn would require that all
have reliable information about the others' military activities in the

region and that all contribute to procedures to build mutual confidence, such as public notification of routine military operations. A formal organization would be useful, perhaps indispensable, for these purposes, but the region has none. Reassurance also may require negotiated limits on the military forces in the Strategic Quadrangle, which, during the Cold War, the United States consistently opposed.[20]

Once the American government decided how to carry out the policy of reassurance in the Strategic Quadrangle, it would then have to obtain support for it. East Asian governments do support the policy. But while they want the United States to stay in the region, few are eager to announce this to the world. Most are understandably reluctant to say publicly that they do not trust their neighbors.[21] The Japanese do say that they want the Americans to stay. They go further. They underwrite part of the cost of the American military presence in the region and have a large stake in it. The Japanese-American Security Treaty, and the American forces that support it, relieve Japan of the need to defend itself unaided. Without them, Japan would have to spend considerably more on defense to protect itself. It also would have to confront the question of whether to acquire nuclear weapons. A more heavily armed—and especially a nuclear armed—Japan would alarm its neighbors. Thus the American presence is Japan's guarantee of membership in good standing in the region.

Yet the present security arrangements have Japan paying, in effect, to deter itself, and the Japanese may not be content to do so forever. Someday they may conclude that with the demise of the Soviet Union, they no longer want or need American protection in security in affairs.[22]

In the end, the citizens of the United States itself may turn out to be the most skeptical of the need for a continuing American presence in East Asia. North America lies thousands of miles from the region's center of military gravity. What is of direct concern to the Chinese and the Japanese is remote for Americans. North America was, of course, no closer to the Asian mainland during the Cold War than it is now, and the United States then regarded the balance of power in the region as bearing directly on its own interests. But then the Soviet Union was seen as a threat everywhere; for forty years Americans proved willing to support forces whose aim was to prevent a Soviet attack. It remains to be seen whether they can be persuaded to pay for the less familiar, less intuitively urgent task of reassurance.[23]

Post–Cold War East Asia did present one potential threat to American interests of a more familiar kind: the prospect of Communist North Korea acquiring nuclear weapons. The Korean peninsula is perhaps the most strategically sensitive place in the Strategic Quadrangle. It is Japan's nearest neighbor and former colony. The United States stations troops there. Korea has common borders with both Russia and China. All four powers participated, directly or indirectly, in the Korean War of the 1950s.

At the end of 1991 the two Korean states seemed to be moving toward a rapprochement, especially on issues concerning nuclear weapons. In December of that year they signed an agreement on political reconciliation, and soon thereafter North Korea agreed to submit its nuclear facilities to international inspection, as required by the Non-Proliferation Treaty (NPT) of 1968. In March 1993, however, Pyongyang reversed itself, announcing that it would withdraw from the NPT and bar inspectors from its nuclear sites. This was almost certainly related to the international inspectors' discovery that small amounts of plutonium were unaccounted for in North Korea and might have been diverted to make nuclear explosives. Protracted negotiations with the United States followed. The American aim was to convince North Korea to allow the inspection of both the facilities it had acknowledged to have nuclear purposes and undeclared sites the international community suspected of also being devoted to such purposes.[24]

The nuclear problem on the Korean peninsula was, in part, a holdover from the Cold War. It stemmed, ultimately, from the division of the country and the threat to the status quo posed by the Communist regime in the north—the same set of circumstances that had led to war in 1950. The same dictator—Kim Il-sung— who had launched the attack in 1950 was in power and threatening to acquire nuclear weapons in 1994.

But while a holdover from the past, the threat of a North Korean bomb was also a post–Cold War issue. The end of that conflict left North Korea without the patronage of the world's two largest Communist countries, the Soviet Union and China, whose support had sustained it for the better part of four decades. Kim had reason to fear that his regime would suffer the fate of East Germany: collapse and absorption by the other economically more dynamic and politically more legitimate Korean state.[25] Although not given to sharing his motives with others, the North Korean dictator appeared to have decided, in an effort to avoid this fate, to use the threat of acquiring nuclear weapons to extract diplomatic concessions and economic support from the outside world, in particular from South Korea, Japan, and the United States.

Moreover, the North Korean threat to the United States was of a distinctly post–Cold War kind: not a frontal assault on a pro-Western government by the forces of communism as part of a global conflict, but rather nuclear weapons in the hands of a rogue state that would use its nuclear arsenal to terrorize its neighbors for its own narrow purposes or sell bombs to other equally dangerous regimes. Indeed, North Korean nuclear weapons would produce precisely what the post–Cold War American military mission of reassurance was designed to prevent: a dangerous political and military chain reaction within the region. Japan and South Korea would strengthen their armed forces, perhaps even equipping themselves with nuclear weapons. This would alarm other Asian countries, in particular China, which would respond in similar fashion.

The problem of North Korean nuclear weapons produced a political alignment in the region that demonstrated the differences between the Cold War and post–Cold War eras in yet another way. In 1950 the United States and Japan were allied with South Korea against North Korea, the Soviet Union, and the People's Republic of China. In 1993 still nominally Communist China and post-Communist Russia joined the United States, Japan, and South Korea in opposing in principle a North Korean bomb.

Opposition in principle, however, seemed unlikely to dispose of the matter. Ensuring that the Korean peninsula remained free of nuclear weapons would likely require unprecedentedly close cooperation among the four powers of the Strategic Quadrangle. Two diplomatic undertakings in other parts of the world illustrated what was likely to be needed.

One was the international coalition that evicted Saddam Hussein's army from Kuwait. As with North Korea, this was a regime acting in violation of international law and in defiance of the international community. The task the multinational coalition undertook was more taxing than deterrence: It involved reversing an invasion that had already occurred. Similarly, an international coalition might at some point be called upon to seize or destroy North Korean nuclear weapons already assembled. And as in the Persian Gulf, while military operations might be conducted under the nominal auspices of the United Nations, the task of assembling and leading the coalition against North Korea would inevitably fall to the United States.

The second international precedent pertinent to the Korean nuclear problem is the unification of Germany. This was accomplished under a diplomatic rubric known as the two-plus-four negotiations. It included the two German states and the four outside powers whose role in the country stemmed from agreements made at the close of World War II: the United States, Great Britain, France, and the Soviet Union. If the political status of the Korean peninsula is to be changed peacefully during the 1990s—and given the economic deterioration and political isolation of the Communist North, the alternative would appear to be change that is *not* peaceful—a similar arrangement involving the two Koreas and the four most important outside powers, the four countries of the Strategic Quadrangle, would be necessary.[26]

Thus the task of resolving what could be a nasty, messy, dangerous political, economic, and perhaps military crisis on the Korean peninsula, like the more diffuse aim of substituting a policy of reassurance for the more traditional military mission of deterrence, may at some point require the kind of international cooperation, perhaps under the auspices of multilateral institutions, the historic absence of which has distinguished the politics of the Strategic Quadrangle from that of Europe.

POLITICAL CONFLICTS

The United States is the political child of Europe. Its political ideas have their origins in the great civilizations and the great events of

English and continental history: the Enlightenment, the Reformation, the struggle between monarchs and nobles and between secular and ecclesiastical authority. The ideas are drawn from the canonical texts of liberal political thinkers, Montesquieu and Locke in particular. The product of these influences, and of the American experience itself, is a strong and abiding devotion to the principles of individual rights and democratic governance.

Not surprisingly, this devotion has left its mark on relations with other countries throughout American history, including the period of the Cold War. The conflict with the Soviet Union was an ideological struggle, a clash of political ideas and governing practices. The struggle had that character, however, principally in Europe, where both sets of contending ideas were born. In Asia the Cold War was different: There the United States was less devoted than in Europe to defending democracies. There were few—indeed for most of the four relevant decades there was none save Japan—to defend.

The democratic tradition, with its emphasis on personal liberty, popular sovereignty, and individual rights, if not nonexistent on the western side of the Pacific, has not flourished there. China is an ancient civilization but no evidence of ancient Chinese democracy has yet been discovered.

To be sure, there were American allies and clients in the region besides Japan. Neither South Korea nor South Vietnam, however, in defense of which the United States fought two major wars, was a democracy; nor was Indonesia, with which the United States maintained friendly relations, nor, for most of the period of the Cold War, was Thailand or the Philippines, with which Washington had ties that were not merely friendly but close. Nor, by any standard, was the People's Republic of China a democracy or a country whose government was solicitous of the rights of those it governed, during the two Cold War decades when Beijing and Washington were aligned.

The Cold War brought the United States together with all of them. The requirements of security in the region, as Washington defined them, overrode American political convictions. All were governed by authoritarian rulers who nonetheless shared some of America's purposes in Asia and who were, therefore, "friendly tyrants."[27] Washington put aside its distaste for their methods of rule for the sake of solidarity in the face of the Soviet Union.[28]

Yet in the wake of the Cold War, democracy and human rights became increasingly prominent in American policy toward two of the other countries of the Strategic Quadrangle. In part this was because of the increased importance of democracy in American policy everywhere, which, in turn, was the natural result of the end of the Cold War. As security came to be a less dominant concern, other sources of American international conduct came to the fore. Democracy is so deeply embedded in the political genes of the United States that it was inevitable that it would play an expanded role in American foreign policy.

With one of the other powers of the Strategic Quadrangle, Russia, the promotion of democracy actually became the centerpiece of American policy. The first leader of post-Soviet Russia, Boris Yeltsin, committed himself to making his country a Western democracy. The United States undertook to support him. Washington led an international effort to provide financial assistance to support the transformation of Russia's centrally planned economy to one operated according to market principles.[29] The American policy was based on the belief that a market economy would give critical support to a democratic political system, which would, in turn, assure that the new Russia would be a good neighbor in East Asia and Eastern Europe and, perhaps, ultimately a global partner of the United States.

In the last decade of the Cold War, some Asian countries redesigned their political systems along democratic lines. In 1986 Ferdinand Marcos of the Philippines was overthrown by a democratic movement. In South Korea in 1987 the reign of the generals gave way to government by democratically elected officials. And in 1988 the ruling Kuomintang lifted martial law on Taiwan and an official opposition party was allowed to participate in politics. Because these countries threw off dictatorial rule, it was easier for the United States to maintain friendly relations with them. There was, however, no comparable basis for post–Cold War relations with the government of China, with which the issue of democracy became a sharply divisive one.

The catalyst of the rise of democracy to the top of the Sino-

American agenda came in the spring of 1989, when the Communist authorities brutally suppressed a large, amorphous popular movement that had arisen spontaneously to press for political change. The movement began with a handful of students demonstrating in Beijing's Tiananmen Square, the heart of the city, against official corruption and in favor of what they termed, without being specific, "more democracy." By the end of May similar movements had appeared in other Chinese cities, and people from other sectors of society had joined the students. Ultimately the demonstrators and their active sympathizers numbered in the millions. Their protests captured the attention of the world's media, whose ranks in the Chinese capital were swollen in mid-May by the arrival of the Soviet leader Mikhail Gorbachev for a summit meeting.

On June 3 the Chinese government cracked down forcefully on the demonstrators, using troops from the People's Liberation Army. An unknown number were killed by what appeared to be random shootings of unarmed civilians. Many more were arrested and imprisoned; some were reported executed. The government mounted a propaganda campaign reviling the protestors, with the aim of enforcing orthodoxy and obedience, a campaign that was, at least in its rhetoric, reminiscent of the terrible Chinese purges of the 1950s and 1960s.

The crackdown provoked a public outcry in the West, especially in the United States, where television coverage had made the demonstrators familiar and heroic figures. In response, the American government imposed a series of sanctions on China, including the suspension of the delivery of military equipment. China policy became the subject of domestic political conflict: The Congress passed a bill giving every Chinese student residing in the United States the right to remain rather than being required to return home. President George Bush, once the American representative in Beijing, vetoed the bill on the grounds that it would unnecessarily annoy China's rulers and that in any event a law was unnecessary to permit the students to stay in the country. After a heated debate his veto was narrowly sustained.

The issue on which discontent with China's political practices then came to focus was trade. At the end of the 1970s, as part of the policy of normalizing relations with Beijing, China had been granted Most Favored Nation (MFN) trading status. Despite its name, this did not involve special treatment. It meant rather that no country's goods were treated more favorably than were China's. After the Tiananmen debacle, and for the next three years, the Democratically controlled Congress voted to deny MFN status to China until its government did more to respect the rights of Chinese citizens. The Republican president George Bush exercised his veto each time, and China retained MFN status.[30]

The battle over MFN became an annual event, a rite of spring in American politics that changed, but did not disappear, when a Democrat entered the White House. In May 1993 President Bill Clinton extended China's MFN status for a year but issued an executive order stipulating that the Chinese must improve their human rights performance in order to receive it thereafter.

The ongoing American effort to secure modifications in Chinese political practices provoked a debate in the United States over the wisdom of making unfettered trade conditional on such changes, changes that had more to do with human rights than with democracy. The two are closely related, and both are alien to Communist political systems, but they are distinguishable from each other. Human rights involve the individual's freedom from oppressive government actions, such as arbitrary imprisonment and torture. (A prominent theme of the bills denying MFN status to China was prison labor, a Chinese practice that is outlawed by international convention.) Democracy involves the freedom to participate in the political process. The Congress did not demand that China conduct free and fair elections in order to receive MFN status.[31]

The proponents of "conditionality" were motivated by a commitment to the promotion of human rights, which has been basic to American politics since the founding of the republic. The Chinese government routinely violated rights Americans regard as fundamental.[32] In the view of its champions, conditionality was not only desirable, it was also feasible. China depended heavily on the American market. By one estimate 38 percent of its exports found their way to the United States. This gave the American government considerable leverage, which President Bush, they believed, lacked the courage or vision to use.

To complicate the issue, two different types of conditionality were advocated. The measures that the Congress passed regularly tied market access for China to its internal political practices; but there were also congressional proposals to make trade conditional on changes in Chinese *international* practices, in particular its commerce in weaponry. China was suspected of selling ballistic missiles in the Middle East and providing technology helpful in making nuclear weapons to Pakistan, Iran, and Algeria.[33] Senator John Glenn wrote that the United States "should not routinely grant MFN trading status to any country that flouts its nonproliferation commitments."[34]

One of the strongest arguments against conditionality came from the Chinese government itself, which announced that "no foreign country, organization, or individual has the right to make irresponsible remarks or interfere" in internal Chinese affairs.[35] Other Asian governments echoed Beijing's denunciations of the United States on this score, sometimes arguing that Western political models were not necessarily suitable for their region.[36]

Few Americans were prepared to concede that the United States had no right to impose conditions on trade, or that a billion Chinese did not deserve to enjoy the rights that the Declaration of Independence had proclaimed to be universal. But opponents of conditionality did argue that it was a tactic that would fail. China would not, they predicted, meet American demands. Rather than comply with them, China would forgo access to the American market because the defense of its own sovereignty was of fundamental importance to its rulers and because they believed they would gain access to the American market without making the concessions the Congress was demanding.

Economic estrangement from China would, after all, hurt the United States as well. Trade between the two countries had grown from $5 billion in 1983 to $35 billion in 1992. Interrupting it would penalize both American consumers and American workers. Moreover, those skeptical of conditionality argued, China had both other sources of capital and other markets in which to sell its products. No other industrial democracy showed any sign of following the American lead in linking trade with politics in dealing with China.[37]

Another argument against making trade conditional on human rights held that economic sanctions would be self-defeating because expanded trade was in fact the most effective method for *promoting* political liberalization in China. Economic contact with other countries, according to this position, had always been a channel through which foreign political ideas could reach the Chinese people. The Chinese government seemed to agree, complaining periodically of the "spiritual pollution" from the West.

More important, according to this argument, trade is the ally of human rights by promoting the growth of a private economy, which was extraordinarily rapid in China after 1979. A private economy is, in turn, the basis of a more tolerant and ultimately more democratic political system. This is so because a private economy is itself an island of relative liberty, an area of activity free from direct government control and thus something that orthodox Communist governments suppressed. It is true as well because democracy requires the existence of civil society, a sphere of social activity and political debate beyond the reach of the government, a sphere in which political debate can take place and from which democratic challenges to power can be mounted. The core of civil society is a private economy.

Finally, the spread of democracy generally is associated with a firmly established middle class and a relatively high per-capita income, both of which depend on economic growth, which trade with the United States helped to promote in China.[38]

Thus, according to this argument against conditionality, the United States can serve the cause of democracy and human rights in China most effectively by encouraging the trends that Deng's 1979 reforms set in motion, trends that China's economic engagement with the rest of the world strengthens. In fact, China was a far less repressive place in the 1990s than it had been from the 1950s through the 1970s, in large part because the explosive growth of a private sector there had weakened the government's grip on society.[39]

Richard Nixon's historic visit to Beijing in 1972 came in the final years of the massive, Mao-inspired spasm of violence and repression known as the Cultural Revolution. Two decades later it was virtually unthinkable that the Communist government would—or could—order anything like it. Moreover, a degree of personal freedom was available to ordinary Chinese that had been undreamed of in the Maoist era. "China might not be as free in some areas compared to the U.S.," one private Chinese business- man told a reporter for *The Wall Street Journal,* "but it's freer than some other countries."[40]

Although the Clinton administration entered office in 1993 committed to the kind of conditions on trade with China that the Congress had advocated under President Bush, it proceeded to back away from that position. After the renewal of MFN status in 1993, it made a series of friendly public gestures to Beijing, in- cluding a meeting between the American and Chinese presidents at the summit meeting of the forum for Asia-Pacific Economic Coop- eration (APEC) in Seattle in November 1993, while at the same time privately trying to coax Beijing to make concessions on human rights that would permit the administration to maintain trade without appearing to abandon the cause of human rights altogether.[41]

Finally, on May 26, 1994, President Clinton severed the link between trade practices and respect for human rights. He said that the Chinese had not achieved "overall significant progress in all areas outlined" in the previous year's executive order. Nonetheless, he continued, the decision to "delink" offered "the best opportu- nity to lay the basis for long-term sustainable progress in human rights and for the advancement of our other interests with China."[42]

This will not, however, make the issue of human rights in China disappear from the agenda of American policy in the Strate- gic Quadrangle. Tensions between deeply held American beliefs and powerfully rooted Chinese practices are certain to be an en- during feature of Sino-American relations, which, under the best of circumstances, will be marked on the American side by the uneasy coexistence of economic engagement and moral disapproval. The American people are unlikely to grant China an exemption from normal American political standards, especially in the absence of the kind of threat to the United States that, in the Cold War, had justified the suppression of those concerns for the sake of geo- political solidarity. A poll in December 1993, for example, found that 65 percent of the American public wanted improvement in

Chinese human rights practices to be the condition for continuing trade. Only 29 percent favored maintaining good relations despite Chinese human rights violations.[43]

On the other hand, China is not on the verge of becoming a democracy. The patterns of conduct that caused outrage in the United States will surely continue into the twenty-first century no matter how rapidly the Chinese economy grows. The Communist government will continue to insist on silencing organized activity on behalf of the kind of democracy that Americans favor and that, if it ever came to China, would abolish Communist rule even in its relatively benign and circumscribed form of the 1990s.

Nor is the extensive Chinese system of prison labor camps known as "lao gai" likely to be dismantled speedily. Even in a country where free labor is cheap by world standards, this system is probably profitable.[44]

A third continuing source of Sino-American friction on the question of human rights will almost certainly be the status of Tibet, where Beijing's rule since 1950 has been particularly harsh. The Chinese assaulted Tibet's Buddhist culture, destroying monasteries and forbidding religious observance. They flooded the region with Han Chinese settlers[45] after driving the Dalai Lama, Tibet's spiritual leader, into exile in India with many of his followers. He in turn conducted a worldwide campaign to achieve political autonomy for Tibet and became a prominent symbol of the global struggle for human rights, especially after receiving the Nobel Peace Prize in 1989.

Ironically, the more open China became, the more the regime relaxed its grip, the more visible and politically provocative these sources of Sino-American irritation became. The liberalization of Chinese life, linked to the revolutionary economic changes, gave dissidents greater scope for airing their views and foreigners increased access (at the height of the Maoist period they had had none) to Chinese prisons and Tibetan cities.[46]

Yet another source of Sino-American acrimony was the status of Hong Kong. A British colony since 1898, by agreement between the governments in London and Beijing Hong Kong was scheduled to return to Chinese control in 1997, when the ninety-nine-year lease the British had acquired was due to expire. The Chinese government pledged not to tamper with Hong Kong's robust market economy or to impose heavy-handed political direction, a promise expressed in the slogan "one country, two systems." But there was no guarantee that the transition to rule from Beijing would be smooth.

Because Hong Kong had been Britain's responsibility for so long, it status received relatively little attention in the United States. But given popular American concern with democracy in China and a reflexive sympathy for small countries, repressive policies in Hong Kong after 1997 could aggravate Sino-American relations.

There was one center of Chinese culture in which democracy was plainly thriving but that, for that very reason, had the greatest potential for changing Sino-American relations radically for the worse and for reshaping the politics of the Strategic Quadrangle in the post–Cold War era: the island of Taiwan.

Taiwan was the main object of contention between Washington and Beijing during the first two decades of the Cold War. The rapprochement of 1972 was possible because they agreed not to permit their disagreement about its status to obstruct cooperation against the Soviet Union. The Shanghai Communiqué of 1972, issued jointly by the two governments, affirmed their common position that there is but one China, a position to which the Kuomintang government in Taipei also had subscribed. The two countries tacitly agreed that the final resolution of the island's relationship to the mainland would be decided by the Chinese themselves in both places.

As the Cold War ended, relations between Taipei and Beijing were improving. Trade and investment had replaced the artillery barrages of the 1950s as the principal form of contact across the Taiwan Strait. By the end of 1990 Taiwan had become the third largest source of offshore investment on the mainland, which, in turn, had become Taiwan's third largest market. But Taiwan's process of democratization in the 1980s gave Taiwanese independence increased prominence. The opposition Democratic People's Party made this goal an important part of its program.

While the island has been autonomous under American protection since 1950, formal, juridical independence was wholly unacceptable to Beijing. The Communist government has suggested that a Taiwanese declaration of independence would provoke a military response from the mainland. That, in turn, would precipitate a crisis in Sino-American relations. It would be difficult for the United States to withhold support for Taiwan's independence if it were declared in order to consolidate democracy. But in Beijing such support would be regarded as an act of hostility. In the worst case, East Asia would once again become the scene of the kind of military confrontation that defined Sino-American relations throughout the 1950s.

Neither the United States nor China desires such an outcome. No country in Asia, with the possible exception of North Korea, would welcome it. That, however, does not guarantee that it would not happen.

ECONOMIC PROBLEMS

"It is now likelier than not," announced *The Economist* in late 1993, "that the most momentous public event in the lifetime of anybody reading this survey will turn out to have been the modernisation of Asia."[47] The surging economic growth of East Asia, most of it in Japan and China, is one of the defining events of the last part of the twentieth century. It caught the eye of American officials. "No region in the world is more important to the United States," Secretary of State Christopher said of Asia, where "we see most clearly that economic policy stands at the center of our foreign policy."[48]

The United States helped to make possible the East Asian economic miracle. Trade and investment require a stable political foundation. The American navy and air force in the western Pacific served as the guarantors of political stability. After 1945, the Pacific Ocean became a highway for an ever-expanding volume of commerce. Businesses in Asia, the Pacific, and North America could make use of one of the great trade routes in world history, secure in the knowledge that the American armed forces were patrolling it.[49]

The United States made a more strictly economic contribution to the Asian miracle as well. An open international economic order such as the one to which the United States and its Asian trad-ing partners belonged—an order in which trade and capital flow more or less freely across international borders—does not come into existence spontaneously. It must be organized and supported. The task of doing so has historically fallen to a single, dominant power. Great Britain was such a power in the latter part of the nineteenth century; the United States became the world's economic "hegemon" after 1945. As such, it supplied a currency that came into common international use, a large market in which other countries could sell their goods, and capital that found its way to places where it was scarce but could be used productively.[50]

The open international economic order of the postwar period was one in which the Western Europeans and Latin Americans also participated, but the countries of East Asia took particular advantage of it. Of course, the characteristics of their societies—dedication to hard work, relatively benign labor relations, skill in translating new technologies into commercial products—were in no small part responsible for their economic success. International economic conditions were essential as well, however. The prevail-ing pattern of economic growth in East Asia emphasized exports, and this was possible only because of the trading system that the United States supported.

In addition to contributing to it, the United States also bene-fited from Asia's remarkable economic progress. The benefits were partly political. The growth of the economies of Japan, China, and other countries of the region aligned with the United States strengthened the anti-Soviet coalition in the region; and the attrac-tion of the Communist model weakened as their example made it clear that fidelity to market principles, rather than to central plan-ning, was the path to economic success.

The surging economic growth in the region also brought eco-nomic gains to the people of the United States. A wider variety of products became available in North America at lower prices than if all of East Asia had remained poor and backward. Similarly, as Asians became richer, they bought more from the United States. American exports to the region grew steadily during the last decade of the Cold War.

The market economies of East Asia, however, sold more than they bought in the United States. This imbalance, which was chronic, touched a nerve in the American public, particularly the largest and most durable trade imbalance, the one with Japan.[51] For Americans this imbalance was first a source of annoyance, then anger, and ultimately alarm. Japanese imports, many believed, were destroying American jobs; after all, every American who bought a product made in Japan was passing up a comparable product made in the United States, thus hurting Americans employed in the pertinent industry. The problem became all the more severe in American eyes as Japanese firms entrenched themselves in visible, high-wage industries, many in the manufacturing sector, such as automobile production.[52]

Professional economists argued that American anxieties about trade were misplaced: Economic progress and the generation of wealth stem from competition, which inevitably displaces workers from less to more efficient firms and industries; trade balances per se denote nothing about a country's prosperity; and American trade was in imbalance overall due to macroeconomic factors—the low rate of savings above all. Their arguments, however cogent, failed to stem the growing feeling among Americans in the final years of the Cold War that the United States was becoming weaker and that Japan, which was growing stronger, was at least partly responsible for this.

Japan's perceived prowess in industries that American companies had previously dominated was seen as both a symptom and a cause of what became an American preoccupation at the end of the 1980s: national decline.[53]

As the end of the Cold War removed the need for Japanese-American solidarity against the Soviet Union, objections to Japanese trade practices came to dominate American policy toward the country that had been, during the Cold War, the closest Asian ally of the United States.

From the 1950s through the 1970s, Japan's trade surplus had been only a minor irritant in American policy in the Strategic Quadrangle. Wartime rules of diplomacy applied; squabbles within the anti-Soviet coalition were set aside for the sake of waging the conflict. Moreover, at the outset of this period Japan was not an industrial giant. It specialized in textiles and inexpensive consumer electronics, which hardly threatened the commanding heights of the American economy.[54]

In the 1980s popular displeasure with Japanese trade practices assumed greater significance in overall American policy. Japanese firms made inroads in industries that turned out to be politically sensitive: not only automobiles, but also advanced consumer electronics and computer hardware, involving the most sophisticated manufacturing technology. At the end of the decade, a recession and the cumulative effects of two decades of stagnant real incomes for much of the workforce made the American public increasingly sensitive to what seemed to be a foreign assault on its standards of living. Polls showed that a rising proportion of the American public regarded Japanese economic competition as "threatening" to the United States.[55] As the trade deficit with Japan became a more salient political issue, three different approaches to balancing the account with Japan were attempted.[56]

One such approach, favored by professional economists, was to adjust the rate of exchange between the dollar and the yen. With a weak dollar American products would be less expensive in Japan and Japanese would buy more of them; Japanese products, similarly, would be more expensive in the United States and Americans would buy fewer of them. This experiment in economic logic did not succeed. Beginning in 1985 the yen appreciated, ultimately doubling its value vis-á-vis the dollar. Yet the Japanese trade surplus did not decline in proportion to the drop in the value of the dollar. Indeed, it scarcely declined at all. Moreover, the trade deficit with Japan persisted even as the American deficits with other countries responded to the falling dollar by dwindling.[57]

The efforts to deal with the trade imbalance with Japan had a second focus: the United States itself. From an economic standpoint, the heart of the problem—if indeed the trade deficit *was* a problem—was located in American domestic economic policies. The United States saved too little and consumed too much, hence its overall trade deficit.

This second approach drew upon the debate about American decline. This debate generated a body of commentary that attributed the economic difficulties of the United States not only to the macroeconomic imbalances that produced the trade deficit, but also to the system of corporate finance and ownership that valued short-term profitability rather than long-term growth as well as to the shortcomings of American society, in particular a system of public education that failed to impart economically useful skills to its graduates.[58] An outpouring of books, articles, and task force reports, combining alarm and exhortation, diagnosed the nation's ills and proposed remedies for them.

There was little disagreement about the diagnosis. But the task of implementing the policies that followed from it could be described by the phrase that Clausewitz had used to characterize war: simple but difficult. It was easy enough to say that Americans should save more and spend less, invest more patiently, and study harder—and many did say these things, sometimes eloquently. It was difficult, however, to *do* them, and especially to do them quickly. Even if they could have been done quickly, the economic gains they would have produced would have been decades in coming.

And so American attention turned to a third way to correct the trade imbalance with the Japanese: changing Japan. This approach drew strength from the conviction that it was, after all, Japanese practices and policies that were responsible for its chronic trade imbalances—not only with the United States but also with the rest of the world. American impatience with the Japanese surplus was reflected in legislation designed to reduce it. In 1988 the Congress passed a law requiring the president to take retaliatory action against countries with trade imbalances acquired through unfair practices. In 1989 the Bush administration found Japan to be in violation of the law's provisions.

Negotiations between the United States and Japan to narrow the trade gap became a permanent feature of the relationship, as had arms control negotiations with the Soviet Union during the second half of the Cold War. In noticeable ways Japan did change. Some barriers to trade came down, due, in the opinion of both Japanese and American observers, to foreign pressure—*gaiatsu* in Japanese.

Providing intellectual ballast for the ongoing effort to produce change in Japan itself was a body of literature compiled by writers who came to be known, collectively, as "Japan revisionists."[59] They argued that Japan's chronic trade surpluses stemmed from three differences between Japan and the advanced economies of Western Europe and North America.

First, the Japanese government channeled credit to support favored industries. It was adept at what governments are not supposed to be able to do: "picking winners" in the Darwinian competition that is the international marketplace. Second, Japanese industry, often with indirect government help, penetrated and dominated foreign markets in selected industries, underselling the competition so as to drive it out of business. This was possible because the Japanese aimed at market shares rather than short-term profits.[60] Third, and most disturbing from the American point of view, Japan protected its own market with a variety of measures, all of them in violation of the spirit of free trade although not necessarily the letter of what is the international commercial equivalent of law: the General Agreement on Tariffs and Trade (GATT). Japanese agriculture, construction, consumer electronics, and computers were all heavily protected.[61] The country resisted foreign direct investment; total foreign investment in the United States was many times greater than the foreign investment by other countries in Japan.[62]

Revisionism had an unusually wide political significance because of the politics of trade issues in the United States. For most of the postwar period, protectionist sentiment, which is perpetually strong at the grass roots, was kept in check by a powerful bipartisan coalition of business leaders, government officials, journalists, and academics, all of whom supported the principle of free trade. On issues of trade the political cleavage was not between Republicans and Democrats, or between liberals and conservatives, but between those most attentive to and active in political affairs— the "elite"—and the rest of the country.[63]

Two factors united the elite consensus. One was the conflict with the Soviet Union and the need for political solidarity with America's trading partners in order to wage it. The second was the widely shared conviction that there was no intellectually respectable case for opposing free trade. The revisionists' arguments, regardless of whether they were correct, passed the political test of respectability. Indeed, with the advent of the Clinton administration, that case came to have a practical effect on American policy.

The Clinton administration completed the transition to a post–Cold War American policy in the Strategic Quadrangle by placing trade at the center of the relations between the United States and Japan. It did so, ironically, by discarding what was, on paper, the most ambitious effort to change Japanese practices in order to correct the trade imbalance between the two countries, the Structural Impediments Initiative (SII) of 1990. The SII's underlying premise was that the Japanese surplus had been caused by "structural" features of the Japanese economy: its lack of antitrust laws; its retail system, which excludes foreign products; its modest expenditures on infrastructure, which, if they were increased, might attract products from abroad. The SII was designed to change all this.

It produced few visible results. Critics accused the Japanese government of using the SII as a pretext for doing nothing about its trade surpluses. Whether this was justified or not, it was certainly true that the changes the SII prescribed, involving, as they did, alterations in long-established customs and institutions and strongly held beliefs, could scarcely be accomplished overnight.[64]

The Clinton administration sought immediate results. It adopted another approach, called by its opponents "managed trade." This involved setting numerical indicators for measuring progress in the hoped-for expansion of American exports to Japan. The precedent was a 1986 agreement between the two countries specifying that American-made semiconductors would have 20 percent of the Japanese market in five years. This goal was achieved.[65]

Americans saw this approach as a useful way to increase Japan's imports without attempting to rearrange Japanese society. The Japanese objected, however, as did professional economists and governments of third countries on the grounds that managed trade runs directly counter to the law of comparative advantage, the scientific basis of the doctrine of free trade that was first outlined by the English economist David Ricardo in the early nineteenth century. He demonstrated that nations maximize their wealth when they specialize in what each can produce with greatest economic efficiency compared with others, and then trade freely among themselves. Under a regime of managed trade, the flow of products between countries is determined on political rather than economic grounds.

Like the Sino-American conflict over human rights, Japanese-American friction over trade is unlikely to disappear. The Japanese economy is powerfully geared to exports; the United States has been its most important market. The disposition to equate the trade balance with overall national economic health, whatever its status in economic theory, seems firmly embedded in the American psyche.[66]

Even more than the dispute with China over human rights, the Japanese-American conflict on trade is likely to have consequences beyond the bilateral relationship and beyond East Asia. Because Japan and the United States are the two largest economies in the world, the rules of engagement they establish for each other are likely to be adopted elsewhere in the international economy. Managed trade between them will encourage managed trade elsewhere. It will be especially tempting for the United States to negotiate similar targets with other East Asian countries, because they too maintain chronic export surpluses. The economies of China, Hong Kong, Singapore, and South Korea differ from that of Japan in important respects, but all have based their strategies of economic growth on selling manufactured products abroad, especially in North America.[67]

The members of the European Union, although opposed in principle to managed trade, have not welcomed many products from Asia and, closer to home, tightly controlled the volume of exports from the formerly Communist countries of Europe. Indeed, the wealthy industrial countries face the prospect of a flood of cheap imports in the twenty-first century from countries with low labor costs, increasingly sophisticated industrial bases, and governments committed to strategies of export-led growth: China, which is embarked along that path; India, the world's second most populous country, which began a program of economic liberalization in the 1990s; and perhaps ultimately from Russia and other former Soviet republics. If the richest countries do not trade freely among themselves, they are unlikely to trade freely with these new entrants into the international economy.[68]

At the extreme, the trend toward managed trade could lead to the formation of distinct trading blocs. The European Union provides the basis for a European bloc, and the North American Free Trade Agreement could play a similar role in the Western Hemisphere. In East Asia, the logical core of a regional grouping is Japan.

None of the powers of the Strategic Quadrangle desires such an arrangement. Japan has no interest in retreating economically into its own region, nor does China or any of the other countries of East Asia wish to give Japan the power that would come with the creation of a yen bloc. Nor do their trade patterns suggest a natural basis for such an arrangement. Intra-Asian trade is increasing in the 1990s, but so is the trade of East Asian countries in markets outside the region.[69]

Purely economic considerations weigh against the fragmenting of the international economic order into separate, self-contained regional blocs; that would make all countries less affluent than they would be if trade and investment were global in scope. And during the Cold War, political considerations had the same effect: opening American markets to Asian products was a way of strengthening the coalition against the Soviet Union, which had the highest priority for the United States in East Asia. But with the end of the Cold War, solidarity with the market economies of Asia no longer occupies so important a place in American policy in the Strategic Quadrangle.

CONCLUSION

How will America's relations with the three other powers of the Strategic Quadrangle and its approaches to the major issues at the center of its relations with them—security, human rights, and trade—evolve into a coherent policy for East Asia? They may not. The government may conduct its bilateral relations with each of the major powers in the region separately from one another, with none having an appreciable effect on the other two. It may pursue a security policy in the western Pacific, a human rights policy toward China, and trade policy toward Japan, but no overall policy for East Asia as a whole.

Nonetheless, there will be a pull toward interconnections among the various policies and thus toward a new common denominator for American policy in the Strategic Quadrangle. Public policy—and foreign policy is no exception—abhors a conceptual vacuum. Policymakers need guidelines to follow. They also need public support, which requires justifications for what they do. The broader and more general these justifications are, the more coherent, easy to conduct, and ultimately successful foreign policy is likely to be. There are at least three candidates to replace the Cold War as the basis for American policy in East Asia.

One is the primacy of *security*. This would continue, in modified fashion, the way American foreign policy was organized during the Cold War. The United States would maintain a military presence to reassure the countries of the region. Diplomatic cooperation to keep nuclear weapons out of the hands of the North Korean government would be important, as would the task of managing such instability as the internal weakness of the North Korean regime may create. In the interest of keeping the region stable, the United States would downplay its differences with China and Japan.

While stability in East Asia is desirable, it lacks the powerful resonance in public opinion that confronting a major adversary has. A common danger, such as the Soviet Union in the Cold War, can override economic and political quarrels. The vaguer and less urgent goal of stability is unlikely to exert the same discipline on American policy in the region.

The second approach involves the *primacy of economic considerations,* in which the size of Japan's economy and the rate of growth of China's make participating in the region's economy the highest priority of American policy. Deploying military forces for the purpose of reassurance would be attractive because it would complement the American economic presence in East Asia. Under this second set of policies, the prospect of economic gain would keep the inevitable American concerns about the political practices of China's Communist regime from inhibiting trade and investment there and would spur the United States and Japan to negotiate rules that would perpetuate trade between them. The aim of integrating the eastern part of Russia into the commerce of the

Pacific rim is very much in keeping with the spirit of this second organizing principle for post–Cold War American foreign policy in the Strategic Quadrangle.

There is a continuing demand for this approach in Asia. The region's leaders want an American military presence in some form and in particular want continued access to the American market. But this second approach would make demands that the American public finds uncongenial: paying for a military mission for which there is no apparent precedent in American history but that appears suspiciously like the distinctly unpopular role of "world policeman"; tolerating the violation of rights deemed fundamental and universal; and accommodating trade practices that many believe harm Americans.

Disengagement is a third possible American approach to East Asia, one shaped by the differences between the United States and the other three powers of the Strategic Quadrangle. These differences can reinforce one another and lead to the estrangement of the United States from the other three and from the region itself.

Angered by China's treatment of political dissidents, the United States might withdraw MFN status, which would sharply reduce trade between the two countries, inflicting economic costs on both. Sino-American political relations would deteriorate. So too, in all likelihood, would relations between Tokyo and Washington, because Japan would not join the United States in imposing trade sanctions on China. American frustration with Japan would increase, a fact that would in turn hamper efforts to work out mutually acceptable trading rules between them. American relations with Russia will depend more on events in Europe than on developments in Asia; but no future Russian government is likely to side with the United States on the question of human rights in China or join Washington in condemning Japanese trade practices.

These interlocking disputes could create a political climate in the United States in which support for military deployments in East Asia weakens. Americans would be loath to tax themselves to deploy forces whose purpose was to reassure countries with which the United States was sharply at odds on political and economic issues. Japan and China would come to seem, to the American public, increasingly ungrateful, if not actually hostile, to the United States.

Under such circumstances, the idea of military and economic disengagement—of keeping no forces west of Pearl Harbor and of concentrating the nation's economic attention on Europe and the Americas—would receive a more favorable hearing in the United States than during the Cold War. Disengagement from the region is conceivable for the United States in a way it is not for the other three powers of the Strategic Quadrangle. The American presence in East Asia rests ultimately on political decisions, which, unlike the facts of geography on which the participation of the other three countries is based, can be reversed.

Disengagement, however, is improbable. It would be a radical departure from the American policy not only of the post-1945 era but of the entire twentieth century. The United States was a power in East Asia well before 1945, at least since 1898 and arguably since 1853, when Commodore Matthew Perry sailed his "black ships" into Tokyo Bay. Disengagement also would risk triggering political instability whose effects ultimately would be felt on the opposite—North American—side of the Pacific and would cut off the United States from the fastest-growing part of the world. However different from the Cold War the post–Cold War era turns out to be, its international politics will be dominated by considerations of power and wealth. The fear of the first and the lure of the second will keep the United States engaged in East Asia, which means that, at the outset of the twenty-first century as at the end of the twentieth, the United States will be an active participant in the Strategic Quadrangle.

Notes

1. Always in the background as well was the American nuclear arsenal, part of which was carried by a fleet of submarines that moved between the west coast of North America and the Asian mainland and much of which could be aimed at targets in the Soviet Far East. In Korea, 43,000 American troops were stationed until the end of the Cold War, part of a continuous presence after the Korean conflict in the 1950s. There were 47,000 American servicemen and women in Japan and 16,000 in the Philippines.

   The post-Vietnam deployment of military forces in East Asia more or less reconstituted the American military position of 1945. Immediately after the defeat of Japan, the American military dominated the Pacific and had acquired bases around the rim of East Asia but was largely absent from the Asian mainland.

This position relied on American strengths. Air and naval forces depend more on technological virtuosity and less on the capacity to mobilize troops in large numbers and to absorb casualties than do land armies. For just this reason the American people, like the British before them, have traditionally been more willing to support a powerful navy than a large army.

2. This is perhaps an exaggerated appraisal of the Soviet view. But Mikhail Gorbachev ceased to challenge the American presence in the region, and his predecessor may privately have preferred it to the likely alternative—a militarily more powerful Japan.

3. The original postwar trade relationship between the two countries, insofar as it was recognized as one-sided, with greater Japanese access to the American market than American exports had to Japan, was justified on Cold War grounds. Washington considered it important to build up Japan economically, as a bulwark against the Soviet Union, even at the expensive of commercial reciprocity. By the 1970s Japanese economic strength was not in question. Then American unhappiness with Japan's trade practices came to the surface.

4. It was Gorbachev who, before the collapse of the Soviet Union in 1991, fulfilled Beijing's three conditions for the normalization of Sino-Soviet relations: the reduction of troops on the border between the two countries; the end of Vietnamese military and political domination of Cambodia; and the withdrawal of the Soviet army from Afghanistan. See Chapter 1 in this volume.

5. Cited in "Gearing Up,"*The Economist,* February 20, 1993, p. 20.

6. Only 6 percent was forward deployed in Asia. Cited in Richard K. Betts, "Wealth, Power, and Instability: East Asia and the United States After the Cold War,"*International Security,* 18, no. 3 (Winter 1993/1994): 50. The sharpest reductions of the Cold War era had come in the early 1970s, when American ground forces withdrew from Vietnam.

7. Cited in David B. H. Denoon, *Real Reciprocity: Balancing U.S. Economic and Security Policy in the Pacific Basin* (New York: The Council on Foreign Relations, 1993), p. 17.

8. This is a theme of Paul Kennedy, *The Rise and Fall of the Great Powers* (New York: Random House, 1987), pp. 447–458.

9. See John Fialka, "U.S. Fears China's Success in Skimming Cream of Weapons Experts from Russia," *The Wall Street Journal,* October 30, 1993.

10. See below, pp. 175–176.

11. Vietnam, the Philippines, Malaysia, and Brunei had conflicting claims. Betts, "Wealth, Power, and Instability," p. 65. See also Denoon, *Real Reciprocity,* pp. 26–27.

12. If the growth rates of the 1980s and 1990s were sustained into the next century, China's sheer size—it would have the largest economy as well as the largest population in the world—would be of concern to its neighbors. In this sense, as Richard K. Betts has noted, China's status in Asia is comparable to Europe's "German problem" after 1871, when the newly united and economically dynamic Germany proved too large for the existing patterns of European international relations to include peacefully. Betts, "Wealth, Power, and Instability," p. 61.

13. For the role of buffer, the distance between the United States and the other countries of the Strategic Quadrangle was an advantage. Distance made the

United States less threatening and thus more acceptable to each of the other parties. In the 1950s and 1960s, when American troops were fighting in Korea and Vietnam, the distance between North America and the Asian mainland had counted as a military liability. In the 1980s it came to be something of a political asset.

14. Michael Howard, "Reassurance and Deterrence: Western Defense in the 1980s," *Foreign Affairs* 61, no. 2 (Winter 1982–3). Howard argued that in the early 1980s in Europe, the requirements of deterrence and those of reassurance had come into conflict. The conflict stemmed from the Atlantic Alliance's decision to deploy American-controlled intermediate-range nuclear-tipped missiles in Europe. Military specialists considered these weapons necessary to reinforce the credibility of the American commitment to defend Western Europe. Many Europeans, however, especially in the Federal Republic of Germany, found the missiles provocative. To them the missiles were alarming, not reassuring.

15. Quoted in James A. Winnefeld et al., *A New Strategy and Fewer Forces: The Pacific Dimension* (Santa Monica, CA: The Rand Corporation, 1992), p. 40.

16. Warren Christopher, "America's Pacific Future," address presented at the University of Washington, Seattle, November 17, 1993.

17. The phrase is Jonathan Pollack's, cited in "Gearing Up," p. 20.

18. Japan amassed considerable military force while keeping defense spending at or near 1 percent of its gross national product simply because its GNP grew so rapidly.

19. See the introduction to this volume.

20. The differences in the composition of the two opposing forces stood in the way of negotiating arms control agreements in the Asia-Pacific region. On the European continent, and in the case of the two major nuclear arsenals, forces were roughly similar. In East Asia, by contrast, the United States was and is predominantly a naval power, while Soviet military might was concentrated in land forces. Negotiating arms control agreements involves striking roughly even balances between and among the military forces of different countries. In Europe this was an exercise in balancing like with like. In East Asia it is a matter of equating apples and oranges, and thus more difficult to do.

   During the Cold War the asymmetry did not prevent some, notably Russians, from touting the merits of naval arms control in the Pacific. The United States resisted. Because it enjoyed naval superiority, the equality that arms control accords customarily enshrine would have required larger reductions on the American side. And while the doctrines governing most American nuclear and nonnuclear forces during the Cold War held that American interests were adequately served by military parity with the Soviet Union, the U.S. Navy considered superiority in the Pacific necessary to carry out its missions there. On naval arms control see Andrew Mack, "Superpower Arms Control in the Pacific," in Miles Kahler (ed.), *Beyond the Cold War in the Pacific* (San Diego: University of California, Institute on Global Conflict and Cooperation, 1991).

21. Lee Kuan Yew of Singapore is an exception. "If Japan can carry on with its current policy, leaving security to the Americans and concentrating on the

economic and the political, the world will be better off. And the Japanese are quite happy to do this. It is when America feels that it's too burdensome and not worth the candle to be present in Asia to protect Japan that it will have to look after its own security. When Japan becomes a separate player, it is an extra joker in the pack of cards." Fareed Zakaria, "A Conversation with Lee Kuan Yew," *Foreign Affairs* 75, no. 2 (March/April 1994): p. 123.

22. There is also a potential contradiction between the aim of reassurance—to quiet anxieties about Japanese military power by preventing incentives for its expansion from arising—and a Cold War goal of American policy in East Asia that has survived the end of the conflict: transferring to Japan a larger share of the burden of keeping the region secure.

23. Having the Japanese pay for the task of reassurance does not guarantee that American armed forces will carry it out. The American public might then view its forces as mercenaries, in which case U.S. support for keeping troops in Asia would almost certainly dwindle.

24. On this issue see *North Korea's Nuclear Program: Challenge and Opportunity for American Policy* (Washington, D.C.: The United States Institute of Peace, 1994).

25. One way of trying to stave off collapse was to institute the kinds of economic changes that China had made beginning in 1979. Chinese officials reportedly urged such changes on their North Korean counterparts, who declined to adopt them, perhaps because they were convinced that this would dilute their power or even lead, in the end, to the German outcome.

26. Although the four powers of the Strategic Quadrangle, and indeed all the other countries of East Asia, were united in opposing North Korean acquisition of nuclear weapons, a potential for division existed between the United States on the one hand and the East Asians on the other over the tactics employed to accomplish this aim. Washington saw the issue in global terms. It would therefore seek not only to deny nuclear weapons to North Korea but to do so in a way that would not encourage other countries elsewhere to try to get them. For this reason the United States would be reluctant to reward North Korea for giving up its nuclear ambitions. The East Asians, by contrast, approached the issue from a regional perspective. Rewarding Pyongyang was more likely to seem worthwhile to them if it assured a nuclear-free Korean peninsula.

27. See Daniel Pipes and Adam Garfinkle (eds.), *Friendly Tyrants: An American Policy Dilemma* (New York: St. Martin's Press, 1991).

28. The United States supported friendly tyrants as well on the theory that if they fell from power, their successors might well be both less friendly to the United States *and* less respectful of liberal political norms. Mao Zedong, Fidel Castro, and the Ayatollah Khomeini, each of whom replaced a pro-American strongman, all turned out to be distinctly *un*friendly tyrants.

29. The American-sponsored campaign of support for Russia created a potential source of strain between the United States and Japan. The Japanese were more skeptical than the Americans that the Russian government was capable of using wisely whatever money was raised; in addition, unlike the United States, Japan had a territorial grievance against Russia as the successor state of the Soviet Union. The Americans did not regard the return of Japan's

"Northern Territories" as a necessary condition for dispensing funds to Moscow.

30. For details of the MFN controversy see Harry Harding, *A Fragile Relationship: The United States and China since 1972* (Washington, D.C.: The Brookings Institution, 1992), pp. 265–269, 275–280.

31. One of the issues over which the United States was consistently at odds with China linked the two: the right of political dissidents to express their views, which often included the advocacy of democracy.

32. A less prominent reason for pressing for internal change in China was the belief that, because democracies tend to be peaceful, the more powerful China became, the more dangerous it was apt to be if it retained a repressive political system. See Betts, "Wealth, Power, and Instability," p. 61.

   The campaign to promote human rights could also be seen as the reassertion of the nineteenth-century belief in a special missionary role in China for the United States, with responsibility for making China over in the prosperous, rational, Christian image of the West.

33. The United States also suspected China of selling chemicals used in making poison gas to Iran. In May 1993 the United States went so far as to stop, board, and inspect a ship suspected of carrying such chemicals. None was found. See Don Oberdorfer, "Replaying the China Card," *The Washington Post,* November 7, 1993, p. C3.

34. John Glenn, "China's Dangerous Arms Exports," *The Washington Post,* December 3, 1993, p. A29. The two different bases for imposing conditions on trade re-created the "war of the two Henrys" over American policy toward the Soviet Union in the 1970s. Senator Henry Jackson of Washington favored tying MFN status explicitly to human rights, specifically to free emigration for those who wished to leave. (In practice this meant, for the most part, Soviet Jews.) His preference was codified in the Jackson-Vanik Amendment. National Security Advisor and then–Secretary of State Henry Kissinger favored a loose and implicit linkage between economic relations and Soviet foreign policy. If Moscow conducted itself to the liking of the United States in the international arena, under the policy he preferred, economic engagement would follow. Kissinger and President Richard Nixon believed that the linkage would work the other way as well: If the Soviet Union were enmeshed in a web of ties, it would be less likely to carry out aggressive policies that would risk rupturing them.

35. The statement came on the eve of a visit to Beijing by Secretary of State Warren Christopher that was marked by unusual public acrimony on the issue of human rights. Quoted in Elaine Sciolino, "U.S. Showing Frustration Over China's Human Rights Policy," *The New York Times,* March 9, 1994, p. A11.

   China's nineteenth-century encounter with the West, which included the establishment of Western colonial enclaves along the Chinese coast, the denunciation of which was a staple of Communist propaganda, may have given this assertion particular resonance within China. As David M. Lampton notes in Chapter 2 in this volume, the Chinese government seemed increasingly confident that it could withstand American pressure for changes in its political practice. By contrast, Beijing showed some willingness to negotiate on the foreign policies to which the United States objected.

36. See, for example, Victor Mallet, "Confucius or Convenience?" *Financial Times,* March 5/6, 1994, p. xxvi, and James Fallows, *Looking at the Sun: The Rise of the New East Asian Economic and Political System* (New York: Pantheon, 1994), pp. 312–314.

37. The increasing economic importance of China had political consequences in the United States. Businesses with a direct stake in the continuation of commercial relations pressed their case in Washington, providing a countervailing force to the proponents of conditionality. They constituted the third version since 1949 of an American "China lobby." (The first, in the 1950s, had been supporters of Taiwan; the second, in the 1980s, were concerned about human rights in China.)

38. See Samuel P. Huntington, *The Third Wave: Democratization in the Late Twentieth Century* (Norman: University of Oklahoma Press, 1991), p. 105. China had far to go on both counts to reach the levels of most democracies.

39. It was certainly not a democracy, but China might be said to have changed, to use terminology from the Cold War era, from a totalitarian to an authoritarian regime, one in which a single party monopolized political power but did not dictate every facet of social and economic life.

40. Kathy Chen, "U.S. Human Rights Demands Puzzle the Chinese, Many of Whom Enjoy New Comfort and Freedom," *The Wall Street Journal,* March 7, 1994, p. A7.

41. Oberdorfer, "Replaying the China Card."

42. *The New York Times,* May 27, 1994, p A8.

43. Cited in *The Wall Street Journal,* December 16, 1993.

44. On prison labor in China see "China's Secret Economy," *The Economist,* October 2, 1993.

45. In this respect there is a similarity between Chinese policy in Tibet after 1950 and the Soviet policy toward the Baltic states of Estonia, Latvia, and Lithuania. The three were conquered and occupied in 1940, in the wake of the Nazi-Soviet pact. After the war, in the 1950s, Moscow began to send Russians in large numbers to live there.

46. See Harding, *A Fragile Relationship,* pp. 203–204.

47. Jim Rowher, "Asia Survey: A Billion Consumers," *The Economist,* October 30, 1993, p. 1.

48. Christopher, "America's Pacific Future."

49. One of the missions of the U.S. Navy, as of the British navy before it, was to keep open the sea lanes between the home countries and transoceanic allies (or, in the British case, imperial possessions).

50. The idea that an economic hegemon is required to organize and sustain an open, or liberal, international economic order was first proposed by Charles Kindleberger and has been refined by many others. For a summary of the issue and the literature on it, see Michael Mandelbaum, *The Fate of Nations: The Search for National Security in the 19th and 20th Centuries* (New York: Cambridge University Press, 1988), chap. 6.

51. For details see Denoon, *Real Reciprocity,* pp. 46–55.

52. By normal standards the composition as well as the volume of Japanese-American trade was unbalanced. There was relatively little trade within industries. Although Japan was the second-largest trading partner of the United

States, it bought mainly raw materials from and sold mainly finished products to Americans, which was not true, for example, of trade between the United States and Western Europe. See Edward N. Luttwak, *The Endangered American Dream* (New York: Simon and Schuster, 1993), pp. 94–95, and Fallows, *Looking at the Sun,* pp. 232–233, 274–277.

53. The debate about American decline was set off—inadvertently—by what, in the absence of popular concern about the nation's ability to compete in international markets would have been an obscure, although well-written, scrupulous, and extremely useful work of history, Paul Kennedy's *The Rise and Fall of the Great Powers* (New York: Random House, 1987). Kennedy sketched a historical pattern in which the burden of deploying and wielding great international power over time erodes the economic basis of that power. He suggested that the United States might be suffering from the effects of this syndrome, while noting—presciently—that the Soviet Union was far more seriously affected. The book became a best-seller and touched off a vigorous debate. For a rebuttal see Samuel P. Huntington, "America: Decline or Renewal?" *Foreign Affairs* (Winter 1988–89): 76–96.

54. During that period American irritation with Japanese exports was not nonexistent. There was, for example, a major squabble over textiles in 1969. See I. M. Destler, *Managing an Alliance* (Washington, D.C.: The Brookings Institution, 1976), pp. 35–45.

55. See, for example, David Brock, "The Theory and Practice of Japan-Bashing," *The National Interest,* no. 17 (Fall 1989): 30.

56. An important milestone in the evolution of Japanese-American relations, one that illustrated the rise of economic competition and the related decline of security cooperation as the touchstone of the relationship, was the controversy over the FSX. This advanced jet fighter airplane was to be coproduced by the two countries, but the Congress acted to block it for fear that it would result in the "leakage" of commercially valuable American technology to Japan. See Luttwak, *The Endangered American Dream,* pp. 64–88.

57. Denoon, *Real Reciprocity,* pp. 50–51, and Fallows, *Looking at the Sun,* pp. 256–260.

58. Luttwak, *The Endangered American Dream,* summarizes these critiques. See in particular Peter G. Peterson, *Facing Up: How to Rescue the Economy from Crushing Debt and Restore the American Dream* (New York: Simon and Schuster, 1993).

59. The intellectual origins of the revisionist school lie in the work of the political scientist Chalmers Johnson, especially his book *MITI and the Japanese Miracle* (Stanford, CA: Stanford University Press, 1982). The most widely read of the revisionists was James Fallows, who published a series of articles in *The Atlantic* in the late 1980s and two books: *More Like Us* (Boston: Houghton Mifflin, 1989), which, because its focus was the United States, was as much a part of the "declinist" as the "revisionist" literature, and *Looking at the Sun,* whose subtitle contains its thesis: "The Rise of a New East Asian Economic and Political System."

Karel Van Wolferen, a Dutch journalist resident in Japan, wrote a revisionist account of Japanese politics, *The Japanese Enigma* (New York: Knopf, 1989). Clyde Prestowitz, a one-time American trade official, argued that the

United States had failed to cope effectively with predatory Japanese trade practices in *Trading Places: How We Allowed Japan to Take the Lead* (New York: Basic Books, 1988). Revisionism provoked a literature of rebuttal, of which the most prominent popular exponent was Bill Emmott, first Japan correspondent then editor of the London *Economist*. In *The Sun Also Sets: The Limits to Japan's Economic Power* (New York: Times Books, 1990), and *Japanophobia: The Myth of the Invincible Japanese* (New York: Times Books, 1993), he argued that Japan was not really different from other advanced industrial capitalist states and that, to the extent it was or ever had been, it was becoming more like them all the time. Paul Krugman's *Peddling Prosperity* (New York: W.W. Norton, 1994) offered a different revisionist argument: that the overall condition of the American economy had very little to do with international economic competition.

60. This was, in turn, made possible by the particular Japanese pattern of corporate ownership, which allotted a prominent role for banks that could afford to be patient as American shareholders rarely were.

61. Even among those unsympathetic to the revisionist case there was little dispute that Japan practiced protection. What was in dispute was how fast this was changing, how different Japan was in this respect from other countries, the United States included, and how much difference complete openness to foreign products would actually make in the Japanese trade balance.

62. Denoon, *Real Reciprocity,* p. 56. From the standpoint of Western (and largely Anglo-American) neoclassical economics, Japanese departures from the canons of orthodox economic practice (and there was a debate about just how substantial these departures were) were not altogether surprising. No national economy is run strictly according to the principles of Adam Smith and his intellectual descendants. A far stiffer challenge to this economic orthodoxy was the proposition that these departures actually *increased* Japan's well-being, that Japan had grown rich because of, not despite, straying from proper market practices. Some tried to show that this was so at least to a limited extent, updating the familiar "infant industry" justification for protection by arguing that there were certain "strategic" industries that, if allowed to flourish, would ultimately lift entire economies. See Laura Tyson, *Who's Bashing Whom?* (Washington, D.C.: Institute for International Economics, 1992). If the economic practices that the revisionists identified as distinctly Japanese did not make the country as a whole more prosperous, as neoclassical economic doctrine maintained, why were they undertaken? An answer was supplied by Karel Van Wolferen, *The Japanese Enigma,* who argued that Japan was not fully a democracy and thus the Japanese people could not change the economic practices that injured them as well as Japan's trading partners. See also Fallows, *Looking at the Sun,* pp. 211–212.

63. See Michael Mandelbaum, "U.S. Global Role Vital for U.S. and Globe," *Newsday,* November 28, 1993.

64. See Luttwak, *The Endangered American Dream,* pp. 55–59.

65. According to a later version of the accord, American industry "expects that the foreign market share will grow to more than 20 percent . . . by the end of 1992." *The Financial Times,* March 23, 1994, p. 4. See also Fallows, *Looking at the Sun,* pp. 64–65.

66. The American anger abated somewhat, but did not disappear, during the American economic recovery and the Japanese recession of 1993–1994.

67. China's trade surplus with the United States reached $18 billion in 1992. Taiwan's application to join the GATT stalled over the issue of its barriers to trade. South Korea's trade with the United States was in rough balance, but it was even more difficult for foreigners to invest there than in Japan.

68. On this issue see Robert D. Hormats, "Making Regionalism Safe," *Foreign Affairs* (March/April 1994).

69. Miles Kahler, "United States Interests and Economic Regionalism in the Pacific," paper prepared for a conference entitled "Reconceptualizing U.S. Policy Toward East Asia," sponsored by the Council on Foreign Relations and the University of California Institute on Global Conflict and Cooperation, March 11–12, 1993.

CHAPTER FIVE

Who Will Shape the Emerging Structure of East Asia?

RICHARD H. SOLOMON

The title of this timely volume reflects the fact that four major powers have interacting interests and foreign policies in East Asia; and the economic vitality of the region warrants this focus on the future dynamics of the Strategic Quadrangle. The East Asian economies are increasingly an engine of global development. With the end of the Cold War, however, patterns of policy and interaction in the region are increasingly difficult to discern—but also of undiminished relevance to the United States and the other nations of the Pacific Rim.

In concluding this wide-ranging assessment of the policies and perspectives of the United States, Russia, China, and Japan toward East Asia, it is thus important to consider which of the major powers will shape the emerging structure of this burgeoning region. We are today in a relatively "open" period of history following the collapse of the Soviet Union and the freeing up of much of the globe from the polarized structure of the Cold War decades. Yet it is not clear which nations, if any, will succeed in imparting a new pattern on the Asian region—or whether global economic trends or subnational forces will upset the plans of the major players.

QUADRANGULAR INTERESTS, BUT STILL A BILATERAL GAME

The analyses in this volume make it clear that East Asia and the Pacific remains a region in which, for the near term, the United

States has the resources, the influence, and the national interests to shape the strategic and economic environment as much as any of the four major powers. Whether, in fact, we will grasp the reins leading to the future is a matter of political leadership and domestic political will. China is the other major power that will actively try to shape the region's future, but its influence will be played out over the long term—assuming its current high level of growth is maintained for several decades and the resources generated by the dramatic expansion of its economy are translated into instruments of commercial, political, and military influence.

Russia, as Robert Legvold's chapter makes clear, is unlikely to be a major factor shaping the basic equilibrium in East Asia. Its post-Soviet preoccupations are largely domestic and economic, and the country has lost the ideological focus and coherent military capabilities of the Soviet era that led Moscow to project its influence into a region distant from the European center of Russian national life. Moscow's security preoccupations are most likely to remain in Eastern Europe or in the southern tier of newly independent states in the "near abroad," many of which are of the Islamic world. To the degree that Russia might become an influence in East Asia, it would probably be in the context of a resurgent, ultra-nationalist shift in its domestic politics, with a figure such as the right-wing politician Vladimir Zhirinovsky reasserting territorial claims against China and Japan or transforming currently neutral relations with Europe and the United States—once again—into a hostile political-military confrontation.

Japan will continue to be a major economic player in the region, and in the world. However, as the country does not hold a strategic vision of itself as an out-in-front leader in East Asia, Tokyo will not feel compelled to convert the country's economic wealth into the political and military components of leadership. Contemporary Japan lacks a political party or leader who articulates a go-it-alone foreign policy; and in the domestic political fluidity that has followed the demise of Liberal Democratic Party dominance of the political scene, it is notable that virtually all contenders for power—even the first Socialist party prime minister, Tomiichi Murayama—stress the desire to maintain close relations with the United States. Thus, Japan is most likely to continue to "lead from behind" in East Asia, preferring to shelter its commercial weight and security interests behind American strategic leadership.

Trade tensions in the U.S.-Japan relationship will persist, but if handled with reasonable sensitivity and skill on both sides, they are unlikely to escalate to the point of rupturing this durable strategic partnership. This is the message in the Clinton administration's moderation of its initial high-pressure approach to "framework" trade talks with Tokyo designed to gain measurable increases in American access to Japan's domestic markets and consequently reduce the bilateral trade deficit. Yet the decades-long U.S. struggle to open Japan's economy will persist, as will tensions over Japan playing a more proactive international role as a partner of the United States. Periodic threats of trade sanctions and frustrations at Japanese resistance to contributing more manpower and money to international peacekeeping and humanitarian assistance operations will constrain the élan of the relationship.

The one contemporary issue that could significantly threaten the Washington-Tokyo tie would be serious mismanagement of current tensions over the North Korean nuclear program. If the confrontation were to degenerate into a military conflict, *and* if Japan were unwilling to work with the United States in the context of the security treaty to contain or counter a military challenge from Pyongyang, the U.S.-Japan tie could be fatally fractured.

In Chapter 3 Mike Mochizuki notes that the United States remains the one country with which Japan shares the broadest range of interests. And the four decades of Cold War partnership have established an association that is likely to continue to be a durable foundation element in the East Asian strategic equation. For reasons of history, economic self-interest, and security conception, Japan would find neither China nor Russia an agreeable strategic partner. The legacy of the Pacific war still constrains the Japanese from trying to establish for themselves an independent position of leadership in East Asia. Some in Japan have been tempted by Malaysian prime minister Mahathir's notion of a coalition of East Asian states, led by Japan, forming a caucus or grouping to counter economic pressures from the United States, Canada, Australia, and New Zealand. But such a coalition would severely strain Tokyo's relations with the United States, which remains its security guarantor and major market.

Thus, the future structure of East Asia—to the extent that national governments will play a determining role—is most likely to be shaped by the interaction of policies formulated in Washington and Beijing.

SINO-AMERICAN RELATIONS:
CONTINUING STRUGGLE, OR RENORMALIZATION?

The normalization of relations between China and the United States in the 1970s—set in motion by Henry Kissinger's secret trip to Beijing in 1971 and President Nixon's meeting with Chairman Mao the following year—marked the second major structural transformation in Cold War–era international relations. (The first, of course, was the collapse of the Sino-Soviet alliance in 1960.) The near breakdown in normal Sino-American relations eighteen years later—after the Tiananmen events of June 1989—in combination with the breakup of the Soviet Union that same year fundamentally altered the dynamic of international relations in Asia, as in the rest of the world. Can bilateral relations between Washington and Beijing be reconstituted today without the sense of shared threat from another major power that brought them together during the Cold War?

That question will be answered by the complex interplay of a range of factors, the most salient of which will be domestic economic and political trends and developments in both countries. What one can say today is that despite the deep distrust on both sides of the Sino-American relationship that was induced by the shock of Tiananmen, both leaderships—half a decade later—are trying to prevent persisting tensions from precipitating a downward spiral into renewed hostility and overt confrontation.

As chapter 2 documents, China's senior leaders see the United States as the most likely challenger to their country's emergence as a global power. Deng Xiaoping, not long after Tiananmen, observed that tensions with the United States constituted a kind of new "Cold War"; and senior officials have seen Washington's stress on human rights issues as threatening party leadership and political stability in China. American pressure on human rights is seen as a counterpoint to the enticement of economic development that they fear may contribute, over time, to a domestic process of "peaceful evolution" and weakening of Communist Party rule of the country. And for the longer term, the United States, with its global military reach and its alliances with Japan, South Korea, the Philippines, Thailand, and Australia, is seen as the most likely power to stand in the way of China's claims to islands in the East China Sea and major portions of the South China Sea.

Compounding the complexity of Sino-American relations, however, is the realization among China's leaders that the sustained growth of their economy requires access for some time to U.S. markets, technology, and investment, as well as training opportunities in American universities. Moreover, cooperative if not friendly relations with the United States maintains the stable international environment that is seen as necessary for the country's development. They are also a hedge against security problems that might emanate from such developments as a shift in Russian foreign policy or the remilitarization of Japan.

Many Chinese are thus highly ambivalent about the United States. They seek positive relations in the short run but privately assume there will be problems in the future. The period ahead, for China's leaders, will be a time of delicate maneuvering among these conflicting trends and interests as they single-mindedly pursue the goal of China's emergence—after nearly two centuries of dynastic decay, domestic revolution, foreign interventions, and war—as a unified nation and a powerful, wealthy center of global influence.

The playout of these factors will be significantly shaped by China's domestic politics. The country is approaching the succession to Deng Xiaoping's remarkable two decades of leadership, during which he wrested control of the country from Mao Zedong's wife, Jiang Qing, and the other members of the Gang of Four and transformed the chairman's disastrous economic policies into one of the current world's most dramatic development successes. Will the successor leadership remain unified? It seems likely that Deng's development strategy of market-oriented opening to the world combined with domestic political discipline, economic reform, and decentralization will be sustained. But will his successors find a way to respond to growing public pressures for responsive leadership; or will there be another mass political explosion as occurred in 1989, fueled by popular resentment at official corruption, the effects of inflation, and uneven distribution of the benefits of growth? It seems likely that there will be future unrest, but that its dynamics will be different—perhaps less centralized and less visible to foreign television coverage.

Will the national center of leadership in Beijing work out an effective balance of power with the rapidly growing coastal and southern provinces that are the engines of China's dramatic takeoff? And will the social transformation of this long-enduring peasant empire, with its dynamic centers of change now in the cities and in growing links to the world beyond China, include controls over state power that will minimize prospects for the abuses and misjudgments of leadership that were so costly in human, political, and economic terms in Chairman Mao's time?

Despite these uncertainties, the Chinese as a people have a strong sense of themselves as a civilization and as a center of power in East Asia. Virtually any leadership in Beijing will use the resources now being generated by the country's economic takeoff to strengthen China's capabilities for regional—and global—leadership and for the pursuit of the country's national interests. The Chinese have always played for the long term; and unlike the Japanese, who have been content to pursue their interests in coalition with another major power (the United States), the Chinese are unlikely to be easy coalition partners of any other major power, as the Russians discovered in the decade of the Sino-Soviet alliance. Thus, Beijing will work methodically in the decades to come to regain China's position of international leadership that is assumed to be the country's inheritance and destiny—as is rooted in five thousand years of dynastic history and as was denied China for more than a century by the impact of the West in East Asia.

THE UNCERTAINTIES OF AMERICAN LEADERSHIP

While the United States is the world's single remaining superpower, it is also true that the United States, after the decades of Cold War struggle, has lost much of its enthusiasm for global strategic leadership. With the collapse of the Soviet Union, the sense of threat and challenge that provided the rationale for global engagement and for decades of defense spending at more than 5 percent of gross domestic product (GDP) has now diffused. The Clinton administration's determination to focus on domestic issues—with economic revitalization and health care reform as its highest priorities—has been accompanied by sharp cutbacks in defense spending. By 1995 the country will be spending 3.7 percent of GDP on military capabilities, a lower level than the 4.4 percent just before the Korean War in 1950. Although the national economy today is more than three and one-half times larger than it was in 1950, and while technological advances of the Cold War era now give the military capabilities we do maintain significantly more "bang for the buck," the national mood is one of reluctance to incur the costs of international leadership. Foreign economic assistance, for example, has been reduced by a quarter since the end of the Cold War.

Despite Clinton administration efforts to redefine the conception of American foreign policy from one of "containment" of communism to "enlargement" of the sphere of democratic and market-oriented states, there is now a growing mismatch between lingering notions of foreign policy activism and the capabilities to support rhetoric with resources. This disparity ultimately will be resolved either by a change in the rhetoric or by an international crisis that will force a reallocation of domestic priorities and resources toward more defense and foreign operations.

The Clinton administration's current approach to East Asia seems less influenced by the desire to avoid foreign involvements than its policies toward other parts of the world. This reflects awareness of the critical security issues associated with our position in the region, as well as realization that the boundary between domestic and international concerns has been breached by the forces of economic and social globalization. The president's commitment to domestic job creation led him to see in East Asia the linkage between domestic economic expansion and the extension of American market access to the most rapidly growing region of the world. Thus, the administration has built on the Bush administration's support for APEC—the Asia-Pacific Economic Cooperation initiative of late 1989—by raising it at the Seattle APEC ministerial meeting in November 1993 to a yearly convocation of regional heads of state. Its stated objective in fostering this leadership dialogue is to build greater consensus on economic policies that will further open domestic markets and spur another cycle of regional growth—the underpinnings of a "Pacific Community."

The administration also has supported the development of a regionwide security dialogue by backing the formation of an ASEAN Regional Forum (ARF) in association with the yearly ASEAN postministerial meetings. The first ARF was held in July 1993, and while the dialogue will continue, it is unlikely that the forum will become the core of a collective security system. Collective security has never worked in modern East Asia. The Co-Prosperity Sphere produced a disastrous war; the Sino-Soviet Alliance fell apart; SEATO never got off the ground; and the Soviet call for an Asian collective security system had no takers. The Clinton administration, like its predecessors, will attempt to sustain the American security role in the region, despite the deep cutbacks in domestic defense spending, by affirming the bilateral alliances established in the Cold War years and by strengthening U.S. military access to ports and airfields in a number of the ASEAN states. It also has grasped leadership of the challenge of nuclear proliferation in North Korea, a critical issue for the future of the American security role in East Asia.

What does all this add up to for relations with China? The administration came to office with a commitment to the punitive China policy that had been developed after Tiananmen by Democratic party leaders in the Congress. After eighteen months of pressing China on human rights concerns with the threat of withdrawal of Most Favored Nation (MFN) trading status, the president, in May 1994, dropped the linkage between human rights and MFN in favor of a less confrontational approach. As he noted in announcing this shift in policy:

> China has an atomic arsenal and a vote and a veto in the U.N. Security Council. It is a major factor in Asian and global security. We share important interests, such as in a nuclear-free Korean peninsula and in sustaining the global environment. . . . China is also the world's fastest-growing economy. Over $8 billion of United States

exports to China last year supported more than 150,000 jobs. . . . Extending MFN will avoid isolating China and instead will permit us to engage the Chinese not only with economic contacts but with cultural, educational and other contacts . . . that I believe will make it more likely that China will play a responsible role, both at home and abroad.[1]

Underlying this effort to reconstitute more normal relations with Beijing, however, are areas of serious concern that will continue to impede restoration of the cooperative ties that developed with increasing cordiality throughout the 1970s and 1980s. Apart from continuing Chinese human rights abuses, a growing bilateral trade imbalance that in 1993 exceeded $22 billion reflects constraints on American access to Chinese markets, indifferent Chinese efforts to protect Western intellectual property, and illegal Chinese exports of textiles and goods produced by prison labor. As in the case of Japan, these commercial issues will sustain tension in the relationship and limit Sino-American economic cooperation— as in the U.S. insistence that China's membership in the new World Trade Organization come only in the context of expanded access to China's domestic markets and adequate enforcement of its laws protecting foreign intellectual property.

Security cooperation is one area where the Sino-American relationship might again find some common direction, yet in the absence of a shared threat from a major power, uncertainties persist here as well. The Clinton administration is attempting to reengage Chinese leaders on strategic and security issues through a program of enhanced military exchanges. Beijing has offered limited and low-visibility cooperation on the issue of North Korea's nuclear program, but has been reluctant to side overtly with the United States and others on a critical security issue close to its own borders. Should China seem to break with the United States in the handling of this challenge, it could seriously undermine the president's rationale for a more cooperative policy of "engagement" with China. As well, Beijing's sustained, if moderately paced, program of military modernization—at a time when most nations are cutting back on defense spending—and arms exports and nuclear cooperation with sensitive countries in the Middle East and Gulf such as Iran will be sources of continuing friction and mistrust.

The Washington-Beijing connection thus has modest elements of cooperation that can be developed with determined efforts by both leaderships; yet it is a fragile relationship that is vulnerable to strains that can be induced from numerous sources. Failure to address the market access and other issues underlying the trade imbalance could renew congressional pressures for economic sanctions, as could some new and highly visible act of political repression on the part of the governing authorities in Beijing. The Taiwan issue is currently quiescent, but is of growing concern to Beijing as pro-independence forces on the island gain greater strength. Mishandling of this loaded issue by any of the parties involved could pose difficult choices for all concerned. The approaching return of Hong Kong to Chinese sovereign control will test Beijing's willingness to handle reversion within the framework of the Sino-British agreements, especially those related to political control of the territory. A military crisis in the region—most likely in the near term over the North Korean nuclear program, but in time over Beijing's efforts to assert control over contested territories in the East and South China seas—could force the two sides back into confrontation. And if Beijing were seen to be actively collaborating in the nuclear and missile armament of a challenging power, such as Iran, in areas of high sensitivity to the United States and its allies, serious strains could be induced into the relationship.

A REGIONAL POWER BALANCE AND A "PACIFIC COMMUNITY"

The most promising future one can anticipate for the coming period in East Asia is that of a loose balance of power among the states of the Strategic Quadrangle embodying areas of political and economic cooperation—with the U.S.-Japan alliance as the stabilizing core of the region. Such a pattern will help sustain the remarkable economic growth that has persisted in East Asia for well over a decade. If the United States uses its resources and influence with moderate activism, it can sustain the confidence of its allies as their security guarantor. It can sustain the movement toward ever more open markets in a way that will forestall the formation of an

East Asian yen-dominated trading bloc and advance the formation of a Pacific Basin–wide economic and political community.

Such a positive future may be all the more likely if policymakers in Washington and Beijing consider the alternative of a serious deterioration in Sino-American relations. Mishandling of security, trade, or human rights issues could lead to a confrontation that would be very costly for all concerned. It was recognition of this fact that led the Clinton administration, in the spring of 1994, to adjust its dealings with China and Japan when both seemed headed for trouble. The United States will maximize its own interests if it is able to find common cause with all the major players of East Asia. If its pursuit of human rights or trade concerns are handled in a divisive way, however, as David Lampton suggests, the United States could find itself the isolated party in the region. Tokyo and Moscow—or Seoul, or the ASEAN countries—will be reluctant to put in jeopardy their now-normal relations with Beijing by supporting American initiatives that seem distant from their own interests. Similarly, U.S. efforts to open Asian markets—which will benefit the long-term growth of the regional economy—must be modulated to reflect the domestic political pressures generated by the explosive pace of this period of technological and economic change.

AND THEN, THERE ARE ALWAYS WILD CARDS

This volume has been structured on the assumption that the interactions of the major powers will be the major factors shaping the future of East Asia. This is a reasonable premise, but we live in an era in which subnational forces are increasingly influential in international affairs and in which global economic, technological, and social forces are eroding the power of even great nation-states to shape their own destinies. The future of East Asia could be determined by factors only cursorily explored by the contributors to this volume.

What are such "wild cards" in the games of the major powers? I have already noted the critical importance to the region of the growing tensions on the Korean Peninsula as a result of North

Korea's nuclear program. A breakdown in U.S. negotiations with the North would lead to a serious confrontation if not military action—with unpredictable consequences for relations among the four major powers. Renewed confrontation in the Gulf over control of energy resources, perhaps the next time with a nuclear-armed Iran, would present difficult dilemmas for relations within the Strategic Quadrangle, especially if China sided with Iran or was seen to have contributed to Iran's nuclear and missile capabilities.

The economies of East Asia, while securely linked to the global economy and to the United States, are increasingly integrated through the rapid expansion of intraregional trading patterns. Intraregional trade as a component of the total world trade of the East Asian economies has grown from around 30 percent in 1970 to around 40 percent in 1990; and it is expected to grow still further throughout the remainder of this last decade of the twentieth century. It thus may come to pass that Prime Minister Mahathir's concept of a trading bloc of East Asian states will acquire economic reality if not institutional form. In such circumstances, American hopes for Pacific Basin–wide economic integration organized around APEC could run afoul of the growth of an East Asian yen bloc of trading nations resistant to U.S. pressures for market opening, the meeting of Western standards of intellectual property protection, labor force and human rights protections, and environmental concerns. Such a development, which seems unlikely today, would undermine American hopes for the growth of a Pacific Community in the twenty-first century.

And finally, one cannot ignore the possibility that subnational forces will have a major impact on the future of relations among the major powers of East Asia. I have already commented on the possible impact of independence-minded forces in Taiwan on Sino-American relations. It is also possible that the growing economic decentralization of China's economy will lead to regional political fragmentation. In addition, non-Han minority groups in Tibet, Mongolia, and Xinjiang may further strain the unity of China—with possibly explosive repercussions for Beijing's relations with the other major powers. So too would political turmoil on the China mainland that led to major refugee movements into Hong

Kong or across the Taiwan Straits, Yellow Sea, or East China Sea toward Taiwan, Japan, or Korea.

The sum total of these factors for the future of East Asia is not calculable. Most likely the economies of the region will continue to grow, and the major powers will see it in their interests to maintain cooperative relations in loose association. But history has not ended; and change is seldom a straight-line projection of current trends. An expression attributed to a Chinese philosopher, but perhaps more accurately associated with Yogi Berra, puts it best: "Prediction is very difficult, especially regarding the future."

Note

1. As quoted in the *New York Times*, May 27, 1994, p. A8.

ABOUT THE AUTHORS

David M. Lampton is president of the National Committee on United States–China Relations in New York City, the nation's oldest not-for-profit educational organization devoted to enhancing mutual understanding among the peoples of the United States and China's mainland, Taiwan, and Hong Kong. Before assuming his current position in 1988, Dr. Lampton was director of the China Policy Program at the American Enterprise Institute in Washington, D.C., and associate professor of political science at Ohio State University. Dr. Lampton is the author and editor of seven books and monographs, among which are *The Politics of Medicine in China; Paths to Power: Elite Mobility in Contemporary China;* and *Policy Implementation in Post-Mao China.* Most recently, Dr. Lampton, with Barber B. Conable, Jr., wrote "China: The Coming Power," which appeared in *Foreign Affairs.* He received his Ph.D. from Stanford University in 1974 and completed undergraduate work at the same institution in 1968, graduating Phi Beta Kappa.

Robert Legvold is professor of political science at Columbia University, where he specializes in the international relations of the Soviet Union and its successor states. He was director of the Harriman Institute, Columbia University, from 1986 to 1992. Prior to going to Columbia in 1984, he served for six years as senior fellow and director of the Soviet Studies Project at the Council on Foreign Relations in New York. He received his Ph.D. from the Fletcher School of Law and Diplomacy in 1967. Professor Legvold's areas of particular interest are the foreign policies of Russia, Ukraine, and the other newstates of the former Soviet Union, US-Soviet relations, Soviet policy in Europe and Asia, Soviet security policy, and the Soviet role in the world economy. With Timothy Colton and other authors, he has most recently completed, *After the Soviet Union: From Empire to Nations* (1992). He is the author of chapters and articles in a number of edited volumes and professional journals. The most recent are: "Western Europe and the Post-Soviet Challenge," in Armand Cless, Richard Rosecranz, and Yoshikazu Sakamoto, eds., *After the Collapse of the East-West Order* (1994); "Russian Developments," in Dick Clark, ed., *Building a Congressional Cadre* (1994); and "The Collapse of the Soviet Union and the New Asian Order," *Analysis: National Bureau of Asian Research* (1992).

Michael Mandelbaum is director of the Project on East-West Relations at the Council on Foreign Relations and the Christian A. Herter Professor of American Foreign Policy at the Paul H. Nitze School of Advanced International Studies of the Johns Hopkins University in Washington, D.C. He is also the associate director of the Aspen Institute's Congressional Project on Central and Eastern Europe and the Former Soviet Union and a regular columnist on foreign affairs for *Newsday*. Professor Mandelbaum received an M.A. from King's College, Cambridge, and a Ph.D. from Harvard University. He has also taught at Columbia University and the United States Naval Academy. He is the author or editor of thirteen books, including *Central Asia and the World* (1994); *The Rise of Nations in the Soviet Union: American Foreign Policy and the Disintegration of the USSR* (1991); *The Fate of Nations: The Search for National Security in the 19th and 20th Centuries* (1988); with Seweryn Bialer, *The Global Rivals* (1988); and with Strobe Talbott, *Reagan and Gorbachev* (1987).

Mike M. Mochizuki is codirector of the Center for Asia-Pacific Policy at the RAND Corporation in Santa Monica, California. He is also associate professor of international relations at the University of Southern California. After receiving his Ph.D. in political science from Harvard University, he was a postdoctoral fellow at Harvard's Center for International Affairs and an assistant professor of political science at Yale University. He specializes in Japanese politics and foreign policy, U.S.-Japan relations, and East Asian security issues. Dr. Mochizuki is editor of the forthcoming book, *Ruling Japan: Conservative Hegemony in the Postwar Era.*

Richard H. Solomon, currently president of the United States Institute of Peace, was assistant secretary of state for East Asian and Pacific affairs (1989–1992) and ambassador to the Philippines (1992–1993). His career began as professor of political science at the University of Michigan and has included assignments on the National Security Council staff, with the RAND Corporation, and director of policy planning in the State Department. His other work on Asian security issues includes the edited volumes *Asian Security in the 1980s: Problems and Policies for a Time of Transition* (1980); *The Soviet Far East Military Buildup: Nuclear Dilemmas and Asian Security* (1986); and the policy statements "Asian Security in the 1990s: Diversity in Defense" (*Dispatch,* vol. 1, no. 10, 1990); and "America and Asian Security in an Era of Geoeconomics" (*Dispatch,* May 1992).

INDEX